IN THE
GREAT
TRADITION

IN THE GREAT TRADITION

In honor of
Winthrop S. Hudson

Essays on Pluralism,
Voluntarism,
and Revivalism

Joseph D. Ban, Paul R. Dekar, editors

Judson Press® Valley Forge

IN THE GREAT TRADITION

Library of Congress Cataloging in Publication Data
Main entry under title:

In the great tradition.

Themes honoring the writings of Winthrop S.
Hudson.
Includes bibliographical references and index.
Contents: On comparing and connecting histories/
Martin E. Marty—Protestant patterns in Canada
and the United States/Robert T. Handy—On the
soul of nations/Paul R. Dekar—[etc.]
1. United States—Church history—Addresses,
essays, lectures. 2. Canada—Church history—Addresses, essays, lectures. 3. England—Church
history—Addresses, essays, lectures.
4. Hudson, Winthrop Still, 1911-   —Addresses,
essays, lectures. I. Ban, Joseph D. II. Dekar,
Paul R. III. Hudson, Winthrop Still, 1911-
BR515.I44   1982   280'.4'0973   82-13034
ISBN 0-8170-0972-8

*"Let me disclose the gifts reserved for age
To set a crown upon your lifetime's effort."*

from T. S. Eliot, "Little Gidding,"
        Four Quartets,
        *The Complete Poems and Plays
        1909–1950*
        (New York: Harcourt Brace Jovanovich, 1952), p. 141.

Contents

I. COMPARATIVE THEMES

> **Martin E. Marty,** Fairfax M. Cone Distinguished Service Professor of the History of Modern Christianity at the Divinity School of the University of Chicago.

> **Robert T. Handy,** Henry Sloane Coffin Professor of Church History at Union Theological Seminary, New York.

> **Paul R. Dekar,** Associate Professor of Christian History at McMaster Divinity College, McMaster University, Hamilton, Ontario, Canada.

II. CONTINENTAL THEMES

III. THEMES ON THE HISTORY OF CHRISTIANITY IN THE UNITED STATES

Introduction

The scholarly contributions of Winthrop S. Hudson have substantially enlarged the treasury of knowledge regarding American religious tradition, the English Reformation, and the Baptist heritage. The contributors intend this volume to be worthy of this historian. Hudson has made a significant contribution to the spiritual and intellectual life of churches in North America and Great Britain as well as to the larger religious and cultural scene.

The organizing principle for this volume honoring Hudson the historian draws upon the themes developed in his various writings. The three major areas include: I. Comparative Themes; II. Continental Themes; III. Themes on the History of Christianity in the United States.

Martin Marty begins the discussion with an essay on the idea of comparison itself. He points to Hudson's contributions to both comparisons and connections. Religion provides an excellent sphere for comparison. This Robert Handy does in exploring the similarities and differences in the Protestant patterns in Canada and the United States. Handy finds pluralism and voluntarism in both countries as well as an intense religious activism. The Union Seminary historian has pioneered in promoting understanding of the religious history of these neighboring nations. This article will sharpen the reader's awareness of how different Canada is from its larger neighbor to the south as well as highlight the ties that bind Christians despite national boundaries. Paul Dekar, in turn, provides a comparative exploration of the public religion, civil piety, and nationalistic dimensions for both English Protestant Canada and the United States. The reader from the United States should take notice of the fact that both Handy and Dekar are historians writing in English about the religious history of English-speaking churches, and thus a major part of religious history in Canada—that of the French-language churches—is mentioned only in passing. This cautionary note, while it may mean little to U.S. readers, is itself a fact of life in Canadian religious circles today.

Peter Kaufman examines the intertwining developments between political culture and Christian piety. This, too, has been an interest of Hudson. Kaufman recognizes the fascination of historians with sixteenth-century dissidents but warns that pluralism is not implicit in the dualism of the sectarian movements. Religious dissent on the Continent is not to be confused with the roots of religious pluralism. Yet this may have been the case in England where the dissenting churches, as represented in Cromwell's New Model Army, provided the opening stages for the pluralism that marks English religious life.

Winthrop Hudson has made substantive contributions to the historical study of Puritanism and the Separatist beginnings of the English Baptist movement. Joseph D. Ban explores the research into the problem of early English Baptist beginnings and the connections, if any, with Continental Anabaptist movements. Ban presents a critical study of recent writing in the field and attempts to demonstrate the validity of the carefully documented studies of Champlin Burrage and to refute the conclusions of Irvin B. Horst.

It is natural for Prentiss Pemberton to return to Hudson's own work on John Locke for an erudite discussion of Lockian ideas on the relationship between the order of nature, the ownership of private property, and the governance of society.

The final section of this volume includes a variety of approaches to the history of Christianity in continental U.S.A. Eldon Ernst again does a masterful study of religious historiography. The telling of the story has itself produced a compelling narrative. Ernst guides us through its development. Jerald Brauer explicates the impact of revivalism and millenarianism upon religious movements that formed the features of Protestantism in the United States. In a time marked by a renewed awareness of the "born-again" experience, Brauer's chapter analyzes the dynamics that helped mold the features of religious expression in the United States. He vividly reminds us of the essential differences as well as the intimate association between revivalism and millenarianism.

Edwin Gaustad explores one of Hudson's favorite themes: "the coercion of voluntarism." How valid is the paradox? Gaustad's analysis deserves careful reading and considerable discussion for the good of the social order and the well-being of the religious community. William McLoughlin investigates a significant century in the political and religious life of the United States. What was the nature of the religious settlement that took place after the American Revolution? McLoughlin's resolution of this question makes for interesting reading. A major shift in the flow of power took place, he asserts. He traces this "trajectory of democratic enthusiasm" to establish his case. Can the origin of a distinctive identity for the United States be placed in the first Great Awakening? What was the relationship between religious movements and the shift of the flow of power? How did theology influence the emergence of a democratic society? McLoughlin's chapter certainly provokes serious thought regarding the role religion has played in the development of existing political structures.

Leonard Sweet describes the later and somewhat different religious phenomena, the Union Prayer Meetings. The reader will naturally make comparisons with other chapters in this volume, as well as with Hudson's writings. Sweet provides us with a vivid portrait of a movement that had considerable impact on the towns and cities of the nation, yet is relatively unknown to many. Here was piety attempting to heal a nation that moved steadily toward tragic division. Grant Wacker closes this volume with a thoughtful analysis of the influence of an earlier Rochester theologian, Augustus Hopkins Strong. Wacker's treatment opens up significant issues in current theological and historical discourse. It is fitting that the chapters in this volume honoring Winthrop Hudson actually open up issues that will be discussed heatedly in the coming years.

It has been said that the theological professor's most important function in professional formation arises from what the mentor is observed doing rather than from the information conveyed in formal courses. Winthrop Hudson, for many, has provided a significant example of the Christian life during troubled, even turbulent, decades. To his students and peers he exhibited the promise and reality of grace. In his courses, articles, books, and conversations Hudson communicated a breadth and depth of intellectual curiosity that was contagious. He assisted many a graduate student's initial explorations into religious, cultural, and intellectual history. Hudson alerted many thoughtful persons to the realization that North American religious and political life faced a day of reckoning. This humane scholar enabled his students to share in the wisdom of former times and gain a perspective that saw beyond the acrimony that marked many recent decades in American life. Many a former student bears witness that the example of Winthrop Hudson helped nourish in him or her a commitment to service in a suffering world, a faithfulness to the rich traditions of Christianity, and honesty in ac-

11

knowledging the limitations of our individual and corporate identities.

The chapters of this book appropriately reflect the continuing
appreciation of the many contributions Winthrop Hudson has made
to us.

Joseph D. Ban

Paul R. Dekar

McMaster Divinity College
McMaster University

Winthrop Still Hudson

A Biographical Sketch

Winthrop S. Hudson has earned deserved recognition for his valued contribution to the study of church history. He was graduated in 1933 from Kalamazoo College, a Baptist-related institution known for excellence. His theological studies were completed at Colgate Rochester Divinity School in 1937, the year of his ordination as a Baptist pastor. He completed the Doctor of Philosophy degree in history at the University of Chicago in 1940. His pastorates included York, New York, and Normal Park, Chicago. In 1942 he became an instructor at Colgate Rochester Divinity School. Then, from 1944 to 1947, he taught History of Christianity in the British Isles at the University of Chicago. Though a tenured associate professor, he returned to Colgate Rochester Divinity School where he came to be appointed the James B. Colgate Professor of History of Christianity. He was elected Distinguished Seminary Professor in 1977–1980. During the period 1970–1977 he simultaneously held appointment as Professor of History at the University of Rochester. Currently he serves as Adjunct Professor of Religion at the University of North Carolina, Chapel Hill.

His contributions to the field of church history range far beyond his classroom and writing. This distinguished scholar served from 1949 to 1972 as a member of the board of managers of the American Baptist Historical Society. He served as the society's president from 1952 to 1962. During his term as president *Foundations, a Baptist Journal of History and Theology* was launched. The motto of the journal, "That those things which cannot be shaken" (Hebrews 12:27, KJV), indicates the interest of its founders in the recovery of Baptist roots. Winthrop Hudson was also deeply involved in the American Baptist Board for Theological Studies.

This scholar has also been credited with facilitating the move of the Samuel Colgate Historical Collection from Hamilton, New York, to Rochester and, as well, the relocation of the American Baptist Historical Collection from Chester, Pennsylvania, to Rochester. These combined collections now form one of the major Baptist historical libraries in the world.

Not only was this seminary professor an impressive teacher and a widely read author, but also his total work was undergirded by painstaking research. This included three terms as a Fellow of the Folger Shakespeare Library and, in 1975, the honor of being named a Senior Fellow of the National Endowment for the Humanities.

The April-June, 1980, issue of *Foundations* (volume 23, number 2) now with the broadened scope of ". . . history, theology and ministry," devoted an entire issue to honoring Winthrop S. Hudson. Readers of this volume will want to consult that journal for significant articles plus a complete bibliography, which we have not replicated here. It is sufficient to note that since his first published work, *John Ponet (1516?-1556): Advocate of Limited Monarchy*, in 1942, Winthrop Hudson has published many books and scholarly articles.

The best known of his publications include *The Great Tradition of the American Churches*, published in 1953 and reprinted in 1963; *American Protestantism*, 1961, in paperback in 1963; and *Religion in America*, 1965, revised 1973 and 1981. Judson Press has published *Baptist Concepts of the Church*, 1959; *A Baptist Manual of Polity and Practice* with Norman H. Maring as joint author, 1963; *Baptist Convictions*, 1963; and *Baptists in Transition: Individualism and Christian Responsibility*, 1979. Hudson's newest publication, *The Cambridge Connection and the Elizabethan Settlement of 1559*, published in 1980, demonstrates the thoroughness of research in original sources, the subtlety of analysis, and the clarity of expression for which all of his writings have become noted.

The Editors

IN THE
GREAT
TRADITION

I

Comparative Themes

On Comparing and
Connecting Histories

Martin E. Marty

"Thinking without comparison is unthinkable," wrote Guy E. Swanson in his argument that all historians write comparative history.[1] In the broadest sense, there is no writing of history without making comparisons. The historian compares his or her own time with the period under scrutiny. Researchers have to compare early and later moments in the development of their subjects' careers. If there are hints of moral judgment in the tone—for example, if they imply in their chronicles that Hitler was an evil person—they will inevitably be writing with comparisons of other people or higher standards in mind.

When modern historians plead for the writing of comparative history, however, they have a somewhat more narrow concept in view. They are trying to break out of the notion that one can understand a phenomenon by examining it in a petri dish formed by its own locale in an isolated moment in history. Usually that laboratory container for isolation is the nation. In American studies this means that most history has concentrated on the American story apart from its provenance, contexts, and consequences.

Many have called for comparative history, but in the American religious field few have done anything about it. Winthrop Hudson is an exception, and he would be first to admit that he has not done much. Since so few of the rest of his colleagues do anything at all, however, it is certainly appropriate to begin with reference to Hudson's efforts and achievements and to move out from there to ponder the limits of comparative studies beyond the Hudson corpus. Let it also be noted that by concentrating on the Anglo-American correlations and influences, Hudson himself is doing less comparative history than what I might call connectional history. In a more pure sense, comparative history tends to lift out two stories and illumine them even though they do not have much direct influence on each other through a period. An example of this is the well-regarded work of George M. Fredrickson, *White Supremacy: A Comparative Study in American and South African History*.[2] The South Africans and the Americans hardly knew each other, had little contact with each other; yet a comparison of their separate treatments of black slavery throws light on each half of the Fredrickson story.

Hudson has struggled valiantly to keep the connectional ties between at least English and American religious history alive. Mention that "the denomination" is an American invention and someone will remind you that in many times and many places Hudson has already refuted that point by showing both the occasions for the rise of denominationalism in England and the development of the term there. Because he is interested in what Alan Simpson in another connectional study calls *Puritanism in Old England and New*[3] and in topics like the rise of religious liberties in the English-speaking world, he would appear to have an easy task. In both those cases, there is a single story with two locales, and not to connect them is to shortchange those who come for understanding.

Despite the obviousness of the ties, Hudson has not always been free to make the point. A *festschrift* is as good a place as any to confess one's own complicity in frustrating the subject's good intentions. An instance: in his Preface to *Nationalism and Religion in America: Concepts of American Identity and Mission*, Hudson appends some English readings and explains their location.

> The selections in the Appendix illustrating the English heritage were originally compiled as an opening chapter to provide perspective and background for American developments. It soon became apparent that this extensive block of material at the outset of the volume would be more confusing than illuminating. There will be many readers, however, who will wish to turn to the Appendix for fuller explication. . . .[4]

It did not "soon become apparent" at all. Hudson's editor, the author of this essay, and the publisher, Harper & Row, spent considerable energy convincing him to go along with the notion of moving his up-front material to down-rear. They had certain assumptions about the curiosities and competences of the members of a potential clientele for the book, and these assumptions suggested that books about America designed for American classrooms had to begin straight out with American themes.

In the symposium to which Hudson contributed the essay "How American Is Religion in America?" his squelching editor, the present writer, as they say, directly followed Hudson with a seconding of the motion, a forthright claim in agreement that comparative history was exemplary.

The historian of religion in America today is beginning to find that he can best understand his culture and make a contribution to others' self-understanding by enlarging the milieu concerning which he asks historical questions.

Ideally, this editor-historian went on, the whole world should be that milieu. Now and then a superperson might write a comparative study between America and the East or the Third World. "But to picture sustaining such an approach as a lifework seems staggering and, in its own way, artificial." Yet one must locate some larger-than-American province. The proposal then was for a province called "the West" or "Atlantic community," which in the modern case at least meant the field of nations in which industrialization (following or coming along with political democracy) had occurred. To make the case, Hudson's colleague drew upon nineteenth-century writers like John Williamson Nevin, who in 1845 called attention to the continental context:

It is preposterous to suppose that in the most speculative portion of the whole Christian world these errors stand in no connection with the general movement of the world's mind, or that they do not *need* to be surmounted by a fresh advance on the part of truth.

"*How* to tell the unified or interrelated story is the difficult question." The world was already too full of "mere generalists," and "church historians in particular have to resist the temptation to become experts on everything." The question was, "Why should the partly accidental experience of national isolation and the ideology of innocence which grew up around its religious experience be determinative?"

Hudson's colleague came up with the proposal that one could do topical slices that allowed for necessary specialization. Behind this was Jacob Burckhardt's proposal for method: "We shall confine ourselves to observation, taking transverse sections of history *(Querdurchschnitten)* in as many directions as possible." Among the possibilities were and are:

revolutions, the rise and fall of colonial and imperial projects, the development of constitutionalism, the progressive separation of church and state, kinds of romanticism and reaction to Enlightenment, industrial development and revolution, the actual interaction and transfer of people in emigration-immigration, religious revivals and awakenings, missionary expansion . . . , the rise of humanitarianism and the abolition of human slavery, a variety of assaults on Christian dominion and ideas, the rise of cities and the accompanying problems for religious institutions, the growth of modern nationalism, the foretastes of Christian ecumenical movements, and some theological interaction.[5]

21

That was an ambitious but valid and valuable program, but few have followed up on it. The proposer himself did not, having executed only one comparative book, *The Modern Schism: Three Paths to the Secular*,[6] before retreating to the safe limits of the national model for subsequent work.

The calls for comparative history and the claims for its advance are common. In a review of Fredrickson, C. Vann Woodward could say:

> Left for a long time to amateurs, comparative history has lately captured growing attention from professionals. It was the main theme of a recent convention of the American Historical Association, and it is the subject of all the articles in the latest number of the organization's official journal.[7]

Woodward cites an article by Raymond Grew, who edits a journal that is itself indicative of the promise in this field—*Comparative Studies in Society and History.*

> To look at other cases is to see other outcomes. By considering them, the historian wins some freedom from the tyranny of what happened and develops that awareness of alternatives—of a missing revolution, of banks that were not formed, of parliaments that did not meet, of populations that failed to increase—that underlies some of the most provocative of historical questions. We are easily blinded by the obvious . . . only comparison establishes that there is something to be explained.

Because of Grew's experience, he brings credentials to the call for comparison and merits more attention. He can cite the influence of greats like Marc Bloch and Lord Acton in the lineage of theorists, just as he keeps at a distance the philosophers of history (as opposed to working historians) like Oswald Spengler, Pitirim Sorokin, and Arnold Toynbee, whose comparative study of civilizations has not fared well in the eyes of historians.

For Grew, comparing religious topics is one of the promising areas. "Institutions that go by common names of church or party or bank may, in fact, perform quite different functions in different societies or at different times." Yet as with churches or banks or anything else, American institutions too rarely get compared.

22

> In the writing of American history it is surprising, as John Higham has commented, not that comparison "should at last have begun to flourish, but that it should have been so long delayed." So great . . . is the need that "comparative history" is often taken to mean comparison between nations, which has the paradoxical effect of reinforcing the tendency to consider nations the major unit of analysis.

Wrote Grew, "Deliberately used, comparison can aid historians at four stages of their work: (1) in asking questions, (2) in identifying historical problems, (3) in designing the appropriate research, and (4) in reaching and testing significant conclusions." Grew strenuously insists, however, that there is no "comparative method" and even feels that "comparative history" is a term "better avoided." Even Bloch spoke of *histoire comparée* and not *histoire comparative.* "For historians to think comparatively, to compare histories, is to do what we already do—a little more consciously and on a somewhat broader plane. It is not to embrace some new type or genre of historical investigation." So he comes to a point that Hudson's lifework, even when he seems to be dealing only with America, certifies: "There is . . . no paradox in insisting that the study of a single case can be comparative."[8]

Against such a background, Hudson's own catalog of illustrations, agenda, and pointings to connections in the theme essay is appropriately modest. "How American Is Religion in America?" is a question that admits of no answers unless one "thinks comparatively," as Grew suggests all historians must. "In the field of church history, our provincialism has obscured many of the interrelationships that have bound us to Europe." For a program he suggests study of the European rootages of denominations, the transatlantic character of evangelicalism, the institutions of a voluntary society, the two-way traffic across the Atlantic, literary influences of a reciprocal character, the importation of Continental biblical criticism, theology, spirituality, the social gospel, and the like—all in the interest of moving beyond a claim for American uniqueness that "leads to a narrow and provincial understanding of ourselves" and to "nativism and jingoism . . . cultural and intellectual isolationism . . . messianic impulses" and the like. On the positive side the connectional study, the relocation of American religious history in its Angloid and Continental contexts, should give us "a sense of continuity, perspective, and insight" as well as an awareness, for Christians, of the way they are part of "the whole church of Christ both past and present."[9]

The Hudson footnotes, however, suggest that by 1968, when he published his address, there were still few titles to cite. On voluntary societies he pointed to Charles I. Foster, *An Errand of Mercy: The Evangelical United Front,* and it still merits pointing to as a case for comparison and connection. In a string of Washington Gladden books, one is entitled *England and America* (1898),[10] and that is it. All the other footnoted works deal with intercontinental topics but only with single-nation models.

For all the enthusiasms of Woodward, Grew, and Higham, and

for all the regularity with which they point to the religious themes, religion is not part of any large comparative genre among American historians (and American religion is even less so a subject of curiosity for contextual studies by Europeans). For a 1982 issue of *The Journal of Religion* I have compiled and commented upon scores upon scores of significant works on American religious history reviewed in two major secular and two "church history" journals. The list suggests a marvelous range of topics, but few comparative works.

The first book cited is one of the rare exceptions. Robert T. Handy at least crossed one border, for the sake of a series, to deal with a second nation whose story has become familiar to him. Yet Handy himself would admit, with the reviewers, that his *History of the Churches in the United States and Canada*[11] is more a publication of two parallel stories than a critical comparison of similar phenomena in the two nations. He moved so much further than most generalists on American history that he left little room for complaint, but now it is legitimate to hope that he will produce at least a substantial comparative essay based on what he·learned while doing research for the book.

No other "general" works, no discussions of public and civil religion and the American revolution, have self-conscious comparison built in. One work on "colonial themes," Ernest Stoeffler's small, edited work *Continental Pietism and Early American Christianity*[12] implies more than it delivers, because "Continental" here means groups of Continental provenance, whose stories become of interest after their arrival. A major topic area was "revivalism and conversion and millennialism," but for all the promise of the category, only Richard Carwardine's *Transatlantic Revivalism: Popular Evangelicalism in Britain and America, 1790–1865*[13] includes more than the United States locale. If we use books like Fredrickson for models, however, it is impossible to see Carwardine as a comparer; he chiefly concentrates on two stories and points to their moments of overlap and interconnection.

Naturally, the section on fundamentalism, evangelicalism, pentecostalism, and the charismatic movement showed some signs of flourishing activity. The first of these was largely an American movement, though not without international implications and derivations; yet nothing of a comparative character has appeared. Evangelicalism will certainly be treated increasingly as a product of an expanding Atlantic community, but the journals located no such works as yet. And pentecostalism offers rich possibilities for American/Third World comparison and connection, but no American historian has been ambitious enough to do the tracing of entwinements.

By its very nature the topic of Christian missions is international. During the last half of the 1970s two works of such sufficient importance that the four editors had them reviewed moved a bit beyond provincialism. John A. Andrews, in *Rebuilding the Christian Commonwealth: New England Congregationalists and Foreign Missions,*[14] concentrated on New England but at least showed awarenesses of the Sandwich Islands and other foreign shores. And, of course, China and America had to be intertwined in some essays in John Fairbanks's edition of *The Missionary Enterprise in China and America.*[15] If missionary history is reawakened, as Fairbanks thinks it will and must be, we shall, of course, see more connectional and comparative history involving Americans. Sometimes America provides the milieu for interculturalism, as in Cornelius J. Jaenen's *Friend and Foe: Aspects of French-Amerindian Cultural Contact in the Sixteenth and Seventeenth Centuries.*[16] Yet such books count in a list of comparative works only to the extent that they show curiosity about the current history of the "sending" nation, for example, in Jaenen's case, France.

George Eaton Simpson in *Black Religions in the New World,*[17] a synthesis of his lifework on Latin America, the Caribbean, and North America, moves further than almost any other work in connecting stories, but his is the only such book in the "black religion" category. Surprisingly, there has been little international or interplace research on women and religion. Almost all the books in the burgeoning field of Eastern, occult, and new religions, though they deal with imports, spend only a page or two on the Asian or ancient contexts and all the rest on what happens in America. Even intellectual history seldom sees American development in a larger context. A partial exception, because it pays attention to Bacon and then the Scottish Enlightenment, is Theodore Dwight Bozeman's *Protestants in an Age of Science: The Baconian Ideal and Antebellum American Religious Thought.*[18]

Social religion, politics, church and state, education, the life cycle, and even "miscellaneous" turned up little more. A few of the biographies demanded and drew upon intercontinental themes, including, of course, Edwin Scott Gaustad's *George Berkeley in America.*[19] Few other cosmopolitan figures were subjects of biography, however. And none of the denominational works followed up on Hudson's first call, i.e., to write on the European setting of denominations. In fact, there were few historical works on main-line denominations, and those that dealt with "homegrown" ones like Mormonism, concentrated on the domestic scene. I did not follow

25

up on the hundreds of titles dealing with ethnicity, though many of them include religious dimensions and most of them must have some reference to the European, African, and Asian roots of the ethnic groups.

Nine titles in all can thus be smuggled in under the "comparative" or "connective" tents, and almost none of these deals with our theme in systematic fashion.

The *Journal of Religion* essay includes 123 titles. Fredrickson has few counterparts in the field of religion, and the observations by Grew, Higham, and others that comparison is flourishing are not valid in one of the areas they thought most promising—religion. If the essay overlooked some titles reviewed by the journals, or if the editors of those journals passed over some books that deserved review, these must be so few that neither they nor I need to duplicate ready-made versions of apologies for sins of omission.

If the calls for comparison are so frequent, the reports on promise so rich, yet the performance so thin, then this may be the proper time and place to review quickly the case for comparison and then to make some proposals as to why so little has occurred among religious historians.

All historians tell stories. They may be fashionable enough to borrow "synchronics" from anthropologists to supplement their "diachronic" approach—in order to compare stories. They may use computers to enhance the data of their stories, but in the end they will provide some sort of narratives from the past, and the computer data usually imply some sort of comparison.

The significance of stories emerges only in the context of comparison of some sort. How does the child know the scope of horror or the delight of security from a single fairy tale, or how does the historian bring in moral judgments implying good people and bad people without comparison? How does the historian become suspicious enough to do detective work, which historians call "research," unless he or she has experience in comparing authentic and inauthentic materials?

The historians' need for comparison grows out of their need to
26 have models, more or less as sociologists do. When S. S. Acquaviva or Michael Argyle[20] as sociologists want to show trends in religious observance or to speculate on the situation of desacralization, they present comparative data from numbers of cultures. This is fairly easy for many kinds of sociologists to do, as they can lift out statistics on, say, church attendance from many cultures and nations without always having to tell the story of the context as historians do. Yet historians need "models" as much as sociologists do, if they are to

know what to ask, what to find significant, and how to tie together the plot of their stories.

These models come not only from differing times—no one complains about an absence of curiosity about that among historians—but also from different places. The great object of concern has been the fact that places, to modern historians, mean nations. The nation itself is a modern invention demanding comparative study, and it has religious dimensions that make such comparison a proper subject of religious history, as Carlton J. H. Hayes and others, including Winthrop Hudson, have shown.[21] Nations as religious complexes do not always follow denominational lines. Switzerland and the Netherlands are anomalies in Europe since they are complexes of ethnic and religious or sectarian components. That is one of their assets for comparative study. But the nation also has to be treated with care because it can impose periods and significances on religious history. Many an American religious history—one thinks of Abdel Ross Wentz's work on Lutheranism, for instance[22]—has fallen into the trap of letting national history set the terms for religion. If the late nineteenth century was the period for big corporations, then it must have been the period for big church bureaucratization and so forth. Such capitulations to national history often lead religious historians away from deep thought about the inner dynamics of the phenomena with which they deal. One special problem with connecting religion and nation is that religious tendencies tend to look epiphenomenal. One tells the story of Iran and attaches Shi'ite Islam to it without studying Islam and seeing how Iran is but one of the passing nations in which Islam finds life.

There are, most partisans of comparison agree, special reasons for religious historians to move beyond merely single-nation models. Religion is supposed to make transcendent claims, to include prophetic notes that lead prophets to call into question the pretensions of nations. Historians are not likely to trace out those elements unless they are at least aware of the differences between nations, including differences between those that have a single faith. Thus, to compare American and Third-World Christianity in a time of "imperialist" and "anti-colonialist" charges illumines the way religion is tangled with national claims in both contexts. To sound jingoistic for a moment: sometimes American Christians are charged by, say, people from India with including no prophetic note. They do not stand apart from or above their nation, say the Indians who, on second glance, seem to "transcend" nationalism only because they transcend *American* nationalism. They may be very much tied up with their own nation's destiny.

Religion is an excellent sphere for comparison because in most

27

cases it claims to be ecumenical. The members of the Christian churches purport to have a common history yet have lived in hundreds of nations. By doing comparative work, one can better learn what is Christian about this *Una Sancta*. One can pursue the central drama of a faith best by extricating it from its career and destiny in a single nation. Shi'ite Islam in Iran is far from being the whole of Islam and Spanish Catholicism far from being representative of all Catholicism, but this fact cannot be shown by those who fail to do comparative work.

If history profits from comparison and religion is a prime subject, then American religious history should be doubly prime. As Hudson and others have pointed out, America's claim to be a "chosen" nation, based on English claims that "God is so much English," or "we of England are the saved people," looks different when one listens only to provincial claims for election. The self-designation becomes qualified, if not absurd, when one hears Spaniards, Netherlanders, Swiss, Germans, Baltic and Balkan peoples, and Eastern European Christians making the same claim just as cogently and strenuously.

American religion is such an excellent topic for comparison because—and here again Hudson has beat us to the point—it is derivative. Almost all its denominations come from Europe, its religious impulses from Asia and Africa, or whence else its immigrants came. Even the homegrown groups tend to test themselves internationally at once. Within their first decade, Latter-Day Saints were in the Scandinavian nations and England, and Ellen Gould White immediately took her Adventism to Switzerland and New Zealand. Comparing Mormon and Adventist faiths in two locales informs the story of the faith.

Hudson's call for comparison, implied in his question, "How American is American religion?" came from his maturing as a historian after World War II when American distinctiveness and uniqueness were modish topics. Daniel J. Boorstin and other "consensus" historians were talking about American "givenness" and distinctiveness.[23] What was lost on so many budding historians was this: that to make and to back the claims for distinctiveness, people like Boorstin had to be cosmopolitan, had to inform themselves about other nations' distinctivenesses. Today, thanks to the recovery of ethnic, racial, and other forms of sub- and international history, the issue of American distinctiveness is less urgent, but comparison remains a promising field.

Why has the promise been denied? Why can one think of only a dozen out of many hundreds of titles by American historians of religion fifteen years after Hudson was doing his questioning and calling? Certainly the fields for comparison have only grown, and so have the motives for it. The reasons are complex, but we can point to some of them.

First is the way the American academy is organized. Few history departments allow themselves the luxury of comparative studies. Some individual historians may moonlight in the field, and their students profit from the perspective their teacher gains from such forays beyond the national model. But one glance at a curriculum will show that the students who proceed to Ph.D. work and teaching will not often find positions that will encourage them to transmit to their students an interplace model. They will be specialists in Russian history, American history, Ugandan history, or whatever. Religion departments, if they make room for a historian, will expect expertise in several eras and locales. The "American church historian" will teach general courses on the whole history of the church, for example. But honors courses and advanced seminars again follow national specialties.

As with the academy, so with research projects, funding, sabbaticals, and opportunities. It is difficult for the specialist in Slovakian or Brazilian religious history to convince the National Endowment for the Humanities or the American Council of Learned Societies or Guggenheim people that he or she can also have expertise in things American *and* elsewhere. Reading committees and referees will lack competence to pass on interplace models of research and may even carry prejudices against them. One is dreaming to imagine that the income of historians will be of a sort that permits them to do the grand tour of archives in many countries on their own.

I suppose one should be honest and mention that language is a problem. One would not feel confident writing on religion, of all things, without possessing competence in the language of its expression. While writers of American religious history who have been through the Ph.D. mill will (ordinarily) have had to demonstrate competence in French and German, it is not likely that competence means true skill. The passing of years between sabbaticals will mean an atrophy of linguistic abilities. Americanists may have devoted so much to England not only because most of the interconnecting 29 between the early seventeenth century and the mid-nineteenth century was Anglo-American but also because the documents were in English in both cases.

As one surveys the bleak landscape of comparative or connectional studies in American religious history *and* . . . , there are some consolations. There is no question but that historians, who have had interplace familiarity develop as a result of integrative graduate work, travel, teaching experience, or accident, use insights from that experience to gain perspective for American stories. But those are small consolations.

Perhaps Fredrickson is a model for religious historians. His topic, his obsession one might almost say, is slavery. There is no such thing as slavery in the abstract, in disembodied form. It is incarnate in places like the nineteenth-century American South and South Africa. By becoming expert on slavery, Fredrickson can find his choice of nation not quite arbitrary, but still not so commanding that he comes to be known chiefly as, say, a historian of South Africa. Some historians have worked on comparative utopianism or revolution or the frontier.

In the future it may be that, following Foster and Carwardine, historians of evangelicalism will carry their stories systematically beyond America. If the long advocated "women's history" gets beyond call toward synthesis, after an era of monographs, one must hope that comparative studies of women in American and German or Italian or Argentinian history will emerge.

For now there is not much to do but to enjoy the calls issued and the clues left by rare souls like Winthrop Hudson, and to go looking for oases on the sere landscape of comparative, connective, "interplace" history. Until then, we are likely to have to answer, when we are asked what we think about comparative history in religion, as Gandhi did when asked what he thought of civilization:

"I think it would be a good idea."

NOTES

[1] Guy E. Swanson, "Frameworks for Comparative Research: Structural Anthropology and the Theory of Action," *Comparative Methods in Sociology*, ed. Ivan Vallier (Berkeley: University of California Press, 1971), pp. 141, 145.

[2] George Fredrickson, *White Supremacy: A Comparative Study in American and South African History* (New York: Oxford University Press, 1981).

[3] Alan Simpson, *Puritanism in Old England and New* (Chicago: University of Chicago Press, 1955).

[4] Winthrop S. Hudson, *Nationalism and Religion in America: Concepts of American Identity and Mission* (New York: Harper & Row, Publishers, Inc., 1970), p. xii.

[5] Martin E. Marty, "Reinterpreting American Religious History in Context," *Reinterpretation in American Church History*, ed. Jerald C. Brauer (Chicago: University of Chicago Press, 1968), pp. 207-212. Reprinted by permission of The University of Chicago Press.

[6] Martin E. Marty, *The Modern Schism: Three Paths to the Secular* (New York: Harper & Row, Publishers, Inc., 1969). This is perhaps the appropriate place for Hudson's "squelching editor," to explain what happened to his own dreams of writing on "The Atlantic Community" and not only on American church history.

Guiding fifty completed dissertations was an informing experience—only one or two students could be talked into doing comparative work, and these were in what might be called "missionary history." The others found it possible to tell their stories while concentrating on single places, or else instinctively had their eye on curriculum, vocation, market, and granting systems. He himself later spent some years in administration and found it necessary, on a reduced load, to concentrate. Obligation in Chicago prevented him from even applying for grants to do research overseas (or, for that matter to apply for grants to do research anywhere beyond what could be accessible in Chicago), and this ruled out the constant confrontation with fresh sources one must need to write with confidence. And the demands made on him—and his whole agenda has been based on these demands—were in all cases but one uniquely American. That one exception, a comparison of "national church" ideas in England and America, resulted from a conference arranged by Professor William Hutchison of Harvard, a valiant attempt by a far-seeing comparative-minded historian. The experiment produced only two or three published papers, and the one just mentioned has languished in the quieter bibliographies. Finally, the "demand" has grown into a lifework, a multi-volume history of religion in twentieth-century America, a work that allows for little systematic comparison. *The Modern Schism* then stands alone, as a kind of tract-length illustration of what might have been had the Atlantic Community remained the subject. I hope that forays into Continental and British Isles religious history and curiosity about Third World destinies will inform the multi-volume work and similar writing in the decades ahead.

[7]C. Vann Woodward, "Herrenvolk Democracy," *The New York Review of Books*, March 5, 1981, p. 28.

[8]Raymond Grew, "The Case for Comparing Histories," *American Historical Review*, vol. 85, no. 4 (October, 1980), pp. 769, 764, 765, 767, 769, 777.

[9]Winthrop S. Hudson, "How American Is Religion in America?" *Reinterpretation*, ed. Brauer, pp. 153ff., especially noting pp. 155ff., 167.

[10]Charles I. Foster, *An Errand of Mercy: The Evangelical United Front* (Chapel Hill, N.C.: University of North Carolina Press, 1960); the Gladden book is cited by Winthrop S. Hudson, "How American Is Religion in America?" *Reinterpretation*, ed. Brauer, p. 160.

[11]Robert T. Handy, *A History of the Churches in the United States and Canada* (New York: Oxford University Press, 1977).

[12] Ernest Stoeffler, *Continental Pietism and Early American Christianity* (Grand Rapids, Mich.: Wm. B. Eerdmans Publishing Co., 1976).

[13]Richard Carwardine, *Transatlantic Revivalism: Popular Evangelicalism in Britain and America, 1790–1865* (Westport, Conn.: Greenwood Press, 1978).

[14]John A. Andrews, *Rebuilding the Christian Commonwealth: New England Congregationalists and Foreign Missions* (Lexington: University of Kentucky Press, 1976).

[15]John Fairbanks, ed., *The Missionary Enterprise in China and America* (Cambridge, Mass.: Harvard University Press, 1974).

[16]Cornelius J. Jaenen, *Friend and Foe: Aspects of French-Amerindian Cultural Contact in the Sixteenth and Seventeenth Centuries* (New York: Columbia University Press, 1976).

[17]George Foster Simpson, *Black Religions in the New World* (New York: Columbia University Press, 1978).

[18]Theodore Dwight Bozeman, *Protestants in an Age of Science: The Baconian Ideal and Antebellum American Religious Thought* (Chapel Hill, N.C.: University of North Carolina Press, 1977).

[19]Edwin Scott Gaustad, *George Berkeley in America* (New Haven, Conn.: Yale University Press, 1979).

[20]See S. S. Acquaviva, *The Decline of the Sacred in Industrial Society* (New York: Harper & Row, Publishers, Inc., 1979); and Michael Argyle and Benjamin Beit-Hallahmi, *The Social Psychology of Religion* (London: Routledge and Kegan Paul, 1975).

[21]Carlton J. H. Hayes, *Nationalism and Religion* (New York: Macmillan, Inc., 1960); for Hudson, see *Nationalism and Religion in America*.

[22]Abdel Ross Wentz, *A Basic History of Lutheranism in America* (Philadelphia: Muhlenberg, 1955).

[23]Daniel J. Boorstin, *The Genius of American Politics* (Chicago: University of Chicago Press, 1953), pp. 66, 158, 29-35, 163-170, 8-10, 10-22, 22-29 for various discussions of the "givenness" theme.

Protestant Patterns in Canada and the United States: Similarities and Differences

Robert T. Handy

Throughout his long and fruitful career Winthrop S. Hudson has emphasized the initial and continuing importance of transatlantic connections, especially with the British Isles, in the history of religion in North America. As an author who has written significant works dealing with both American and European Christianity, he has protested an American provincialism that "has obscured many of the interrelationships that have bound us to Europe." He urges the student of religion in America to examine the larger context of its religious life, for then one

> is astonished to discover how continuous and intimate have been the interplay of influences. A comparative study of religious developments at home and abroad quickly reveals that there is scarcely anything in the whole gamut of religious life in America that does not have its equivalent and usually its antecedent in Europe, and most often in the British Isles.[1]

An important though often overlooked part of the larger context of American religious life is Canada, where the transatlantic connection which has impinged on both lands has been even more visible than in the United States. In Hudson's words,

> English-speaking Canada and the United States, while politically separate, have in most other respects constituted a single society. Both have much in common, including regional differences. Both are products of the British colonial system in the New World. Both have encountered similar problems and have been subject to much the same influences. Both have major non-British segments in their population.[2]

Hudson also stresses the closeness and intimacy of religious ties between the two countries. Following up some of the themes he has suggested, along with those mentioned by others who have engaged in some comparative study of the Canadian and American religious scenes, this essay is devoted to a discussion of similarities and differences in the patterns of Protestant life and thought in the two lands.

The similarities have been and remain many and significant. Though the differences will be discussed here in some detail, they should be seen in the context of the striking similarities. There is much evidence for this—many individuals have "felt equally at home in both countries";[3] theological students educated in the one land have fulfilled their careers in the other; ministers have filled pulpits on both sides of the border; theological educators have moved to and from American seminaries and Canadian theological colleges.[4] Major Protestant denominational families have had long histories on both sides of the border, especially the Anglican, Methodist, Presbyterian, Congregational, Baptist, Lutheran and United Church—along with a number of historically smaller denominational groupings, such as the Mennonite and, more recently, the Pentecostal. In both countries there have been struggles to disestablish formerly privileged traditions which had been fully or partly established by law and publicly financed in certain colonies, provinces, or states.

Church historians of both nations have signaled, directly or more often indirectly, similarities as they have written about the mission of the churches to vast frontier regions, about awakenings and revivals in both rural and urban settings, and about the massive support for the foreign mission enterprise of the last two hundred years.[5] Though they have defined them somewhat differently, both nations have prided themselves on their patterns of religious freedom. Both are religiously pluralistic, but admittedly the spectrum of denominations in the United States, whose population has generally averaged about ten times larger, is much wider. With religious liberty and multiformity has gone voluntarism in religion. Drawing on his knowledge of the American scene, Sidney Mead has analyzed and defined voluntarism, whereby "the several religious groups became voluntary associations, equal before, but independent of the civil power of each other."[6] Voluntarism has long been a significant force in both religion and politics in Canada; as Robert Kelley, focusing on the mid-nineteenth century, put it in his important work *The Transatlantic Persuasion*, "Voluntarism, for the next several years the key term in Canadian politics, demanded that all churches be supported by the donations of their members."[7]

Along with pluralism and voluntarism in both lands has gone an intense religious activism; the dependence of the churches on their own resources for survival and growth has required a high level of activity and has inclined them to emphasize the activist over the contemplative side of the Christian traditions. As one American church historian put it, "Amazing activity in Christian service at home and abroad has been the chief glory of American Christianity," while another observer underlined the activism of religion in the United States by noting the low level of concern for the contemplative life among both Protestants and Catholics. "There is a marked absence among us of persons living the contemplative life," the then dean of the Harvard Divinity School once wrote.[8] The similarities are clear; in his pioneer effort to write the overall history of Christianity in Canada, H. H. Walsh commented at a number of points on the activist nature of Canadian church life, and in his concluding paragraph he summarized by saying, "Thus it would seem that activism, born of frontier revivalism, is still the authentic note of Canadian Christianity."[9]

In view of the political differences between these two North American nations, the similarities in religious patterns are striking; John Gwynne-Timothy once explained that "in a general sense, Canada had chosen, by the middle of the nineteenth century, to hold by the British political system and the American religious system."[10] At least for the nineteenth and into the early twentieth centuries, the religious system seemed to be working. De Tocqueville's comment on the American scene as he perceived it in 1831 has become famous: "There is no country in the world where the Christian religion retains a greater influence over the souls of men than in America."[11] One wonders if the memory of those words consciously or unconsciously influenced S. D. Clark's judgment more than a century later: "In few countries of the Western world has religion exerted as great an influence upon the development of the community as it has in Canada."[12] Thus, though the religious patterns of both lands are richly diversified, Protestant visitors and migrants across the border find quite similar ranges of ecclesiastical, liturgical, homiletical, and congregational practices.

Though the emphasis must fall first on the similarities, within this context it is also illuminating to seek to identify and understand the differences. Some of them are rooted in the obvious differences of geography, size of population, sources of immigration, political realities, and chronology (for example, in certain ways Canadian Confederation in 1867 was the equivalent of the American Federal Union in 1789). But scholars who have undertaken comparisons of the religious histories of the two countries have ventured some judgments and generalizations; ten points of comparison form the body of this essay. As is often true in such summaries, a number

35

of the points are interrelated; the significance of some of those listed earlier may be further illumined by some that follow.

1. While in the formation of the United States a revolutionary tradition which had important roots (among others) in the Enlightenment was victorious, in the continuing British provinces of North America this tradition was stoutly resisted. Few interpreters of American religion have called attention to the Enlightenment roots of the new American republic more strongly than has Sidney Mead, who declared that "most of the effectively powerful intellectual, social, and political leaders were rationalists."[13] In Canada, however, both the revolutionary spirit and the influence of the Enlightenment were largely rebuffed in both the English- and French-speaking British colonies of North America. As H. H. Walsh once put it, not only were the American and French revolutions generally rejected, but also

> perhaps even more significant in creating a basis for a common Canadianism was a third rejection, that of the Enlightenment. The closest either of the Canadas came to the Enlightenment, which has played such a prominent role in shaping reform movements in the rest of the new world, was during the rebellious era of the 1830s.[14]

The initial differences in philosophical and political starting points have surfaced from time to time in the anti-Americanism which has been a part of Canadian life. Certain differences in the religious tone of the two lands arise in part from these divergent historical roots.

2. Directly related to the first point is a second: the emergence of differing patterns of church and state in the two nations. In the United States the clauses on religion in the First Amendment to the Constitution, providing that "Congress shall make no law respecting an establishment of religion, or prohibiting the free exercise thereof," went into effect in 1791. The influence of the philosophy of Enlightenment was strong in that statement, which has frequently been interpreted in the light of Thomas Jefferson's image of the "wall of separation" between church and state. A number of the legal establishments of religion in the southern states disappeared in the late eighteenth century; by 1833 the last of the three New England establishments was brought to an end.

In Canada, though some of the same forces making for the separation of church and state were at work, notably pluralism and voluntarism, there has been no official constitutional statement like the First Amendment, nor has a concept like the "wall of separation" been generally accepted. There were indeed bitter struggles against established and privileged churches, most dramatically in the battle to secularize the Clergy Reserves, which were lands set aside, especially in Ontario, for the support of religion, then often interpreted to mean the Church of England. After long and bitter struggles, complicated by the political connection with Britain, the law that settled the issue in 1854 declared that "it is desirable to remove all semblance of connection between Church and State."[15] By providing for the continuation of stipends for life to the clergy then receiving them, and allowing them to commute the estimated total lump sum due them to their churches, the principle was to some extent compromised by the law. So, as John S. Moir has summarized the matter,

> Canada has rejected the European tradition of church establishment without adopting the American ideal of complete separation. Here no established church exists, yet neither is there an unscalable wall between religion and politics if for no other reason than that much of the Canadian constitution is unwritten.

Hence Canadians "assume the presence of an unwritten separation of church and state," he adds, in an "ill-defined—and difficult to define—relationship" which is peculiarly Canadian.[16]

When the Parliament of Canada passed the "Canadian Bill of Rights" after the middle of the twentieth century, it did declare that, along with other rights, freedom of religion has "existed and shall exist without discrimination by reason of race, national origin, colour, religion or sex"; yet this is not a parallel to the First Amendment, for, as M. James Penton has explained, "there is no restraint on the powers of either the Parliament of Canada or provincial legislatures in the way there is on those of Congress or American state legislatures." He goes on to say that "instead of there being 'a wall of separation between church and state,' in Canada there is what may be described as a quasi-establishment."[17]

Edward R. Norman puts the matter in somewhat similar terms. He suggests that the three stages of development in the relationship of church and state can be discerned in the Anglo-American world: public confessionalism, the "establishment" of nonsectarian Christianity, and strict neutrality on the part of the state. "Now it would appear that Britain, Canada, and the United States are still very largely in the second stage of development—the stage where nonsectarian religious opinion is accorded a sort of established status," he concludes. "The laws and customs of all three nations continue to be shot through with supports for religious belief and actual aids, direct and indirect, to the churches." He views Britain as closer to the original confessionalism and the United States as making some slight advances into a fuller practice of stage-three neutrality, but finds that "Canada is pretty centrally in the middle zone."[18] While

Americans generally believe that the proper safeguard for religious freedom is the formal separation of church and state, the Canadians find their religious freedom secure with a different understanding of what separation is.

3. This leads directly to another closely related point: in a number of Canadian provinces, denominational schools are subsidized by public funds, something which has not happened in the United States except in isolated instances, despite many pressures. The British North America Act, which enabled the formation of the Dominion of Canada in 1867, put jurisdiction over education under provincial authority, but with the specific provision that no right or privilege with respect to denominational schools would be affected. There have been many conflicts over the public funding of denominational schools in both lands, but the solutions have been quite different. In Canada, the patterns vary from province to province. For example, in Newfoundland, the schools are denominationally controlled; in Quebec a dual school system is maintained; in Ontario, Saskatchewan, and Alberta there is legal provision for Roman Catholic separate schools; while the situation in British Columbia is most like that of the United States.[19]

It has been at the level of post-secondary education, however, that intense church-state conflicts have erupted in Canada. Norman finds that "second only to the clergy reserves controversy, it was the university question which most sharply focused the clash between religious pluralism and the establishment principle in British North America."[20] Political and religious passions ran high in Ontario when the secular University of Toronto was created in 1849 and the appropriated endowments of the Anglican King's College were applied to it. Later in Manitoba, however, a new pattern was worked out whereby denominational colleges affiliated with secular, provincial universities and thus gained access to public funds. In the last few years this has meant that even denominational theological colleges have been aided by such funds.[21]

4. While American Protestant life has been characterized as having an anti-historical bias and being marked by a disregard of history, interpreters of the Canadian scene have stressed the churches' devotion to historical tradition and continuity. Sidney Mead has observed that the American denominations of left-wing sectarian background appealed "over all churches and historical traditions to the authority of the beliefs and practices of primitive Christianity as pictured in the New Testament." As groups representing such backgrounds grew in size and influence in the late eighteenth and early nineteenth centuries, this perspective became widely pervasive. A number of swiftly growing denominations were influenced

by "the idea of pure and normative beginnings to which return was possible; the idea that the intervening history was largely that of aberrations and corruptions which was better ignored; and the idea of building anew in the American wilderness on the true and ancient foundations."[22] These ideas were reflected in much American preaching and were especially evident in the rise of the indigenous Christian (Disciples) denominational family.

Interpreters of Canadian church history, however, do not find much evidence of such ideas in Canada. Goldwin French, for example, finds that Mead's analysis does not fit the land to the north. While admitting that the continuity and partnership of Canadian churches with the historic tradition of Western Christianity has led on occasion to irrelevant controversies and has encouraged doctrinal conservatism, French nevertheless has found that such links have had the "positive merit" of inhibiting "the emergence of that sense of historylessness so characteristic of nineteenth-century American Protestantism." Quoting from *The Lively Experiment,* he reports that few Canadian preachers would have argued, as did John Cotton,

> that any church was a near replica of what would be established "if the Lord Jesus were here himself in person". Significantly, too, no major Christian denomination would claim with the Disciples of Christ that it was "picking up", the "lost threads of primitive Christianity".[23]

Too much should not be made of this point, for exceptions to the overall general trends could be found in both lands, but the basic distinction seems sound.

5. The fifth point is closely linked to the previous one: Canadian church life has tended to be more conservative and churchly than that of the United States. The British North American provinces that did not support the American revolution and then received thousands of Loyalist migrants clung more firmly to European traditions than did the states to the south. Efforts to combine traditional and indigenous influences have been more characteristic of Canadian religious history than the yearning for fresh starts and new departures that has been a conspicuous part of the religious life of the *novus ordo seclorum* south of the border. French has observed that "in this light the destiny of Canada was not to figure as a great 39 experiment, cut off from the history of its peoples, but to prolong and blend its traditions in a new context."[24] John Webster Grant has further emphasized this Canadian Christian commitment to deep-rooted traditions in such summaries as this:

> A corollary to this constant reference to an existing Christendom was the virtual lack of any suggestion that the task of the churches in Canada might be to institute a new Christian society that would

be an alternative to older ones and perhaps even render them obsolete. The recurrent theme of a new Christendom led in the United States to almost endless experimentation. In Canada, by comparison, church life was strikingly devoid of the bizarre or even the novel.[25]

Grant illustrates the lack of innovativeness by noting that Canadian religious controversies were usually reflections from the outside and that suspected heretics were popularizers of critical ideas imported from Europe.

The relationship between this point and the second one is evident. S. D. Clark has commented that "the close alliance between the state and the church in Canada has preserved more fully the influence of religion within an established ecclesiastical system," contrasting that with the American system, and John S. Moir has theorized that

Canada . . . has preserved churchism to preserve itself. Whenever military, economic, political or cultural absorption by the United States threatened, as in 1776, 1812, 1837, 1911 or even 1957, Canada has turned to its counter-revolutionary tradition for inspiration. And ecclesiasticism is a traditional part of that tradition.[26]

Again, this point must not be pressed too far. There has been much traditionalism in American religious life and considerable boldness and daring in Canadian.

6. The theological life of Protestantism in Canada has been more under the domination of European, especially British, scholarship than has that in the United States. Gerald R. Cragg lamented that

Anglo-Canadian theology has been painfully diffident, content to repeat what others have formulated, and hesitant to write anything at all. To Edinburgh and to Glasgow, as to Oxford and Cambridge, we are immeasurably indebted. It is unfortunate that our gratitude has so effectively stultified our originality.[27]

Grant has spoken on the same point: "Many writers have called attention to the scarcity in the Canadian church of intellectual originality and mystical imagination, although learning and piety were always highly valued."[28] A striking, graphic illustration of the hold of the British theological tradition on Canadian Protestant thought has been given by H. Keith Markell: the new Divinity Hall in Montreal, completed in 1931 under the direction of the Joint Board of the Anglican and United Church theological colleges, was decorated with the portraits of eleven British Christian notables—ten English and one Scottish.[29]

American Protestants, much larger in number, can point to a more fully developed theological tradition, from such figures as

Edwards through Bushnell, Hodge and Nevin to Rauschenbusch and the Niebuhrs,[30] but must yet come to terms with Mead's observation that theological structure is the outstanding failure of religion in America.[31]

7. The major denominational families have followed somewhat distinctive historical paths in the two nations so that despite their similarities—an emphasis made early in this essay and to be kept in mind throughout—peculiarly "American" and "Canadian" characteristics have long been discernible, both with respect to the denominations themselves and to the larger Protestant scenes of which they form a part. The denominational spectrum in Canada has not been as wide as would be expected in a land much smaller in population. Some seven denominations contained the overwhelming majority of Canadian church members in the nineteenth century: Roman Catholic, Anglican, Methodist, Presbyterian, Congregational, Baptist, and Lutheran. But in both lands, despite many changes and the arrival of new religious bodies, the denominational patterns that emerged in the nineteenth century have persisted. In 1961 in Canada, for example, six denominational families claimed an estimated following, active or nominal, of over 90 percent of the population: Catholic, United (virtually all Methodists and Congregationalists and over half the Presbyterians formed the United Church of Canada in 1925), Anglican, Presbyterian, Baptist, and Lutheran, so that Grant could report that "the religious affiliations of Canadians had been fixed, by and large, several decades before confederation."[32] In America, the two denominations that became the Protestant giants by mid-nineteenth century remain easily the numerical leaders in the late twentieth century.

The denominational families that have been conspicuous in Canada over the last two centuries were also active on the American scene, but they developed along somewhat different lines and were combined in quite different proportions; the probing of these realities provides many clues to the differing church histories of the two countries. Early in the nineteenth century there were close ties, sometimes organic, between the denominational families. As the century unfolded, however, many of the ties weakened as a number of Canadian churches came to look less to the United States and more to Great Britain for models and guidance. In view of the history of Loyalist migrations from the south following the American revolution, it is understandable why Church of England folk tended to look across the Atlantic to Mother Church; not until after mid-century did a sense of *Canadian* Anglicanism begin to take hold. Goldwin French typified the Anglican clergy of early nineteenth-century Canada in these words:

Frequently they were educated in the ancient English or Irish universities, and they brought with them an awareness of social distinctions, and a taste for civilized pursuits that necessarily affected their work. For them, the real world was the settled rural order of England, Ireland, or the old colonies, from which they came.[33]

The links between American and Canadian Methodism were originally very strong, but the turning point came with the war of 1812-1814, when the American invasion of Canada provoked a nationalist reaction. Closer ties with British Methodism were formed, and the episcopate disappeared, consistent with the English pattern. Canadian Methodism was much divided; a main theme in its nineteenth-century history was its struggle to bring together its various divisions into one church, finally achieved in 1884. The Congregational churches, strongest in the Maritimes, had developed from the outset from both British and American sources; but largely under the impact of both the American revolution and the war of 1812–1814, the tradition had become divided and weakened until help came from England in the person of Henry Wilkes, aided by various missionary societies.[34] Presbyterians also came to Canada both from the United States and the British Isles, especially from Scotland, but again, after the turmoil from 1775 to 1815, "Presbyterianism in the colonies of British North America acquired a strongly British flavour."[35] Or to say it the other way around, "American influences had been purged from Canadian Presbyterianism a long generation before Confederation, thanks to a combination of religious and political conservatism."[36] A similar story can be told about the Baptists; their beginnings in Canada can be viewed primarily as an extension of Baptist work from the south, and the ties remained close, with some Baptist associations straddling the border. The war of 1812-1814 served to disrupt some of these links, but the connection remained closer than in some of the other denominations.[37] The story of Canadian Lutherans, who like the Baptists are a small group on the Canadian scene, is even more complex, and the ties with American Lutheranism remained close; indeed, the largest Lutheran body in Canada today is a member of the Lutheran Church in America.[38] In general, however, the trend for denominations to look to Britain rather than to the United States was strong in the nineteenth century.

42

Meanwhile, in the American context these same denominational families were being influenced and reshaped by their American experiences. Three of them (Baptist, Methodist, Presbyterian), for example, were being torn apart during the struggle over slavery so that at the same time that Canadian denominational families were moving toward internal unity, their American analogs were dividing. In the States the spectacular growth of two black Baptist and three black Methodist bodies after the Civil War introduced a factor quite unlike anything on the Canadian scene, where blacks have remained a small minority of the population.[39] American Lutheranism was being redirected by the vast influx of German and Scandinavian peoples in the nineteenth century, whereas Canadian Lutheranism remained relatively very much smaller. But of particular importance in understanding the differing religious histories is the fact that by mid-nineteenth century two American denominational families had become giants among the Protestant bodies, and have remained so—Baptists and Methodists. Their spread and influence strongly affected the overall tone of American Protestantism and sharpened its inner tensions as the revivalistic styles they adopted were both widely imitated and yet in some quarters stoutly resisted. Hence, though revivalistic evangelicalism is also an important topic in Canadian history, it was not as influential a force across such a wide spectrum of denominations as in the United States; as French has aptly noted, "At no point did any denomination dominate the Canadian religious scene in the degree that Methodists and Baptists dominated American Protestantism."[40] Not only did the sister denominations develop along somewhat distinctive lines, but also the overall denominational mix was quite different in the two nations.

8. The historical understanding within each country that it was a Christian nation came to have quite a different meaning and tone. This also relates to the matter of different denominational mixes, but at this point the reality of the Roman Catholic church, by all odds the largest single church in both lands, must be considered. That church had already become the largest single religious body in America by mid-nineteenth century. But through the nineteenth and into the following century, it was to a considerable degree a church of immigrants and, though it did have some regional concentrations, was widely distributed geographically. At least until World War I, it was seeking to demonstrate that it had become "naturalized" and was at home in American culture. After that time, it took on some of the aspects of a national church and now claims an inclusive membership of nearly fifty million—more than twice the size of the two largest Protestant denominational families combined.

In Canada, though the Roman Catholic church has long had English-speaking components in all the provinces, it has, of course, also had its French-speaking concentration in Quebec. At the present time, that church claims an inclusive membership of more than ten million, nearly half the population of Canada, and is nearly five

43

times the size of the next largest denomination, the United Church of Canada.

Through the nineteenth and early twentieth centuries in America, Protestants, though denominationally divided, were collectively in the majority, were convinced that theirs was a "Christian" (by which they meant a "Protestant") nation, and were confident that the religious future belonged to them. As the new century dawned, the white Protestant leadership of the land anticipated that it would be a Christian century, one in which the Anglo-Saxon people would become dominant in the world scene. In part because of Protestant divisions and subdivisions, however, they often transferred their hopes for the unity and destiny of the whole people under God to the nation. The voices of Catholics, blacks, and others who questioned this white Protestant interpretation of the nation's destiny were angrily shouted down by the majority, until in the later twentieth century the various minorities have grown, matured, and developed firm bases for pressing their own interpretations of the American present and future.[41]

In the Canadian situation, however, neither the English Protestant nor the French Catholic element has been able convincingly to offer an overall religious interpretation of their one land. Whereas Americans have often given a providential interpretation to their founding and destiny as a nation, often in the form of a "civil" or "public" religion,[42] the Canadians have regarded the Confederation of 1867 more as a political or economic matter. Grant has declared that "Canadians have always recognized the secular origins of their nation."[43] N. K. Clifford has traced nineteenth-century Protestant efforts to present a vision of Canada as "His Dominion," but he concludes that they failed because the churches were unable to articulate an ideology of Canadianism acceptable to those of other backgrounds.[44] The dream of Anglo-Saxon world hegemony was certainly not absent from Canadian life; for example, in speaking of Canada's first liberal premier, Alexander Mackenzie (1873–1878), Robert Kelley interprets his commitment to

> a mission which he saw the British and the Canadians carrying forward jointly with the Americans, all being branches of the Anglo-Saxon race. They were a chosen people, he said in 1859 in a carefully prepared address on Anglo-Saxonism, sharing the great mission of spreading Christian civilization through their unique powers of self-governance, and their industrial power.[45]

But there was no way of winning the French-Canadian people to that vision, and an alternate vision of a multiethnic land developed. In French's summary of the matter, "lacking a generally acceptable religious interpretation of national purpose, we were unable to generate in our society the dynamic egoism, so deeply embedded in American nationalism."[46]

Though the shattering events of the last few decades have disclosed the limitations and distortions of the earlier dream of American unity and destiny, it remains an important part of the nation's history, though not without its contemporary overtones. In Canada, political events have highlighted the basic national duality which prevented the earlier development of a similar dream.

9. One of the striking parallels in the religious history of both nations was the emergence of a social gospel to a conspicuous but controversial place in the later nineteenth and early twentieth centuries; we are reminded again that this probing of differences is to be viewed only after stressing the similarities. Grant's summary points to the interrelationships.

> Protestant social concern represented in the main an overflow of the "social gospel" that had come to maturity in the United States about 1895, although there was a constant fertilization of British ideas as well. Social radicalism gained a foothold during the depression years of the early 1890s, but it was stimulated even more by Canada's later crisis of growth. Canadians continued to respond to developments elsewhere, and such American books as Walter Rauschenbusch's *Christianity and the Social Crisis* (1907) and *The Social Creed of the Churches* issued by the Federal Council of Churches (1908) were equally influential on both sides of the border.[47]

The social gospel in both countries reached its peak of influence in the churches at about the same time, just prior to World War I. In both, the social gospel encountered inner divisions, crises, and decline following that war.[48] Both movements had their basic support from similar parts of the socioeconomic spectrum; Grant's judgment that "despite its insistence on concern for labour and the poor, the social gospel was essentially a bourgeois phenomenon" parallels Hudson's view that it "was almost exclusively a manifestation of middle-class idealism."[49]

Certain important differences can be indicated, however. The American social gospel's range of influence across the wider denominational spectrum was more limited, in part because the southern branches of the Methodist, Baptist, and Presbyterian traditions were more resistant to such social emphasis than the northern ones. Conversely, the social emphasis appears to have been stronger in the American Episcopal than in the Canadian Anglican church.[50] But one could not make the claim for the American churches that Allen has done for the Canadian: "No major Protestant denomination in the nation escaped the impact of the social gospel, and few did not contribute some major figure to the movement."[51]

45

In another respect the social gospel proved to have a more lasting effect on the Canadian than on the American scene—in the realm of politics. In the United States the movement did contribute in certain ways to the popularity of Progressivism in the first two decades of the present century, and the movement had some effect in smoothing the way for Franklin D. Roosevelt's New Deal during the Great Depression. In Canada, however, the political effect of the social gospel was more direct; Allen can say of the 1921 election, "The Progressive triumph was, among other things, a triumph of the social gospel."[52] In the depression years persons who had been conspicuous in various wings of that movement, notably J. S. Woodsworth, participated in the formation and growth of the Canadian Commonwealth Federation, which in the next decade became New Democratic Party, carrying Thomas C. Douglas to victory in Saskatchewan, where he formed a successful socialist government with the help of many church people. This political significance of the social gospel seems to be explainable in part because the movement succeeded in influencing radical, rural, and farm labor movements in the prairie provinces, while in the United States the central focus of the social gospel was strongly on the urban industrial worker.

Social Christianity has its conservative as well as progressive and radical aspects; fundamentalist and conservative evangelical Christianity in America did have serious concern for social service and justice.[53] But this was nothing like the political triumph of William Aberhart, pastor of the Calgary Prophetic Church and a famous radio preacher, who combined an appeal to fundamentalists of many types with a program of Social Credit (each adult to receive a monthly cash dividend drawn out of natural resources) which brought him to the premiership of Alberta in 1935.[54] Both the similarities and differences of social Christianity in the two lands are revealing and need further analysis and interpretation.

10. The ecumenical styles of Canadian and American Protestants, despite many similarities, have been characterized by an important difference in approach. In the United States, though there was considerable talk of church union in the twentieth century, the significant developments were along the lines of cooperation and federation. A whole series of cooperative agencies were developed, such as the Foreign Missions Conference of North America, the Home Missions Council of North America, and the International Council of Religious Education.[55] Canadian Protestants were involved in these movements. The agencies were supported by various denominational boards; without initially displacing such agencies, American Protestants decided to develop a federation of denominations. So in 1908 the Federal Council of the Churches of

46

Christ in America was formed by thirty-three American denominations. Thus, American ecumenical efforts early in the century were largely channeled into these cooperative and federative agencies.

The Canadian ecumenical problem was somewhat different. In a vast land with a small population, tiny congregations of the various denominations competed with each other for survival. A drive for church union across confessional lines had begun in earnest by the dawn of the new century. A Basis of Union that seriously engaged the Methodist, Presbyterian, and Congregational churches was ready by 1908. The search for organic union across denominational lines thus took precedence over the cooperative or federational approach. The hope was for a national Protestant church that might attract others into the union; as the preamble to the Basis said, "It shall be the policy of The United Church to foster the spirit of unity in the hope that this sentiment of unity may in due time, so far as Canada is concerned, take shape in a Church which may fittingly be described as national."[56] The high expectations of that period were dimmed as sharp differences of opinion emerged among Presbyterians, and a long, divisive struggle followed. When the union was finally consummated in 1925, a large minority stayed out and continued the Presbyterian Church in Canada.[57] But despite the painful struggle and the scars it left, the union of 1925 was a major event in the history of church union. Grant affirms that, in almost every case,

> unions between comparable groups have been achieved in Canada earlier than in any other Western nation, and the union that brought The United Church of Canada into being almost fifty years ago has not yet been duplicated in Britain, the United States or any other British dominion. This apparently inexorable trend has clearly been a major motif in Canadian church history, although its effects thus far have largely been limited to the middle range of the ecclesiastical spectrum.[58]

The attention given to church union meant that less was given to the cooperative or federative approach. The formation of the Canadian Council of Churches did not occur until 1944, and it was then largely the consequence of a decision made in the United States to merge the Federal Council with other major interdenominational agencies to form the National Council of the Churches of Christ in the U.S.A., which was finally accomplished in 1950. The Canadian Council has not played the role in Canadian church life that the Federal/National Council has in America, but the formation of the United Church of Canada was one of the leading ecumenical achievements of the century.

In overall summary, it can be concluded that national trends in both lands have impinged on their religious histories. Churches which have many similarities have tended to move somewhat in isolation from each other. Though the differences do need to be seen for what they are, they should not be allowed to obscure the deep-rooted similarities among the various Protestant traditions of the two nations. Winthrop Hudson, as both church historian and church leader, has been critical of nationalistic trends in both nations that have brushed aside a long and important history of church cooperation across the border.[59] At the North American Faith and Order Conference in Oberlin in 1957, he urged the importance of close cooperation among the churches of the two countries and presented an amendment to a major action of the Conference to that end, which was unanimously accepted.[60] It is hoped that this historical summary and interpretation of similarities and differences may contribute also to that end.

NOTES

[1] Winthrop S. Hudson, "How American Is Religion in America?" *Reinterpretation in American Church History*, ed. Jerald C. Brauer (Chicago: University of Chicago Press, 1968), pp. 155-156. Reprinted by permission of The University of Chicago Press.

[2] Winthrop S. Hudson, "The Interrelationships of Baptists in Canada and the United States," *Foundations*, vol. 23, no. 1 (January-March, 1980), p. 22.

[3] *Ibid.*, p. 23.

[4] For example, see Robert T. Handy, "The Influence of Canadians on Baptist Theological Education in the United States," *Foundations*, vol. 23, no. 1, (January-March, 1980), pp. 42-56.

[5] For example, see such standard histories of Christianity in Canada and the United States as H. H. Walsh, *The Christian Church in Canada* (Toronto: The Ryerson Press, 1956) and *The Church in the French Era* (Toronto: The Ryerson Press, 1966); John S. Moir, *The Church in the British Era* (Toronto: McGraw-Hill Ryerson, 1972); John Webster Grant, *The Church in the Canadian Era* (Toronto: McGraw-Hill Ryerson, 1972); Winthrop S. Hudson, *Religion in America* (New York: Charles Scribner's Sons, 1965, 1973, 1981); Sydney E. Ahlstrom, *A Religious History of the American People* (New Haven, Conn.: Yale University Press, 1972); Robert T. Handy, *A History of the Churches in the United States and Canada* (New York: Oxford University Press, 1977).

[6] Sidney Mead, *The Lively Experiment: The Shaping of Christianity in America* (New York: Harper & Row, Publishers, Inc., 1963), p. 113.

[7] Robert Kelley, *The Transatlantic Persuasion: The Liberal-Democratic Mind in the Age of Gladstone* (New York: Alfred A. Knopf, Inc., 1969), p. 373.

[8] Lefferts A. Loetscher, *The Broadening Church: A Study of Issues in the Presbyterian Church since 1869* (Philadelphia: University of Pennsylvania Press, 1954), p. 92; Willard A. Sperry, *Religion in America* (New York: Macmillan, Inc., 1946), p. 135.

[9] H. H. Walsh, *The Christian Church in Canada*, p. 391.

[10]Philip LeBlanc and Arnold Edinborough, eds., *One Church, Two Nations?* (Don Mills: Longmans, 1968), p. 41.

[11]Alexander de Tocqueville, *Democracy in America* (New York: Alfred A. Knopf, Inc., 1945), vol. 1, p. 303.

[12]S. D. Clark, *The Developing Canadian Community*, 2nd ed. (Toronto: University of Toronto Press, 1968), p. 168.

[13]Mead, *The Lively Experiment*, p. 36.

[14]"A Canadian Christian Tradition," *The Churches and the Canadian Experience*, ed. John Webster Grant (Toronto: The Ryerson Press, 1963), p. 146.

[15]18 Victoria Cap. 2 (1854), as cited in *Church and State in Canada, 1627-1867: Basic Documents*, ed. John S. Moir (Toronto: McClelland & Stewart, Ltd., 1967), p. 244. See also Alan Wilson, *The Clergy Reserves of Upper Canada: A Canadian Mortmain* (Toronto: University of Toronto Press, 1968).

[16]Moir, *Church and State in Canada*, p. xiii.

[17]M. James Penton, "Religious Freedom and Canadian Law: An Historical Evaluation," *The Canadian Society of Church History Papers, 1980* (mimeographed, 1981), pp. 32, 33, 42.

[18]Edward R. Norman, *The Conscience of the State in North America* (Cambridge: Cambridge University Press, 1968), pp. 184-185.

[19]Gerald M. Craig, *The United States and Canada* (Cambridge, Mass.: Harvard University Press, 1968), pp. 35-36; see also C. B. Sissons, *Church and State in Canadian Education* (Toronto: The Ryerson Press, 1959).

[20]Norman, *The Conscience of the State*, p. 171.

[21]See D. C. Masters, *Protestant Church Colleges in Canada: A History* (Toronto: University of Toronto Press, 1966), especially pp. 89-132; Robin S. Harris, *A History of Higher Education in Canada, 1663–1960* (Toronto: University of Toronto Press, 1976); Charles M. Johnston, *McMaster University*, 2 vols., (Toronto: University of Toronto Press, 1976, 1981); Robert T. Handy, "Trends in Canadian and American Theological Education, 1880-1980: Some Comparisons," *Theological Education*, vol. 18, no. 2 (Spring, 1982), pp. 175-218.

[22]Mead, *The Lively Experiment*, pp. 109, 111.

[23]Goldwin S. French, "The Impact of Christianity on Canadian Culture and Society to 1867," *Theological Bulletin*, McMaster Divinity College, no. 3 (January, 1968), p. 19.

[24]Goldwin S. French, "The Evangelical Creed in Canada," *The Shield of Achilles: Aspects of Canada in the Victorian Age*, ed. W. L. Morton (Toronto: McClelland & Stewart, Ltd., 1968), p. 29.

[25]Grant, *The Church in the Canadian Era*, p. 214. Copyright © McGraw-Hill Ryerson Limited, 1972. Reprinted by permission.

[26]Clark, *The Developing Canadian Community*, p. 181; John S. Moir, "Sectarian Tradition in Canada," in *The Churches and the Canadian Experience*, ed. Grant, p. 132. Paul R. Dekar has questioned the thesis that Canadian Christianity has been less "enthusiastic," more churchly, more conservative, and closer to European patterns than those of the United States. He believes that the utilization of the history of religion's approach to the study of Canadian church history will lead to greater depth and understanding of such "inner happenings" as devotions, worldviews, and values of ordinary members of the various traditions. See "Church History of Canada: Where from Here?" *Theodolite: A Journal of Christian Thought and Practice*, vol. 5 (Summer, 1980), p. 11. Certainly such an approach should be fruitful, and can add much to our understanding of the history of Christianity in North America; at this point I suspect that it may modify and deepen but perhaps not radically alter the broad generalizations on this point that have been offered.

49

[27] Gerald R. Cragg, "The European Wellsprings of Canadian Christianity," *Theological Bulletin*, McMaster Divinity College, no. 3 (January, 1968), p. 9.

[28] Grant, *The Church in the Canadian Era*, p. 13.

[29] H. Keith Markell, *The Faculty of Religious Studies, McGill University, 1948–1978* (Montreal: Faculty of Religious Studies, 1979), p. 11.

[30] Sydney E. Ahlstrom, ed., *Theology in America: The Major Protestant Voices from Puritanism to Neo-Orthodoxy* (Indianapolis: Bobbs-Merrill, 1967).

[31] Mead, *The Lively Experiment*, p. 15.

[32] Grant, *The Church in the Canadian Era*, p. 223.

[33] French, "The Impact of Christianity," pp. 20-21.

[34] Earl B. Eddy, "The Congregational Tradition in Canada," *The Churches and the Canadian Experience*, ed. Grant, pp. 25-37.

[35] Neil G. Smith, "The Presbyterian Tradition in Canada," in *ibid.*, p. 38.

[36] John S. Moir, "American Influences on Canadian Protestant Churches Before Confederation," *Church History*, vol. 36, no. 4 (December, 1967), p. 448.

[37] Hudson, "Interrelationships of Baptists," pp. 22-41, especially pp. 22-27.

[38] E. Clifford Nelson, ed., *The Lutherans in North America* (Philadelphia: Fortress Press, 1975).

[39] See Robin W. Winks, *The Blacks in Canada: A History* (New Haven, Conn.: Yale University Press, 1971).

[40] In *The Shield of Achilles*, ed. Morton, p. 22.

[41] This theme has been developed in many places—e.g., Martin E. Marty, *Righteous Empire: The Protestant Experience in America* (New York: The Dial Press, 1970), and Robert T. Handy, *A Christian America: Protestant Hopes and Historical Realities* (New York: Oxford University Press, 1971).

[42] See Russell E. Richey and Donald G. Jones, eds., *American Civil Religion* (New York: Harper & Row, Publishers, Inc., 1974).

[43] Grant, *The Church in the Canadian Era*, p. 24.

[44] Keith Clifford, "His Dominion: A Vision in Crisis," *Studies in Religion/Sciences Religieuses*, vol. 2, no. 4 (Spring, 1973), pp. 315-326.

[45] Kelley, *The Transatlantic Persuasion*, p. 392.

[46] French, "The Impact of Christianity," p. 34.

[47] Grant, *The Church in the Canadian Era*, p. 101.

[48] Cf. C. Howard Hopkins *The Rise of the Social Gospel in American Protestantism, 1865-1915* (New Haven, Conn.: Yale University Press, 1940); and Richard Allen, *The Social Passion: Religion and Social Reform in Canada, 1914-28* (Toronto: University of Toronto Press, 1971).

[49] Grant, *The Church in the Canadian Era*, p. 103, and Hudson, *Religion in America*, p. 315.

[50] Allen, *The Social Passion*, p. 15.

[51] *Ibid.*, p. 15.

[52] *Ibid.*, p. 218.

[53] Norris Magnuson, *Salvation in the Slums: Evangelical Social Work, 1865-1920* (Metuchen, N.J.: Scarecrow Press, 1977).

[54] See W. E. Mann, *Sect, Cult, and Church in Alberta* (Toronto: University of Toronto Press, 1955), especially pp. 119-122.

[55] Samuel McCrea Cavert, *Church Cooperation and Unity in America: A Historical Review, 1900–1970* (New York: Association Press, 1970).

[56] As quoted by Grant, *The Canadian Experience of Church Union* (London: Lutterworth Press, 1967), p. 20.

[57] A vast collection of literature has gathered around this event and its interpretation; an early basic work was by Claris E. Silcox, *Church Union in Canada: Its Causes and Consequences* (New York: Institute of Social and Religious Research, 1933).

[58]Grant, *The Church in the Canadian Era*, p. 211. Since that paragraph was written, the United Church of Australia has come into being, also uniting Congregationalists, Methodists, and Presbyterians.

[59]Winthrop S. Hudson, "Interrelationships of Baptists," p. 24.

[60]Paul S. Minear, ed., *The Nature of the Unity We Seek* (St. Louis: The Bethany Press, 1958), p. 154.

On the Soul of Nations: Religion and Nationalism in Canada and the United States

Paul R. Dekar

"Canada is a country without a soul."

—*American quoted by Rupert Brooke*[1]

"What is America? A nation with the soul of a church."

—*G. K. Chesterton*[2]

Probably a crab would be outraged if it could hear us classify it as a crustacean and thus dispose of it. "'I am no such thing,' it would say; 'I am MYSELF, MYSELF alone.'"[3] Thus it is with individuals, and so too with nations, the United States and Canada not excepted. The danger in this is clear, for ours is an age not only of nationalism but also of nationalisms run amok. The threat to our common survival is very real.

Throughout a distinguished career, Winthrop S. Hudson has addressed two themes suggested above: the need for comparative study and the relationship between religion and nationalism. He has insisted that "the United States can properly be understood only as an integral part of a larger European society."[4] To delineate precisely how the United States can be so understood, Hudson established an agenda for the next generation of scholars in a seminal essay entitled "How American Is Religion in America?" For Hudson, the need for such study is pressing. Observed Hudson, 53

Canadians do not want to be thought of as Americans. Americans do not want to be identified as Englishmen. Englishmen do not regard themselves as Europeans. Europe is across the Channel. And on the Continent people think of themselves as belonging to distinctive and self-contained national cultures—a French culture, a Norwegian culture, a Spanish culture. This emphasis on individuality has often fostered a false sense of separation and autonomy by obscuring the interrelations and reciprocal influences that have bound these nations together.[5]

From comparative study several benefits derive: service of truth; deepening of corporate and self-identity; recognition of belonging to a community larger than one's own; and, for the Christian, increased awareness of being related in intimate fashion to the whole church of Christ. Without such study, Hudson warned, one becomes easy prey to nativism, jingoism, cultural and intellectual isolation, and messianism.[6]

To avoid these dangers and fully to know ourselves, we must be familiar with the nature and place of religion in public life. Even (and perhaps especially) in modern times nations have tended to claim God as somehow at work in their affairs. However, no consensus has existed among politicians, religious leaders, or the general public concerning the extent of such claims, or how they are to be used. Despite the proliferation of religious studies programs in Canada and the United States and the flood of lively scholarly research on the theme, there has not even emerged consensus as to what questions to ask or how to embark on the search for links between religion and national self-understanding.

To this search the historian Winthrop Hudson has much to contribute. Hudson began his career with English political theory, turned to the story of religion in the United States, and continued with related transatlantic themes, especially English and American identity, mission, and destiny. Recently, he has returned to his earliest interest by looking at the Elizabethan settlement. In this progression Canada does not figure prominently. However, Hudson has not ignored Canadian-United States connections. He has explored the interrelationships of Baptists in Canada and the United States and, in an extended review of Robert T. Handy's *A History of the Churches in the United States and Canada*, decried the nationalistic trends which rend asunder religious ties which otherwise have been close and intimate.[7]

This would not appear to be an auspicious time to explore such volatile subjects as religion and nationalism in Canada and the United States. Economic tensions between the two countries persist, and there seems to be no common perception regarding the nature of the problems or of their possible solutions. Politically, Canada is in the midst of a constitutional crisis which threatens the future of the nation. At the same time, Canadians continue to demonstrate intense fascination with the United States while thinking of themselves as a different and superior kind of America, an authentically American alternative to what is happening in the United States.[8] For its part the United States, spurred on by the so-called Moral

Majority, is reviving old themes of manifest destiny and divine purpose while ignoring any lessons to be derived from its recent history. As for its northern neighbor, the United States continues to oscillate between indifference and extravagant disregard. Yet it is precisely because of these developments that comparative reflection is essential. Hudson's insistence that the links between religion and nationalism be general and flexible helps bring clarity to a subject more frequently characterized by confusion.

False Turn in the Search: The Civil Religion Debate

The image of soul has long referred to moral and spiritual qualities of things. Its use with respect to nations appears to be more recent. Writing in 1827, Thomas Carlyle utilized the notion of soul to describe the wellspring, the center, the ultimate meaning of the nation:

> It is no longer the moral, religious, spiritual condition of the people that is our concern, but their physical, practical, economical condition, as regulated by public laws. Thus is the Body-politic more than ever worshipped and tendered; but the Soul-politic less than ever. Love of country, in any high or generous sense . . . has little importance attached to it . . . Men are to be guided only by their self-interests.[9]

A century later, Rupert Brooke and G. K. Chesterton drew upon the same image to relate autobiographically how during brief visits from the Old World they experienced Canada and the United States. For Rupert Brooke, or at least for the anonymous American who claimed that Canada has no soul, Canada lacked clarity and purity of identity in a transcendent sense. For Chesterton, the United States still possessed soul, which he understood as a spiritual idealism imbibed by each citizen.

Aside from the image of soul, Carlyle's comment pertains to the issue of religion and nationalism. Carlyle wrote during a time of transition and "boundless grinding collision of the New with the Old." For Carlyle the Old included a conception of nationalism as something positive, a natural sense of tradition, of belonging to a place, of having a patrimony. Carlyle accepted that divine providence guides national destiny and provides the basis of Right, Freedom, and Country. In opposition to this Christian notion, a new conception was elevating Country to a status of autonomy and ultimacy. The apotheosis of the state was beginning to supplant the worship of God. A new age of nationalism and competing ideologies had dawned.

Other nineteenth-century writers observed, with varying degrees of optimism and pessimism, the collision of old and new. In *The Ancient City* Fustel de Coulanges explored one example of "the intimate relation which always exists between men's ideas and their social state."[10] In ancient Rome and Greece religion was the basis of civic life. People sought to harmonize earth with heaven. The modern distinction between the sacred and the profane did not exist. A functional analysis of religion found similar expression in de Tocqueville's study of democracy in America, as is suggested by the heading "Religion considered as a political institution which powerfully contributes to the maintenance of a democratic republic among the Americans."[11] Almost prophetically, de Tocqueville warned lest religion in America become "bound down to the dead corpse of superannuated polity." That is, religion should not form alliances with political power such that all distinctions disappear between religion and patriotism or church and state. In a final example, speaking of the English nation incarnate in British North America, Bishop John Strachan averred,

> Here the light of freedom burns with the brightest radiance, and the rights and liberties of man are the best understood and most abundantly enjoyed; and here a lofty sense of independence is of universal growth. From this nation, the cherisher and supporter of religious establishments, have come almost all the lights that exalt modern times. . . . It is to religion that she owes her pre-eminence—it is this that throws a holy splendour round her head, makes her the hope of every land, and urges her to achieve the evangelization of mankind.[12]

For many early critics of modernity the Canadian and American experiments promised the infusion of new life to the older conceptions of religion and nationalism. But the promise has failed. So mourn contemporary counterparts of Carlyle and Fustel de Coulanges, Strachan and de Tocqueville. According to George Grant, for example, the Canadian experiment was to build "a more ordered and stable society than the liberal experiment in the United States." Tradition, morality, recognition of "an eternal order," human freedom, good government—these constituted the key elements of the Canadian search for "an alternative to the American republic built on the northern half of this continent." Now, laments Grant, "this hope has been extinguished, we are too old to be retrained by a new master. We find ourselves like fish left on the shores of a dying lake. The element necessary to our existence has passed away."[13]

Equally compelling is Robert Bellah's elegy for America's vocation. The United States, explains Bellah, was built centrally on "utopian millennial expectations" and an "entire tradition of religious-moral understanding." Just as Christians and Jews have understood their relationship with God through the symbol of covenant, so, too, have Americans understood the relationship of their nation with God in terms of the idea of covenant. That is, there was a common set of religious and moral understandings rooted in a conception of divine order under a Christian, or at least a deist, God. The basic moral norms . . . deriving from that divine order were liberty, justice, and charity, understood in the context of . . . personal virtue as the essential basis of a good society.[14]

In the twentieth century, Bellah laments, Americans have broken the covenant. Just as religious life requires periodic reformation and revival, so, too, must the old vision be renewed. The resulting "new birth of freedom" will generate "a world civil religion . . . as a fulfillment and not a denial" of America's eschatological hopes.[15]

At the heart of the matter is our notion of soul, the idea that there is a religious basis for national life. Bellah's use of the phrase "civil religion" draws explicitly from the writings of Jean Jacques Rousseau. In the eighteenth century Rousseau termed the religious basis of nations "the religion of the citizen" by which he understood those "social sentiments without which a man cannot be a good citizen or faithful subject." This civil religion contrasts with the religion of man, "the religion of the Gospel pure and simple," and priestcraft, "a sort of mixed and anti-social code . . . that destroys social unity." Rousseau desired to attract adherents of the latter, irresponsible practice of religion to a more responsible engagement in civic affairs through the mutual recognition of rights and obligations. Rousseau did not define precisely the relationship between the religion of pure and simple Christianity and civil religion, but he did indicate the religious elements necessary for the commonweal and smooth functioning of the state. These included the existence of God, the life to come, the punishment of wrong, the sanctity of the social contract and the exclusion of religious intolerance.[16]

Rousseau intended to promote responsible engagements in civic affairs, but the unintended consequences of his formulation may have been less salutary. Some see Rousseau as the creator of modern absolutism.[17] Others understand Rousseau more simply, as extolling the classic virtue of patriotism and a positive sense of belonging to a class, a society, a country, a continent, and a civilization.[18] Bellah intimates that the civil religion concept could, potentially, degenerate into perverse worship of the American nation.[19] What Bellah wants to defend in Rousseau's concept is the need for beliefs, symbols, and rituals which enable citizens to understand American experience in the light of ultimate and universal reality.

Bellah clearly understands American civil religion as a differentiated, elaborate, and well-institutionalized religion existing alongside the privatized religion of church, synagogue, or temple.[20] He also clearly intends the concept to be used comparatively and cross-culturally.[21] Although he acknowledges that he has reified and given a name to something that has otherwise existed only semiconsciously, he defends tenaciously his use of the phrase to denote what has generally been accepted as religion. Of course, definitions of religion abound, but Bellah would appear to posit as the attributes of American civil religion these phenomena: (1) some delineation of beliefs; (2) recognized leadership; (3) periodic ceremonies or rituals which transmit and interpret the core beliefs; (4) explicitly defined grounds of membership; (5) some outcome on the behaviour of adherents; and, finally, (6) a coherence of the above characteristics which permit the outsider to name the phenomenon Christian, Buddhist, tribal, or the like.[22]

Thus, Bellah marshals evidence to make the case for American civil religion as something differentiated, elaborate, institutionalized, and subject to analysis. In the first place, the dogmas of American civil religion are, as Rousseau suggested they should be, few, simple, and exactly worded. These include belief in America's sacred origin, the pristine freshness of the New World paradise, and America's vocation as a chosen people. "When God was creating the new heaven and new earth, he began right here in America. . . ." So runs Bellah's vision of America's myth of origin and convenantal responsibility to further God's purposes through the advance not only of individual freedom and happiness in America but also of the good of all people everywhere.

Second, the elaboration of these beliefs takes form in a sacred canon, comprised of foundational documents such as the Declaration of Independence and Bill of Rights, and credal formulations such as the Pledge of Allegiance and national anthem. The intimate relation between the core dogmas, founding documents, and credal statements is made clear in pronouncements by the official and unofficial bards of America's civil religion, for example, President Washington's first and President Lincoln's second inaugural addresses; writings by novelists and poets such as Herman Melville, Julia Ward Howe, and Walt Whitman; the historical accounts of people as diverse as John Winthrop, George Bancroft, or Josiah Strong. Bellah notes that the Protestant clergy long remained central spokespersons for American culture,[23] but he also believes that immigrant and minority groups have appropriated and articulated the core beliefs aright.

Third, Bellah mentions a number of public rites and holy days which provide recognized leaders the occasion to transmit and interpret American civil religion. These include presidential inaugurals; pilgrimages to sacred places such as the Gettysburg and Arlington National Cemeteries, the Tomb of the Unknown Soldier and shrines of martyred Presidents Lincoln and Kennedy; ceremonies marking the national holidays, including Thanksgiving, Memorial Day, the Fourth of July; and relatively minor events such as Veterans Day and Washington's birthday.

The fourth attribute of religion, membership, is more problematic for Bellah. In his 1967 essay "Civil Religion in America" Bellah appears to equate nationality with acceptance of the basic myth-ritual-symbol paradigm. Although there have been times of trial, the "average American" generally has adhered to the American civil religion "without any bitter struggle" between it and the practice of Christianity, ethnicity, or other possible competing loyalties. Subsequently, Bellah's analysis has become more nuanced. Discussing the idea of the United States as an asylum for the oppressed, Bellah cited the Jewish American poet Emma Lazarus, whose words are inscribed on the Statue of Liberty:

> Give me your tired, your poor,
> Your huddled masses yearning to breathe free,
> The wretched refuse of your teeming shore,
> Send these, the homeless, tempest-tossed, to me:
> I lift my lamp beside the golden door.

Bellah also cites early complaints about immigrants, meaning others than Anglo-Saxon Protestants, and acknowledges that for many the promise of America the openhearted receiving the afflicted of the world has proved illusory. Bellah explains this apparent discrepancy between promise and reality by pointing out how many non-Protestants and ethnics have come out as "relatively homogeneous Americans in the melting pot of Americanization." But it is not clear that Bellah succeeds in extricating American civil religion from the matrix of white Anglo-Saxon Protestant identity.[24]

The fifth attribute of religion, behavior, relates to Bellah's optimism regarding the promise of the United States. In Bellah's reading of history, American civil religion provided the ideological basis for liberators such as Washington and Lincoln and prophets such as Henry David Thoreau and William Lloyd Garrison to strive to make concrete in actual practice the rhetoric of "life, liberty, and the pursuit of happiness." Vigorous movements of renewal gave way to fervor of revolution and civil war, which in turn gave way to new efforts to enhance the common good. Decrying the present 59 gospel of materialism and power, Bellah nonetheless discerns evidence in the civil rights and anti-Vietnam war movements during the 1960s that some did continue to alert the nation that it stands under higher judgment.

Finally, the issue of coherence finds expression in the image of soul. Appealing for the renewal of covenant, Bellah states,

> No one has changed a great nation without appealing to its soul,

without stimulating a national idealism, as even those who call themselves materialists have discovered. . . . We [must] have a new vision of man, a new sense of human possibility, and a new conception of the ordering of liberty, the constitution of freedom.[25]

He goes on to call for the revisioning of the common good. Belief and behavior find coherence in the faithful service of people in pursuit of life and the fullness thereof, not for individuals as such, but for people in community.

Bellah forcefully analyzes the phenomenon, observed frequently since de Tocqueville, of religion's immense influence in the United States. Variously designated public religion (Benjamin Franklin), common religion (Robin Williams), or the religion of the republic (Sidney E. Mead), the American case has been generally understood as a particular instance of a universal reality. But Bellah claims more for his construction than has anybody before. Others have regarded American civil religion as genuinely religious,[26] but Bellah asserts that American civil religion is as differentiated, elaborated, and institutionalized as Christianity, Judaism, or Buddhism.

This claim is unfortunate for at least two reasons. First, Bellah provides evidence, summarized above, which fails to substantiate his intuitive thesis. Bellah's formulation cannot be verified historically or scientifically.[27] As with other elusive ideal types, notably Max Weber's "Protestant ethic" and "spirit of capitalism" or Jacob Burckhardt's "civilization of the renaissance," the construction describes no differentiated, elaborated, institutionalized reality as such.

Bellah's claim is also unfortunate because it has diverted the attention of scholars *away from* questions related to the use one makes of claims to linkage between religion and nationalism *to* a search for civil religion. Thus is made the disconcerting contention that civil religions exist wherever they are sought.[28] This simply is not so, as the Canadian case demonstrates.

Canada provides an instructive case because it shares, at least among English-speaking Protestants, many characteristics in religion and politics with the United States. These include a common British heritage; ongoing transatlantic passage of ideas, books, luminaries, and the like; a relatively open border facilitating the flow of population in both directions; institutional religious ties; and distinctive, albeit subtly different patterns of religious freedom, denominationalism, missionary outreach, pluralism, and voluntarism. Religion has been at least as significant an influence forming Canadian society as has been true for the United States. Finally, within English- and French-speaking Canada strong traditions of mission and identity have existed. George Grant, self-proclaimed spokesperson for the Anglo-Canadian variant on the theme, takes for granted that "public religion" is essential for "social cohesion." Whether or not public religion has anything to do with Christianity, Deism, or any differentiated religion, Grant holds that belief in a "higher" divine power is minimally necessary if there is to be constitutional government.[29] This sounds like Canadian civil religion. Right? Wrong. One searches in vain for Canadian civil religion(s). Versions of the idea of God's providential care of Canada have been put forward, but none has been accepted as an ideology, philosophy, or dogmatic framework satisfactory to the majority of Canadians. Until 1982 Canada had no written constitution; a national anthem became official in 1980; its bill of rights is subject to modification by Parliament and a majority of the provinces. Nothing resembles canon or creed. As for sacred rituals, such events as the opening of Parliament and visits to certain government buildings do not have the significance that American counterparts have. The monarchy does have emotional impact for segments of Canadian society, but visits by the royal family do not assume a sacral dimension. There are holidays, but no holy days. The national day, July 1, is less well known than the Fourth of July, while Victoria Day and Thanksgiving are mere "days off" reserved for the family or the opening and closing of cottages. In lieu of the "American melting pot" the acceptance of a "mosaic" image affirms both the reluctance to forge immigrant Canadians of one mold and a preference for divergent Canadian ideals. In sum, the absence of a clear Canadian identity has bred a pattern of indifference and inferiority described by one of Canada's most nationalistic poets, Al Purdy, in "Homo Canadensis":

> And guys like you deserve to be taken over.
> But when you are you'll be 2nd class Americans,
> like Negroes in the south, like Indians here—
> You'll be 2nd class Americans here because
> you were never 1st class Canadians in the first place—[30]

The case for Canadian civil religion, in Bellah's sense of differentiated, elaborated, institutionalized religion, is even more tenuous than for the United States. Yet in English and French Canada, national spokespersons have utilized religious imagery to exert emotional, shaping impact upon the hearts and minds of Canadians. The apparent failure of Bellah's category means only that religion and nationalism have not fused in the sense he intends. But it should be observed that Bellah himself has suggested a more limited meaning for civil religion. This second formulation designates simply the religious dimension of public life. It entails less theoretical baggage than the full paradigm, and it has been more widely ac-

61

cepted. Winthrop Hudson and others have employed it to explore theological and historical religious dimensions of national life with greater precision than does Bellah. Although Hudson's perspective has not figured prominently in the civil religion debate, it does in fact provide a fruitful basis for comparing American and Canadian religion and nationalism. This essay provides an opportunity to redirect the civil religion debate along more productive lines than the slippery search for civil religion. By supplementing Hudson's excellent studies of religion and nationalism in the United States with data from the Anglo-Canadian experience, we may indeed develop a felicitous method for comparative historical study.[31]

Memory of the Forebears

The vast majority of settlers in the original thirteen American states and Maritime provinces thought of themselves as English. The American revolutionists interpreted their war for independence as a struggle to preserve their English liberties. Ironically, the same view was held by loyalist Yankees who fled to New Brunswick and Nova Scotia. However, unlike the settlers of New England, the early Canadian refugees had little to unite them apart from their common loyalty to the memory of England.[32]

This memory was powerful enough. It included the strong conviction that England had a God-given vocation to fulfill, a conviction reinforced through three periods of civil strife. Each conflict produced martyrs, publicists, and a literature which affirmed God's election of England as the first nation to embrace the gospel, the only establisher of it throughout the world, the first reformed and the first to stamp out all vestiges of idolatry, superstition, hypocrisy, and wicked living. As God had been committed to ancient Israel by way of a covenant, so had God with England. As the Geneva Bible, Foxe's *Book of Martyrs*, and an extensive pamphlet and sermon literature emphasized, election had its consequences, for God chose England to be the instrument for promoting true religion and civil liberties throughout the world. In its most succinct form the tradition asserted that God is English.[33] In its most bizarre form, British Israelism, the argument asserts that the British people descend directly from the "lost" tribe of Israel, their monarchs from David and Jesus the Christ.[34]

Observing the centrality of this heritage in the development of early Canadian self-understanding, we must stress that the memory of the forebears had negative and positive consequences. Negatively, it sanctioned the idea, dominant in subsequent Canadian imperialism, that Canada was simply part of a greater empire which would ultimately cover the whole earth with the English language,

English laws, and English Protestantism.[35] Positively, it enabled Canadians to think of themselves as true heirs of Britain and therefore as the providentially established alternative to American claimants to succession. Three examples from the early literature illustrate this positive memory of England in the New World.

The first derives from the pulpits of the national churches, the Church of England and the Church of Scotland. As conservative defenders of British North America, clergy from the established churches frequently preached on public occasions such as the opening of legislature or days of fasting, humiliation, and thanksgiving.[36] In one such venture the Reverend Andrew Brown of the Church of Scotland, pastor of the Halifax Protestant Dissenting Church during the convulsions of the French Revolution, affirmed that God had ordained the present difficulties. Why had God appointed the perils of the time? For the cure of "gross corruptions . . . disorders . . . and national vices." What was the place of British North America in God's scheme? "To listen to the voice of Providence and learn submission to its appointments." The people of Halifax had special cause for thankfulness, for

> no factions have divided our people, or distracted our government. Clubs and cabals are unknown in our settlements. No one has dared to accuse another of disaffection. . . . No people were ever more highly favoured, or blessed with a better opportunity of becoming wise and 'good and happy. Let not the kindness of Providence plead with us in vain. Enjoying safety in the midst of danger, let us observe the dispensations of judgments to other lands, and apply the instructions which they deliver to our own improvement. In a particular manner let us beware of the prevailing vices which have produced the perils of the time—infidelity, licentiousness, and a spirit of innovation.[37]

Nowhere did Brown claim for Nova Scotia divine origin. Nowhere did Brown identify the United States with infidelity, licentiousness, and innovation. Others did, however, as is exemplified by Canada's first nationalist writer, Judge Thomas Chandler Haliburton. In *The Clockmaker* Haliburton assigns to a Tory Squire the task of deflating the quintessential Yankee, Mr. Sam Slick:

> "I think," said I, "this is a happy country, Mr. Slick. The people are fortunately all of one origin; there are no national jealousies to divide, and no very violent politics to agitate them. They appear to be cheerful and contented, and are a civil, good-natured, hospitable race. Considering the unsettled state of almost every part of the world, I think I would as soon cast my lot in Nova Scotia as in any part I know of!"[38]

63

Subsequently Haliburton asserts for Nova Scotia such noble purposes as the cause of "true religion" and "much larning, piety, talent, honour, vartue and refinement."[39] In one passage the question of establishment as a safeguard for the preservation of conservative values becomes explicit. The Reverend Mr. Hopewell relates to Sam Slick and the Squire the final thoughts of George Washington concerning the impiety and blasphemy of excluding religious endowment from the Constitution. Says Washington,

> . . . we ought to have established *a* Church, fixed upon some *one*, and called it a *national* one. Not having done so, nothing short of a direct interposition of Providence, which we do not deserve and therefore cannot hope for, can save this great country from becoming a dependency of Rome. . . . O, that we held fast the Church that we had!—the Church of our forefathers—the Church of England. It is a pure, noble, apostolical structure, the holiest and the best since the days of the Apostles; but we have not, and the consequence is too melancholy and too awful to contemplate.[40]

Aside from the expression of anti-Catholicism, this excerpt reveals Haliburton's widely held conviction that the United States had failed to hold to true religion. Religious toleration had brought into being "endless numbers of sects, more or less absurd, according to the degree of prejudice that was to be pandered to, discontent soothed into complacency, or ignorance extolled into wisdom. . . . Religion was thus daily put on and off like a garment."[41]

Canada was not altogether free of sectarian "vanity" and "pretention," but during Canada's first Great Awakening, between 1776 and 1809, dissenting Congregational and Baptist preachers articulated a position which closely resembled that of the Presbyterian and Anglican divines. The message of Henry Alline, Joseph Dimock, Harris Harding, Edward Manning, and other New Lights went as follows: The Lord God had done a mighty work during America's awakening. But the thirteen colonies had fallen upon evil times and sunk into chaos. God delivered a remnant to the new promised land. Even though a crisis of great severity threatened the people of Nova Scotia, they were surrounded by God's providential care and favor. As a result they had a mission to uphold true religion in "this peaceable corner of the earth." Thus, in his first and longest theological treatise the leader of revival, Henry Alline, recited the signs of the times:

64

> The Great Men and Kings of the Earth grown proud and lofty; all Manner of Debauchery spreading like a Flood; Stage Plays, Balls and Masquerades received as an Indulgence from Heaven; . . . while the Heralds of the Gospel, if any hold forth the Truth, are accounted as mad men and Enthusiasts; . . . cursing, swearing and blaspheming, not only the language of Troops and Mariners but

also of Towns and Countries and received as expressions of Po-
liteness; Drunkenness a common Amusement accounted neither
Sin or Disgrace; the Rich exalted, the Poor trampled in the Dust.
. . .

But, Alline averred, although the "Power of Godliness was
scarcely to be found on earth" in Nova Scotia God's people were
"returning back to the Liberty of the Gospel, and separating from
the Seats of Anti-Christ."[42] Preaching at Liverpool on a day set
aside for thanksgiving in 1782, Alline assured his hearers that God
had screened them from the convulsions of the day: "Yea, and
when we have daily expected the impending cloud, and to share
in the bitter cup, Heaven's indulgent hand has interposed and
averted the blow."Alline continued by urging all "to drink of the
wells of Salvation," and to proclaim "the goodness, the unspeakable
goodness of God to such a people." Colonel Simeon Perkins, who
heard Alline on that occasion, pronounced it "a very good discourse."[43] Others responded positively to Alline's message, as in
1784 when the members of the Maugerville, New Brunswick, Congregational Church, which Alline visited in 1779, declined to follow
their minister, Seth Nobel, back to the United States. The loyalists
explained,

> Are we to throw away the fruits of many years of painful industry
> and leave? . . . the place where God in his providence had smiled
> upon us both in our spiritual and temporal affairs . . . [not] unless
> we could find a place where vice and immorality did not thrive,
> or at least where vital piety did flourish more than here.[44]

As God's favored children, they remained in Canada to be enkindled
as a light unto the nations, to be fitted for the great work of trans-
mitting the power of godliness.

A Covenanted People

In addition to the memory of England, early American and Canadian identity included the tradition of covenant relationship with
God. God providentially cared for his people, but his beneficence
was in some measure conditioned. "It will be a doleful thing,"
explained William Stoughton in 1670, "to be of broken credit with
the Lord, and for the Lord to pronounce us bankrupts. If we frustrate the Lord's expectations, he will cut off ours." This warning
was a constant theme in New England's self-understanding,[45] and
it found expression in Canada as well.

The way of God with God's people was never to abandon them
but, rather, to teach them divine ways, to deter them from wrong-
doing, and to spur them on in doing well. In these three purposes

65

of covenant relationship we find counterparts of John Calvin's understanding of the three functions of the law. Indeed, the covenant served explicitly to provide pilgrim Christians with a framework of moral law by which they might see themselves aright, not through human eyes but in the light of Christ's righteousness.

The first function of the covenant was pedagogical. It taught people what pleases and displeases God by outlining what was expected of them and what they might expect of God. Corporately early settlers of the Maritime Provinces and the Canadas assumed responsibility, through entering into covenants, to walk in the fear of the Lord, to watch over one another, to attend to God's concerns, and early to implant in their children a right notion of religion. Identification with church and community derived from a strong sense of being a people of God with a great debt to God. The following record of the founding of the Congregational church at Chebogue, Nova Scotia, reveals the role of the covenant in developing this sense of peoplehood:

> In the Fall of this Year, (1776) there appeared extraordinary Concern and Engagedness on the Minds of some, and there was a Meeting set up on the Week Time, for Prayer and religious Conference. About this Time also, there was some Persons at Argyle exercised with some serious Concern about the Things of Religion. The People in Jebogue thus seriously inclined, entered into solemn Covenant to walk with God and to watch over one another and to carry on the Concerns of the Redeemer's Kingdom, in about the Space of a Year after their first setting up private Meetings; which Meetings were always held in the Day Time and at the Houses of those that were seriously inclined. The People of Jebogue held meetings on the Lord's Day at this Time, tho' they were destitute of a Minister through all the Summer of this Year.[46]

Naturally, the polity of Baptists, Congregationalists, and Methodists lent itself to the development of an attitude of obligation in the context of church and community. However, Anglicans and Presbyterians imbibed the notion of covenant as well. In this instance, the people expressed their corporate identity through acts of confession, repentance, and thanksgiving. The career of Charles Inglis, first Church of England bishop of Nova Scotia, provides an example. In 1776 Inglis was serving as rector of Trinity Church, New York. The revolutionists had appointed a day for public fasting, prayer, and humiliation. For Inglis this was a timely opportunity to rally the loyalist cause:

> I consented to preach that Day, & indeed our Situation made it highly prudent; tho a submission so far to an Authority that was usurped was exceedingly grating & disagreeable. . . . When the

66

Collects for the King & Royal Family were read, [I expected that] I shold be fired at, as Menaces to that Purpose had frequently flung out—the Matter however passed over without any Accident. Nothing of this Kind happened before or since, which made it more remarkable. I was afterwards assured that something hostile & violent was intended; but He that "stills the Raging of the Sea & Madness of the People," overuled their Purpose, whatever it was.[47]

By thus declaring his patriotic convictions and nerving the loyalist Yankees, Inglis communicated the shared conviction that God does not despise the faithfulness of his chosen instruments nor turn away from them in time of need.

The covenant notion included a legal or deterrent aspect. Quite explicitly church covenants specified what constituted right and wrong. Members met regularly to discipline delinquents on such matters as nonattendance at church, drinking, brawling, dancing, sexual misconduct, hypocrisy, slander, or behaving in an unseemly manner. Sanctions included admonition and excommunication. To cite but one example, the Chebogue covenant discussed earlier stated:

> We do also promise that, by the Grace of God, we will oppose all Sin and Error wherever they appear, both in our selves and others, as far as in us lies; namely, All foolish Talking and Jesting, and Wantonness; All vain Disputings about Words and Things that gender Strife, and doth not edify to more Godliness; Also vain Company-keeping and spending Time idly, at taverns and Tippling-Houses, or elsewhere; Evil Whispering or Backbiting of any Person; also carnel and unnecessary Discourse about Worldly Things, especially on the Sabbath Day; Unnecessary forsaking the Assembling of our selves together in private convenient Conferences, and also on the Sabbath Day; and all other Sins whatsoever, both of Omission and Commission.[48]

Finally, the sense of being a covenanted people fostered the development of what Bishop Strachan called "a community of religious feeling."[49] Arch defender that he was of England and of its national church, Strachan nonetheless became convinced that Britain had proved false to its destiny. A remnant of God's chosen people now existed in Canada and had to stand on its own. This sentiment found voice particularly in 1812 and 1837–1838, with significant consequences for the growth of Canadian nationalism. In 1812 Canadian militia repulsing American invaders sang,

> We're abused and insulted, our country's degraded
> Our rights are infringed both by land and by sea;
> Let us rouse up indignant, when those rights are invaded,
> And announce to the world, "We're united and free!"[50]

67

By 1837 Anglo-Canadian identity was even stronger, as was the sense of divine blessing. "Lord, on our side be seen . . . put down th'invading band" went the words of additional stanzas of "God Save the Queen."[51] The defeat of the insurrection only confirmed for John Strachan God's intent to build up "a Christian society . . . in righteousness."[52] For Baptist editor John W. Maxwell the end of rebellion and infidelity signaled God's expectation that God's bounty of grace should "ripen and grow on earth till it make its subjects fit and meet beings for that new Earth and those new Heavens wherein dwelleth Righteousness."[53]

Concluding Reflections

"Surely we were meant to lead the way to a better pattern of life," observed Nellie McClung in her autobiography *The Stream Runs Fast.*[54] Although she had Canada in mind, she expressed a sense of mission and destiny shared alike by Americans, Anglo-Canadians and, indeed, French-speaking Canadians. "God's last best country" emphasized Carson J. Cameron, Canadian Baptist home missionary, in words strikingly similar to those of Abraham Lincoln who described the struggle to preserve the Union as "the last, best hope of earth" which Americans might "nobly save or meanly lose."[55]

McClung, Cameron, and Lincoln identified their native lands with God's providential care and brought to consciousness what Canadians and Americans have virtually always believed—that religion is the soul of the two nations. The constraint of space precludes further discussion of the theme, but we may observe that American and Canadian data reveal strikingly similar use of religious images to express the congruence of religion and nationalism.

Winthrop Hudson and others have documented that propagandists forged American identity through their claim that the United States had become, by default, the heir of England as the trustee of God's intentions for all people, a claim illustrated by the titles of scholarly narratives, for example, *The Kingdom of God in America, Redeemer Nation, Righteous Empire,* and *A Christian America.*[56] In similar manner scholars have highlighted the theme as it has found expression in Canada.[57] Further analysis using Hudson's additional categories ("a free people," "this mighty empire," and "the renovation of the world") would simply strengthen the case that from colonial times on, Anglo-Canadians, like their counterparts in the United States, understood their mission as one of extending everywhere the glory of God.

Winthrop Hudson stands at the end of one line of interpretation of religion in the United States. As such, he has helped to clarify

68

the collapse of a discredited vision. At the same time, Hudson has reflected deeply on what an apt paradigm might be for "post-Protestant America." His categories of analysis may prove durable in a manner that does not seem likely for Robert Bellah's civil religion proposal. Of course, in many areas Canadians have followed but a few steps behind the lead of Americans, which might suggest that, in a generation, the existence of Canadian civil religion will appear more plausible than at present. This seems unlikely, however, because the collapse of the old vision did not occur in Canada in quite the same way as it did in the United States. Anglo-Canadians institutionalized the dream through the creation of three political parties, including a genuine socialist alternative for Canada, the organic union of three Protestant denominations and political initiatives which continue to differentiate Canada and the United States.[58] However similar the two expressions of religion and nationalism may appear, there are significant differences which bode well for Canada. To cite but one example, whereas from the start the United States created legal barriers to separate church and state, religion and politics have tended to fuse dangerously into ideology. By contrast, Canada rejected formal church establishment without driving a wall between church and state. In consequence, religion has been in a favorable position to voice prophetic judgment upon the nation while at the same time to engage creatively in the corporate life of the nation.

NOTES

[1] Rupert Brooke, *Letters from America* (Toronto: McClelland & Stewart, Ltd., 1916), p. 49. Two comments are in order at this point. First, Canadians have a claim to the designation "American" as legitimate as is that of citizens of the United States. However, no alternative shorthand commends itself. Therefore, in this paper "Canadian" and "American" refer respectively to nationals of Canada and the United States, individually or collectively. Second, I wish to thank Professors John Webster Grant of Emmanuel College; Robert T. Handy of Union Theological Seminary, New York; Melvyn Hillmer of McMaster Divinity College; and Tom Sinclair-Faulkner of Dalhousie University for commenting on early drafts of this essay.

[2] G. K. Chesterton, *What I Saw in America* (New York: Dodd, Mead & Company, 1922), pp. 11-12.

[3] William James, *The Varieties of Religious Experience* (New York: Longmans, Green, & Co., 1902), p. 9.

[4] Winthrop S. Hudson, *Religion in America* (New York: Charles Scribner's Sons, 1965), p. 3.

[5] Winthrop S. Hudson, "How American Is Religion in America?", *Reinterpre-*

tation in American Church History, ed. Jerald C. Brauer (Chicago: University of Chicago Press, 1968), p. 153.

[6] *Ibid.*, p. 167.

[7] Winthrop S. Hudson, "The Interrelationships of Baptists in Canada and the United States," *Foundations*, vol. 23, no. 1 (January-March, 1980), pp. 22-41; review by W. S. Hudson of Robert T. Handy, "A History of the Churches in the United States and Canada," *Union Seminary Quarterly Review*, vol. 32, no. 3 & 4 (Spring & Summer, 1977), pp. 174-179.

[8] William Kilbourn, ed., *Canada: A Guide to the Peaceable Kingdom* (Toronto: Macmillan Company of Canada Ltd., Laurentian Library Edition, 1975), p. xiii; G. Gerald Harrop, "Canada's New Separatist Threat," *The Christian Century*, vol. 98, no. 16 (May 6, 1981), pp. 510-512.

[9] Thomas Carlyle, *Critical and Miscellaneous Essays* (London: Chapman and Hall, 1866), vol. 2, p. 106.

[10] Numa Denis Fustel de Coulanges, *The Ancient City: A Study on the Religion, Laws and Institutions of Greece and Rome*, trans. Willard Small (New York: Doubleday/Anchor Press, 1955; originally 1864).

[11] Alexis de Tocqueville, *Democracy in America*, ed. Phillips Bradley (New York: Random House, Vintage Books, 1954, originally 1835), vol. 1, p. 310.

[12] John Strachan, *Documents and Opinions*, ed. J. L. H. Henderson (Toronto: McClelland & Stewart, Ltd., Carleton Library, 1969), p. 91.

[13] George Grant, *Lament for a Nation. The Defeat of Canadian Nationalism* (Toronto: McClelland & Stewart, Ltd., 1965), especially pp. 1-4, 96-97.

[14] Robert N. Bellah, *The Broken Covenant: American Civil Religion in Time of Trial* (New York: The Seabury Press, Inc., A Crossroad Book, 1975), pp. ix-x. See also pp. vii-xiv, 35.

[15] Robert N. Bellah, "Civil Religion in America," *Daedalus*, vol. 96 (Winter, 1967), pp. 1-21 and repeatedly reprinted. In this essay I refer to this essay as published in Russell E. Richey and Donald G. Jones, eds., *American Civil Religion* (New York: Harper & Row, Publishers, Inc., 1974), pp. 21-44. The quote in this footnote is on p. 40.

[16] Jean Jacques Rousseau, *The Social Contract* (London: J. M. Dent and Sons Ltd., 1916, originally 1762), pp. 113-122.

[17] Hans Kohn, *The Idea of Nationalism: A Study in Its Origins and Background* (New York: Collier Books, 1967), p. 252.

[18] Claude Levi-Strauss, *Tristes Tropiques*, trans. John and Doreen Weightman (New York: Antheneum, 1974), pp. 383-393.

[19] Bellah, "Civil Religion," p. 40.

[20] *Ibid.*, p. 21.

[21] Robert N. Bellah, "American Civil Religion in the 1970s," in Richey and Jones, eds., *American Civil Religion*, pp. 255-272. Bellah and others have done considerable cross-cultural work, reflected in Robert N. Bellah and Phillip E. Hammond, *Varieties of Civil Religion* (San Francisco: Harper & Row, Publishers, Inc., 1980). The civil religion concept has been applied to South Africa, Malaysia, and elsewhere. T. Dunbar Moodie, *The Rise of Afrikanerdom: Power, Apartheid, and the Afrikaner Civil Religion* (Berkeley: University of California Press, 1975); Daniel Regan, "Islam, Intellectuals and Civil Religion in Malaysia," *Sociological Analysis*, vol. 37 (1976), pp. 95-110.

[22] Adapted from John F. Wilson, "The Status of 'Civil Religion' in America," in *The Religion of the Republic*, ed. Elwyn A. Smith (Philadelphia: Fortress Press, 1971), p. 12. Wilson has questioned whether civil religion is a differentiated religion in the sense Bellah intends. See his "A Historian's Approach to Civil Religion," in Richey and Jones, eds., *American Civil Religion*, pp. 115-138, and *Public Religion in American Culture* (Philadelphia: Temple University Press, 1979).

[23] Bellah, *Broken Covenant*, p. 56.

[24] *Ibid.*, pp. 87-111; Robert N. Bellah, "Civil Religion in America," in Richey and Jones, eds., *American Civil Religion*, pp. 34-35.

[25] Bellah, *Broken Covenant*, p. 162.

[26] For example, Will Herberg, "America's Civil Religion: What It Is and Whence It Comes," in Richey and Jones, eds., *American Civil Religion*, pp. 76-88.

[27] See notably John Wilson, as cited in footnote 22, and Martin E. Marty, who observes, "Civil religion does not exist in the same sense as, say, the Roman Catholic Church exists," in his article "Two Kinds of Civil Religion," in Richey and Jones, eds., *American Civil Religion*, p. 139. Also, see chapter 8, "Civil Religion," in his work *A Nation of Behavers* (Chicago: University of Chicago Press, 1976); Henry Warner Bowden, "A Historian's Response to the Concept of American Civil Religion," *Journal of Church and State*, vol. 17 (1975), pp. 495-505; and Robert D. Linder, "Civil Religion in Historical Perspective: The Reality That Underlies the Concept," *Journal of Church and State*, vol. 17 (1975), pp. 399-421.

[28] Philip E. Hammond, "The Sociology of American Civil Religion: A Bibliographic Essay," *Sociological Analysis*, vol. 37 (1976), p. 179. Hammond provides examples, including Queen Elizabeth's coronation, which are more suitably described as public rituals and the routinization of charisma.

[29] George Grant, *Technology and Empire: Perspectives on North America* (Toronto: House of Anansi, 1969), especially pp. 53-58; *Philosophy in the Mass Age*, 2nd ed. (Vancouver: Copp Clark Publishing Company, 1966), pp. 6-8. On similarities and differences more generally, see the Hudson articles cited in footnote 7 and Robert T. Handy, "Protestant Patterns in Canada and the United States: Similarities and Differences," in this volume.

[30] Alfred Purdy, "Homo Canadensis," *The Cariboo Horses* (Toronto: McClelland & Stewart, Ltd., 1965). Reprinted by permission of The Canadian Publishers, McClelland and Stewart, Ltd., Toronto.

[31] Hudson develops his perspective in a number of publications, especially *Nationalism and Religion in America: Concepts of American Identity and Mission* (New York: Harper & Row, Publishers, Inc., 1970); "Fast Days and Civil Religion," in *Theology in Sixteenth and Seventeenth Century England; Papers Read at a Clark Library Seminar February 6, 1971* (Los Angeles: Clark Memorial Library, U.C.L.A., 1971); "Protestant Clergy Debate the Nation's Vocation, 1898–1899," *Church History*, vol. 42 (1973), pp. 110-118; "This Most Favored Nation: Reflections on the Vocation of America," *Journal of Church and State*, vol. 19 (1977), pp. 17-30.

[32] S. F. Wise, "God's Peculiar Peoples," *The Shield of Achilles: Aspects of Canada in the Victorian Age*, ed. W. L. Morton (Toronto: McClelland & Stewart, Ltd., 1968), p. 38.

[33] Hudson, *Nationalism and Religion in America*, p. 163. For a sustained study of the "God is English" theme in Canada, see Terence Dempsey, "The Role of the Church in English Canadian Nationalism: God's Dominion of Canada" (Senior Seminar, McMaster Divinity College, 1979, Canadian Baptist Archives).

[34] For a concise critique of British Israelism, see N. H. Parker, *The Ten Tribes and All That* (Toronto: The Ryerson Press, 1938).

[35] Carl Berger, *The Sense of Power: Studies in the Ideas of Canadian Imperialism 1867-1914* (Toronto: University of Toronto Press, 1970), p. 80.

[36] S. F. Wise, "Sermon Literature and Canadian Intellectual History," *Bulletin, Committee on Archives, United Church of Canada*, vol. 18 (1965), p. 5.

[37] As cited by Wise, "God's Peculiar Peoples," pp. 45-48.

[38] Thomas C. Haliburton, *The Clockmaker*, first series (Toronto: McClelland & Stewart, Ltd., 1958; originally 1835), p. 80.

[39] *Ibid.*, pp. 115, 142.

71

[40][Thomas C. Haliburton], *The Clockmaker, or The Sayings and Doings of Samuel Slick of Slickville*, third series (London: Richard Bently, 1840), pp. 255-257.

[41][Thomas C. Haliburton], *Rule and Misrule of the English in America* (New York: Harper & Row, Publishers, Inc., 1851), pp. 352-353.

[42]H. Alline, *Two Mites on Some of the Most Important and Much Disrupted Points of Divinity, Cast into the Treasury for the Welfare of the Poor and Needy* . . . (Halifax, 1781), as cited by Gordon Stewart and George Rawlyk, *A People Highly Favoured of God: The Nova Scotia Yankees and the American Revolution* (Toronto: Macmillan of Canada, 1972), pp. 159-163.

[43]Henry Alline, *Sermon on a Day of Thanksgiving* (Halifax, 1783), as cited by Maurice W. Armstrong, *The Great Awakening in Nova Scotia 1776-1809* (Hartford, Conn.: American Society of Church History, 1948), p. 57, and Stewart and Rawlyk, *A People Highly Favored*, p. 172.

[44]Stewart and Rawlyk, *A People Highly Favored*, p. 180.

[45]Hudson, *Religion and Nationalism in America*, p. 19.

[46]S. D. Clark, *Church and Sect in Canada* (Toronto: University of Toronto Press, 1948), p. 13.

[47]J. W. Lydekker, *The Life and Letters of Charles Inglis* (London: SPCK, 1936), as cited in *The Cross in Canada*, ed. John S. Moir (Toronto: The Ryerson Press, 1966), pp. 89-90.

[48]Clark, *Church and Sect in Canada*, p. 13. See also David J. Green, "An Investigation into the Role of The Baptist Church as a Moral Court on the Niagara Frontier" (Term paper, McMaster University, n.d., Canadian Baptist Archives).

[49]Strachan, *Documents and Opinions*, p. 93.

[50]Pierre Berton, *The Invasion of Canada 1812-1813* (Toronto: McClelland & Stewart, Ltd., 1980), p. 79.

[51]John S. Moir, *Rhymes of Rebellion: Being a Selection of Contemporary Verses About the "Recent Unpleasantness" in Upper Canada, 1837* (Toronto: The Ryerson Press, 1965), p. 79.

[52]As cited by Wise, "God's Peculiar Peoples," p. 58.

[53]"Rebellion in Upper Canada," *Upper Canada Baptist Missionary Magazine*, vol. 2 (January, 1838), p. 77.

[54]Nellie McClung, *The Stream Runs Fast: My Own Story* (Toronto: Thomas Allen Limited, 1945), p. 134.

[55]C. J. Cameron, *Foreigners or Canadians?* (Toronto: Baptist Home Mission Board of Ontario and Quebec, 1913), p. 5; Lincoln as cited by Sidney E. Mead, *The Lively Experiment: The Shaping of Christianity in America* (New York: Harper & Row, Publishers, Inc., 1963), p. 74.

[56]H. Richard Niebuhr, *The Kingdom of God in America* (New York: Harper & Row, Publishers, Inc., 1937); Ernest Lee Tuveson, *Redeemer Nation: The Idea of America's Millenial Rose* (Chicago: University of Chicago Press, 1968); Martin E. Marty, *Righteous Empire: The Protestant Experience in America* (New York: The Dial Press, 1970); Robert T. Handy, *A Christian America: Protestant Hopes and Historical Realities* (New York: Oxford University Press, 1971).

[57]For example, John Webster Grant, "National Identity: The Background" and N. K. Clifford, "His Dominion: A Vision in Crisis," both in *Religion and Culture in Canada*, ed. Peter Slater (Waterloo: CSSR, 1977).

[58]The creation of a comprehensive medical care programme, the decision not to produce nuclear arms, and Canada's peace-keeping work through the United Nations in some measure reflect implementation of ideals formulated by Protestant pastors cum social gospelers turned national statespersons, for example, Baptist Tommy Douglas and Methodist James Shaver Woodsworth.

II

Continental themes

Sectarian Protestantism
and Political Culture

Peter Iver Kaufman

I

Most would agree that early Christian piety was apolitical. "Nations" might reawaken and carve up idiosyncratically the territories accumulated by Rome, but the new religion was principally concerned with an everlasting kingdom. David's throne now belonged to a messiah who had no particular quarrel with the empire. An interested eye might watch at the peephole as jurisdictions expanded or collapsed, but pagan authorities need not have taken the more basic political indifference of the earliest Christians as a direct challenge to their own legitimacy. The authorities were feared and, for the most part, obeyed as instruments of God's chastening.

Rather suddenly in the fourth century political authorities cultivated a special interest in Christianity. Their attention was repaid in kind, and the story of Christianity's "civil religiosity," as R. Bruce Douglass tells it, began.

> This was not . . . a simple return to civil religion in the earlier sense [the "integrative civic cults of the ancient Mediterranean world"]. With the exception of the enthusiasts in the fourth century who equated the Christianization of the empire with the dawning of the kingdom of God, a distinction was maintained between civil affairs and the ultimate purposes of religion. Even in a perfectly Christianized society, believers would be looking beyond this world to the next. . . . On the other hand, the state, by virtue of becoming an instrument for the Christianization of society, was clearly elevated to a higher status. At least a partial redivinization [of politics] was taking place.[1]

Sorting through the literature of late antiquity and accepted notions of the relationship between Christianity and culture, one could surely collect a bushel of qualifications to add to Douglass's few. But he does not remain long in the fourth century, and neither shall we. His chief concern is that relatively recent concentration on "private religion" imperils civil religion and, with it, the prospect that Christianity can creatively contribute to the structuring of the public realm. Douglass deplores the return to indifference. Yet those who have advocated alternatives have not always been circumspect. The sense that political authority somehow mediates God's grace and will, central to civil religion, has too frequently been transmuted into an idolatrous veneration of political leadership or ideology. More to the point here, historians can be less than discreet in selecting models for the reforming of the political climate or for the structuring of political culture in the history of religious communities.

Douglass has gone a considerable way toward the identification of wholesome civil religion. He formulates two standards that theoretically eliminate the possibility that tyranny and idolatry will be mistaken for legitimate offspring of properly "divinized" politics. Civil religion, according to Douglass, must countenance the "relativization of political society," which prohibits the state from becoming the absolute authority in questions of value. Civil religion must also allow for "the higher forms of religion to which it is subordinate."[2] The second standard is simply the more positive side of the first. Together they encourage religion's direct involvement in political culture insofar as that involvement produces limitations, beyond which reverence for political society will not pass, and provisions for a healthy religious pluralism. Here the historian of religions is set the task of finding and evaluating precedents.

It has become important for historians to illustrate, enlighten, and correct the conversations generated by interest in civil religion, and no one is more welcome into those conversations than Winthrop Hudson. The expanse of his knowledge of "narrow nationalism" charged with religious purpose on both sides of the Atlantic is unrivaled.[3] His own assessment of fast days, religious faith, and political culture is exemplary. Fasts were proclaimed by the Continental Congress during the United States' War of Independence in order to remind constituents of the conditional character of God's favor. As rituals of repentance and rededication, they did not involve fundamental reappraisals of the nation's special place in God's plan for history. But they are memorials to the sober recognition of the limits of political culture. Perhaps fast days are best packed away with the rest of Western democracies' and civil religion's *juvenilia*. For, as Hudson notes, days of national humiliation tend now to confuse rather than inspire citizens. Nostalgia, however, is pardonable. Western democracies stormed the nineteenth century and appear to stumble through the twentieth, confident in their election, by history if not by God, but without a concomitant sense of accountability.[4]

It is not only nostalgia and idle curiosity but also a diligent search for the Western religious contributions to the ordering of democratic ideas and institutions that send students of civil religion, armed with Durkheim, Weber, and Bellah, through Win Hudson's histories. Hudson's work, quite independent of the theorists of civil religion, nevertheless continues to make points, disclose positions, and rediscover rituals significant for the discussion of religion and politics.[5] At the other extreme, historians of Christianity are transparently apologetic, "pointing to [specific denominations'] supposed unique contribution to the inculcation of the holiness and good morals assumed necessary for the being of free institutions."[6] Beyond certain circles, dramaturgy of this kind seldom passes as history. But between these two extremes, historians forage for clues that would connect religious ideas and customs with the discipline of democracy and the political culture of the purportedly free world. Generous attention has been given to the origins of sectarian Protestantism. Historians who frankly and intelligently acknowledge that the structuring of the political order was and remains a religious problem cannot help, it seems, being fascinated by sixteenth-century dissidents who plainly challenged their own premise and thereby disputed the canons of civil religion. This fascination is the subject of what follows.

II

It took little to force the hand of Lord Acton. His pride in the political climate of Victorian England and especially in the constitutional establishment of the twin principles of political and religious liberty poured at the slightest provocation into his various chronicles of other times and places. Provocation was usually provided by the past's immoralities and by power's intolerance of dissent. Acton let loose on all this the Victorian conscience, so central to his understanding of national identity and, derivatively, so significant in his reconstruction of the European and North American experiences with liberty and liberalism. This, of course, is the point of Herbert Butterfield's criticism in *The Whig Interpretation of History*. Authorization is not wanting there for additional studies of the explanatory value of Victorian ideals, which may be found at every turn in Acton's narratives and which nearly compelled him to write a compendious history of liberty. That formidable undertaking, had Acton completed it, would surely have become an impressive hymn of historical science to the political discipline and liberalism of nineteenth-century England. Only tentatively drafted in essays and notes, the project nevertheless features one theme that credits the contention that ostensibly liberal and pluralist societies looked behind progressive political theories of the Enlightenment for the genesis of the principles of their political culture and national identity.

Acton's failure to complete his promised history of liberty seasonally raises crops of conjectures that regularly settle back into the soil to prepare it for the next season's speculations. The observation that survives successive seasons and bears directly both on Acton's reluctance and on my present concern is that history was full of betrayals, more scandalous for Acton as he learned more about them. For every 1789 there was an inevitable 1794. The calendar simply worked against history's idealists and religious ideals. The phrase "1794 against 1789" was Acton's epitaph for the Diet of Speyer, which unalterably reversed the early development of sixteenth-century protests.[7] Protestantism arose spontaneously, according to Acton, to vindicate the offended conscience of Western Europe. Dissent coalesced around the demand for religious liberty, but rapidly "systems of government" developed "externally, by accident" to manage and to restrain the freedoms claimed and substantially acquired.[8] Religious dissidents slipped into unholy alliances with unprincipled politicians. The last representatives of Protestantism's purest ideals, the sectarians or Anabaptists, were condemned in 1529 at Speyer, and the betrayal, in Acton's judgment, was completed.[9]

Speyer's condemnations were to be expected. The violence of incipient Protestantism's response to peasants, who recklessly coaxed social and political consequences from the soteriological promises of the Reformation, threw Luther and other culturally conservative reformers into the arms of princes and magistrates where their religious protests were cradled for generations. Acton believed that Luther's "tremendous vengeance" against the peasants impaired his ability to find and follow the logic of his own ideals in the discipline and discipleship of sectarian Protestantism. Troubled by the failure of evangelicals to achieve a Protestant consensus and to carry Catholicism, as well as by personal failures to control the very process of reformation, reformers appeared to Acton to have turned on their would-be progeny and to have enlisted the governments' cooperation in a wave of persecutions. The awesome amalgam of religious reformation and national or, more appropriately, territorial interest nearly eliminated privileges of conscience in the sixteenth century. The sectarians or Anabaptists, however, stubbornly survived. Acton was convinced that they safeguarded the ideal of religious liberty and escorted it to England and North America where by the nineteeth century it had been enshrined in political constitutions, which conceivably the heroic sectarians, as Acton understood them, would have accepted as the culmination of their efforts.[10]

Although trained by and tremendously fond of his German colleagues, Acton was remarkably preoccupied with English liberalism.[11] In church politics he was closer to Strossmayer and Döllinger than to Manning; yet he suggested that the pope immigrate to England where "the rulers of the church . . . would become familiar with the spectacle of a free and tolerant community, in the light of whose example they would perceive the benefits which liberty confers on religion and learn to distinguish the dross from the ore in systems and professions of freedom."[12] In England, according to Acton, the advanced ideas of sixteenth-century sectarians became "the common property of mankind." "Detached from their theological root," Anabaptists' endorsements of the freedom of conscience "became the creed of a party."[13] What is involved in this trip through centuries and across the English Channel, however, is more than deracination and development. Acton's connections between the Anabaptists huddled unwanted in communities and the accepted ideals of great nations somewhat distorted sectarian piety and exaggerated the legacy of religious separatism. Limited by the unavailability of trustworthy sources, Acton's understanding of sixteenth-century sectarian Protestantism was lamentably flawed. He could hardly have relied on his teachers who, he remarked in mildly judgmental notes, *sibi consulantes*, had been predominantly concerned to rehearse the Reformation's various reformulations of soteriology.[14] Had Acton been better informed, he would not have represented the Anabaptists' "crime" in the sixteenth century and their gift to the nineteenth as the dream that "two religions could coexist in the same place."[15]

Largely to Franklin Littell we owe that better information. Documents and fresh interpretations surfaced as a result of his research during the last few decades and notably advanced contemporary understanding of sixteenth-century sectarian Protestantism as a phenomenon constituted by distinct and often unrelated fellowships, more vivid as a "system" or radical, alternative reformation today than it was in its own century. Separatism was a common and "dominant" theme, according to Littell, a political posture that united, in some measure, otherwise disparate communities of dissenters. Littell, however, not only reported and documented this "dominant" theme, but he also wanted to make these separatists ancestors and progenitors of the ideals associated with the political cultures of Western democracies. This required him to minimize sixteenth-century sectarians' hostility toward the political cultures

79

from which they withdrew. The effect of Littell's work has been to subject the strategy of separation to close and continuing reevaluation,[16] but Littell himself, like Acton, was riveted to the correspondences between the apparent liberalism of the sixteenth-century religious separatists and the political liberalism deemed necessary to keep democracy disciplined and yet responsive to mature dissent.

Littell consequently was prepared to think of the "appalling chasm between Christ and culture" opened by Anabaptists principally as a result of persecution, as a "Manichaean aberration" with little theological standing.[17] What is lost in all this is the rather significant observation that the essentially dualist faith that braced sectarian "democracy" and discipline, a spiritualism inseparable from separatism, as it were, prohibited the extension of sectarian ideals into political culture. Precisely this extension, however, was what Littell has had in mind, notwithstanding the apparent incompatibility of sectarian Protestantism and civil religion. Littell was especially taken with the way sectarians, freed from the steady hand or strong arm of prince and consistory, "talked up" discipline among, and binding upon, all members of their communities. Similarity between this and the "open forum" model of democracy and the town meeting was not lost on Littell. By analogy, he claimed, sectarian ideals and the political culture of democracy could be related and the second alleged as a beneficiary of the first.[18] Clearly he was not insensitive to the provision that sectarian discipline presumed discipleship, that is, a uniform, spiritual, and voluntary reconciliation to divine will. Political culture, however, achieves only a reconciliation or harmonization of wills, at best, through arbitration and compromise. Furthermore, it would be questionable whether a "mixed" assembly of believers and non-believers could expect the spiritual guidance upon which Anabaptist consent and consensus depended. But Littell surmounted these obstacles with a serene confidence that faith in democracy virtually replaced the sectarian faith in spiritual presence as the guarantor of a happy resolve and of a unanimous consent to the outcome of deliberations.[19]

80

It is not surprising that during the chaotic period in which national identity and national purpose were seriously challenged in the United States, Franklin Littell was observed "vigorously promoting the Anabaptist cause, itinerating across the country with a gospel of the contemporary relevance of Anabaptist beliefs like a latter-day circuit rider."[20] But as revelations of official misconduct increasingly tarnished the reputation of the discipline of democracy in the last decade, Littell noted "a special pathos in remembering that for a great many early American Christians the New World was the place where the promises of the New Age, the Age of the Spirit, were to be actualized." The extent to which Littell himself transported that expectation into the twentieth century with his adaptation of sectarian spirituality to political culture may be disputed.[21] But one result of his efforts, and of Acton's earlier invocation of the notion of development to couple sixteenth-century separatism with constitutional guarantees and Whig policies in Victorian England, has been to endorse a civic piety that amounts to the very compound of religious ideals, political process, and national identity deplored in their time by all sectarians.

III

The point at issue is the place of separatism in sectarian life and thought. If the sectarians pioneered the concept of religious pluralism and desired only peaceful coexistence, separation from the community and enmity toward it must have been forced upon them. This is surely Acton's sense of the matter, and presumably it is what Littell means when he proposes that Anabaptist hostility was not "fixed" in its theological foundations. But the sectarian withdrawal from political culture should be construed differently. Anabaptist ecclesiology structured the world of belief as a church of the few saints called from the world of unbelief represented by the many churches of Europe acclimated to the conventions and conceits of the political culture symbolized by "the sword."[22] Religions that subscribed to the idea that a municipality or nation could be "baptized" were altogether discredited.[23] Sectarians angered Protestants and Catholics alike, not with petitions for tolerance and coexistence but by their direct challenge to the developing relationships between church and town council, between religious ideals and political culture. Predictably the sectarians were considered impious, *staatsgefährlich,* and they were hounded as political and religious subversives.

Responding for the sectarians, Leupold Scharnschlager urged solidarity and defiance of efforts to set religious conformity as a standard for municipal or national identity. His *Admonition* and "war cry" *(Fechtgeschrei)* inflexibly prohibited all commerce with political culture. Scharnschlager judged that Christian love departed from persons who endeavored to enrich themselves or to provide for their families in the marketplace. He believed the purchase of a house and the act of adultery to be equally criminal, and this startling equation is emblematic of the *Admonition*'s starched refusal to sanction breaks in sectarian discipline.[24] The intrigues of political culture brought members of Christ into contact with Satan's children. Scharnschlager therefore held that the distinction between

81

the worlds of belief and unbelief must be absolute.[25] The puritan prohibitions that evolved from this distinction were issued from exile and to other ostracized and disinherited dissidents, but the distinction itself was formulated in concert with Pilgram Marpeck when Scharnschlager and Marpeck were at the center of a party of moderate sectarians in one of Reformation Europe's most tolerant cities.

Strategies for the evangelical reform of Strasbourg were under consideration when peasant rebellions erupted in Alsace in 1524 and 1525. The rather sudden social and political adaptation of the concept of Christian liberty must have shaken the aristocratically dominated republic, for the *Reichskammergericht* provisionally halted further innovations.[26] The mass was not eliminated until 1529. But Martin Bucer probably enjoyed greater support than is at first apparent from city officials who were eager to avoid social upheaval.[27] He was successful against the sectarians, who were initially proscribed in 1527.[28] Within six months a fresh message from the *Rat* notified members of their duty to bring sectarians to punishment.[29] Still, it was not until 1533 that Bucer was able to call a synod and effectively to expel from the city what remained of the Anabaptist leadership.[30] Marpeck and Scharnschlager were among the last to leave.

Sectarians had flocked to Strasbourg, and Bucer and his allies were compelled to deal with some of their most articulate spokesmen, *inter alia*, Hans Denck, Melchior Hofmann, Michael Sattler, Sebastian Franck, and Caspar Schwenckfeld.[31] But even as Bucer pressed for consensus among Protestant clergy and for cooperation from the government, the sectarians fought among themselves. Marpeck and Scharnschlager occupied the middle ground between the belligerent Hofmann, who named Scharnschlager as one of his principal opponents, and Schwenckfeld, who was rebuked by Scharnschlager, gently yet at great length, for his advocacy of a new beginning in Christ that did away with all familiar religious forms.[32] Meanwhile Bucer's progress went unchecked. His colleague Wolfgang Capito took an increasingly more active part in identifying and maintaining the points of tension between sectarian Protestantism and the emerging religious consensus of the urban republic. Capito's *Belehrung von Eidverweigerern* contended that the Scripture did not forbid political oaths that annually reaffirmed support of and participation in the civic order.[33] Bucer earlier made the admission that the city was ruled by a "Christian authority," something of a test for loyalty.[34] His principle that the exercise of political authority was not *per se* impious (*oberkeyt nit wider got*) could not have found greater favor among the magistrates and greater opposition among even the moderate sectarians had it been fashioned for these purposes.[35] When Marpeck volunteered the objection that the church was not *of* the world *(nicht von diser wellt)*,[36] Bucer was quick to remind him that the church "nevertheless lives in the world and must truly take account of the needs of this life, foremost among which is authority."[37]

The next round in the debate on this matter belonged to Scharnschlager, who was summoned in 1534 to account for his beliefs.[38] He complained, with some irony, that he was unable to determine whether his summons came from Christians who were disposed to correct him or from magistrates who, *als weltlichs swerdt*, were inclined to punish him.[39] Of course, he realized that the issue had been settled. His implication, that the two functions were incompatible, was trumpeted at the conclusion of his "farewell address" as a blaring protest against the council's abrogation of the "blessed distinction" *(holdselige unnderscheid)* between the powers of the church and those of the unconverted world.[40] Scharnschlager was utterly convinced that the intrigues of political culture rendered impossible unconditional discipleship to Christ. *Liberation from political culture therefore was unquestionably preferable to liberty in it.*[41] The obligations of "Christian citizenship" placed the Christian *(der christen Bürgerschaft)* in unflinching opposition to efforts to inspire municipal identity.[42]

"Christian citizen" was a popular formula among the moderate sectarians and it reflected a widespread sentiment among Anabaptists. Echoing Philippians 3:20, the notion of heavenly citizenship implied that the Christian was but a pilgrim on earth. For Scharnschlager's friend, Marpeck, and for their predecessor in Strasbourg, Michael Sattler, this implication meant simply that the "citizen" of heaven had no claim to the privileges of power.[43] Sattler, it seemed for a short while, might be persuaded to compromise with Bucer and Capito.[44] His sincerity earned their respect, as Capito reported, and the city's reformers made no haste to proceed against his errors.[45] Sattler, however, showed no indication of relinquishing his "Christian citizenship" and of moderating his uncooperative position, and he rapidly became known among evangelical Protestants as the most obstinate of their sectarian competitors *(omnium pertinacissimus)*.[46] All that mattered to Sattler was discipleship to Christ, which required uncompromising dedication to the formation of a sinless community.[47] Capito understood this as "the genesis of a new monasticism" *(ein anfang einer newen moncherey)*, and he was not far wrong.[48] Certainly the articles Sattler composed in 1527 prefigured Scharnschlager's "blessed distinction" and probably carried the point to its extreme. Because he believed that Christ and

83

his kingdom were despised in the world and especially betrayed by the closely coordinated strokes intended to shape simultaneously municipal and religious identity, he was convinced that Satan had overtaken the Strasbourg reform. He announced as he left the city that "there is nothing common between Christ and Satan."[49]

While Sattler's dualism found expression in the literature of the moderate sectarians and the absolute distinction between "Christian citizenship" and citizenship in the urban republic was a commonplace there among Strasbourg Anabaptists, Bucer and Capito became satisfied that the responsibilities of dual citizenship were manageable. What John Yoder branded as the *Staatsoptimismus* of these and other municipal reformers orbited initially around the supposition that the political culture could and should secure the ideal of religious liberty and protect dissenters from the vengeance of the pope and his imperial allies. Optimism cracked in places, and yet it appears as if the security of the Reformation's apparent gains against internal disruptions made the alliance between church and government ever more necessary.[50] By 1535, Strasbourg's council proudly wore the cloak designed for it by Bucer: "We plead guilty and acknowledge ourselves a Christian authority."[51]

The charge, unspoken here, was repeatedly registered by sectarians as they filed from the city. Authority could not, from their perspective, claim to be Christian, for, whether for purposes of protest or public order, the coercion of conscience practiced by authority in its various attempts to associate municipal or regional identity with religious conformity debarred political culture from that set of ponderables that may be dignified by the adjective "Christian." For the sectarians, of course, this was much more than semantic gamesmanship. Coercion, whether in policies devised to rid municipalities of religious dissent or in the baptism of unconsenting infants, was the special mark of Satan's presence. Bucer attacked the notion that infant baptism was a species of coercion.[52] He could hardly deny, however, that coercive measures were part of his plan to clear Strasbourg of dissidents.[53] Sectarians were forced either to conform to the developing religious consensus of the urban republic or to embrace the political consequences of their dualism and to quit the city.

84   Strasbourg's *de facto* experiment with religious pluralism ended with the synod of 1533. After it adjourned, Protestant preachers petitioned the city fathers for the removal of persons "convicted" during the inquiries and yet remaining within the city.[54] Scharnschlager conjectured that if roles were reversed, his accusers, though then a minority, would have continued to enjoy the city's hospitality.[55] It would be a mistake, however, to place great weight

on this admirable position and to suggest that the logic of sectarian dualism, if pursued in political culture, could somehow have become the basis for religious pluralism.[56] Scharnschlager's gesture was based on Anabaptist abhorrence of force. The sectarians' influence was necessarily restricted, but their absolute demands for discipleship and their adaptation of the politically charged concept of citizenship prompt a suspicion that they might have become as imperious as magisterial reformers who claimed the privilege of establishing a comprehensive pastoral ministry for the civic community and who subsequently became politically privileged. Instead, sectarian Protestantism claimed the "privilege" of the persecuted, that is, what A. D. Lindsay once called "the natural exclusiveness of a small group" and "the never-ending audacity of elected persons."[57] This reflected not simply the hardship of exile and homelessness but, more to the point, the rigid dualism that tempted such a fate as well.

Strasbourg, at its most tolerant stage, conformed with Douglass's standards for civil religion. But slowly Bucer and then Capito impressed upon the government the grave political dangers of religious dissent. Their targets, the sectarian Protestants, proved to be the test that the city's permissiveness and pluralism ultimately could not pass, and the leading Anabaptists, who had flocked there, were gone by 1534. But these victims must not be transformed into the pioneers of religious pluralism. Defiance of political authority, despite Acton's insistence to the contrary, was not essentially an assertion of the right of different religions to coexist. Sectarian resistance to religious conformity and the consequent ostracism of Anabaptists were results of the dualism at the very heart of their religious identity. Littell's efforts to rehabilitate contemporary political culture and to manage its pluralism by reconstituting sectarian discipline as a paradigm for political life strike at that heart and tame the sectarians' reckless refusal to meddle in politics. Pluralism is not implicit in Anabaptist dualism. It is the square peg to the sixteenth-century sectarians' round hole, and no amount of well-intentioned hammering will produce a tidy fit. But pluralism is the central affirmation of Western democracies' political cultures, and thus the great challenge of civil religion, as Douglass correctly surmises, is to endorse and encourage religious pluralism as well as to structure political culture as a mediator of divine grace. The experiences of dissenters in municipalities like Strasbourg are replete with lessons for the historian of civil religion. But sectarian Protestantism is an ill-chosen model.

85

NOTES

[1]R. Bruce Douglass, "Civil Religion and Western Christianity," *Thought*, vol. 55 (1980), p. 174.

[2]*Ibid.*, p. 182.

[3]For what follows, see Winthrop S. Hudson, "This Most Favored Nation: Reflections on the Vocation of America," *Journal of Church and State*, vol. 19 (1977), pp. 17-30.

[4]Robert Bellah cites this as the development of "single vision," which simply "dried up" the Protestant imagination from Edwards to Niebuhr, in *The Broken Covenant: American Civil Religion in Time of Trial* (New York: The Seabury Press, Inc., a Crossroad Book, 1975), pp. 72-86.

[5]For example, see Winthrop S. Hudson, *The Cambridge Connection and the Elizabethan Settlement of 1559* (Durham: Duke University Press, 1980), especially pp. 90-150.

[6]Sidney E. Mead, "The Theology of the Republic and the Orthodox Mind," *Journal of the American Academy of Religion*, vol. 44 (1976), pp. 107-108.

[7]Cambridge University Library, Acton, Add. mss. 4995.97. I am grateful for the cooperation of the staff of the manuscript room and for funds from the Department of Religion and from the Research Council at the University of North Carolina at Chapel Hill, all of which enabled me to consult Acton's unpublished notes and journals. Acton was most candid about his disappointments when he was grappling with history's betrayals and less so when he wrote about the nature of history. See, for example, Acton's *Lectures on Modern History* (Gloucester: Peter Smith, 1975); "The Protestant Theory of Persecution," *The History of Freedom and Other Essays*, ed. J. N. Figgis and R. V. Laurence (London: Macmillan and Co., 1910), pp. 150-187; "The Massacre of St. Bartholomew," *The History of Freedom*, pp. 101-149; and "The Rise and Fall of the Mexican Empire," *Essays in the Liberal Interpretation of History*, ed. William H. MacNeill (Chicago: University of Chicago Press, 1967), pp. 214-242. In connection with this presentation of Acton's manuscript notes on sectarian Protestantism and political liberalism, also review Ulrich Noack, *Politik als Sicherung der Freiheit nach den Schriften von John Dalberg-Acton* (Frankfurt am Main: G. Shulte-Bulmke, 1947) and Gertrude Himmelfarb, *Lord Acton* (Chicago: University of Chicago Press, 1952), still the most comprehensive and penetrating study of Acton's thought.

[8]Add. mss. 5402.2.

[9]J. Kühn, *Die Geschichte des speyrer Reichstags, 1529* (Leipzig: M. Heinsius Nachfolger, 1929), pp. 167-168.

[10]Add. mss. 4995.72 and 5412.17.

[11]Acton's manuscript notes are packed with tributes to Continental historians, foremost among whom was Ignaz von Döllinger, Acton's teacher and close friend. Acton remarked in his "Notes on Archival Research, 1864-1868" that Döllinger "initiated" him "into the mysteries of the craft," and he confessed to Döllinger himself, "Ich bin überhaupt nichts als was Sie aus mir gemacht haben." Acton's "Notes" are printed in *Lord Acton, The Decisive Decade*, ed. Damian McElrath (Louvain: Publications Universities de Louvain, 1970), p. 127. His comment to Döllinger appears in *Ignaz von Döllinger—Lord Acton: Briefwechsel*, ed. Victor Conzemius, (Munich: Beck, 1963-71), vol. 1, p. 442. For English historians, Acton had few kind words. He reprimanded Macaulay and Gibbon, and he observed that despite "famous scholars, great libraries, and immense accumulations of manuscripts," England produced no genuine church historians. Add. mss. 4910.14, 5384.78, and 5640.52.

[12]Acton, "Current Events," *Home and Foreign Review* (1863), p. 669. During the

stormy sessions of the Vatican Council, Acton reported from Rome to Döllinger, "Strossmayer [Bishop of Djakovo] hat mit uns gegessen, und meine Frau gewonnen, weil er genau dieselbe Weltanschauung vorträgt, welche die meinige ist." *Briefwechsel,* vol. 2, p. 96. Also consult K. Schatz, *Kirchenbild und päpstliche Unfehlbarkeit bei den deutschsprachigen Minoritätsbischöfen auf dem I. Vatikanum* (Rome: Università Gregoriana, 1975), pp. 95-103, 132-138.

¹³Acton, *Lectures,* pp. 192, 198.

¹⁴Add. mss. 4915.13, 5431.47, and 5640.43-44.

¹⁵*Ibid.,* 4995.171.

¹⁶See, e.g., Walter Klassen, "The Anabaptist Understanding of the Separation of the Church," *Church History,* vol. 46 (1977), pp. 421-436.

¹⁷Franklin H. Littell, *The Church and the Body Politic* (New York: The Seabury Press, Inc., 1969), pp. 133-135. Also consult Littell's *The Free Church* (Boston: Starr King Press, 1957), *From State Church to Pluralism* (Garden City, N.Y.: Doubleday/Anchor Press, 1962), and especially *The Origins of Sectarian Protestantism* (New York: Macmillan, Inc., 1964).

¹⁸Franklin H. Littell, "The Work of the Holy Spirit in Group Decisions," *The Mennonite Quarterly Review,* vol. 34, no. 2 (April, 1960), pp. 82-84. Also note Littell's "The Anabaptist Concept of the Church," *The Recovery of the Anabaptist Vision,* ed. Guy F. Hershberger (Scottdale, Pa.: Herald Press, 1957), pp. 119-134; and "The New Shape of the Church-State Issue," *The Mennonite Quarterly Review,* vol. 40, no. 3 (July, 1966), pp. 179-189.

¹⁹Franklin H. Littell, "A Christian Style of Politics," *Review and Expositor,* vol. 65, no. 3 (Summer, 1968), p. 297; and Franklin H. Littell, "The Work of the Holy Spirit in Group Decisions."

²⁰Donald F. Durnbaugh, "Theories of Free Church Origins," *The Mennonite Quarterly Review,* vol. 41, no. 2 (April, 1968), p. 93.

²¹I am grateful to Dr. Littell for furnishing me with several documents that bear upon this question, among them a typescript of his 1975 address to the College Theology Society of the United States, "The Radical Reformation and the American Experience," from which his remark on "special pathos" is taken.

²²Heinold Fast, "Variationen des Kirchenbegriffs bei den Täufern," *Mennonitische Geschichtsblätter,* vol. 27 (1970), pp. 5-18.

²³Clarence Bauman, *Gewaltlosigkeit im Täufertum* (Leiden: E. J. Brill, 1968), pp. 290-297. Also consult Hans J. Hillerbrand *Die politische Ethik des oberdeutschen Täufertums* (Leiden: E. J. Brill, 1962) and Robert Friedmann, *The Theology of Anabaptism* (Scottdale, Pa.: Herald Press, 1973).

²⁴Leupold Scharnschlager, *Gemeine Vermahnung und Erinnerung, Kunstbuch* (typescript in the Mennonite Historical Library, Goshen, Indiana), pp. 226-227.

²⁵Scharnschlager, *Meldung vom wahren Glauben und gemeinsamen Heil in Christo, Kunstbuch,* pp. 294-304.

²⁶H.-W. Musing, "Karlstadt und die Entstehung der strassburger Täufergemeinde," *The Origins and Characteristics of Anabaptism,* ed. M. Lienhard (The Hague: Nijhoff, 1977), pp. 187-188. Also note Jean Rott, "Strasbourg et la guerre des paysans, les limites de l'action de Strasbourg," *Strasbourg, au coeur réligieux du XVIᵉ siècle,* ed. G. Livet and F. Rapp (Strasbourg: Librarie Istra, 1977), pp. 75-83.

²⁷Thomas A. Brady, Jr., *Ruling Class, Regime, and Reformation at Strasbourg* (Leiden: E. J. Brill, 1978), pp. 198-258.

²⁸*Quellen zur Geschichte der Täufer,* Elsass 1 and 2, Quellen und Forschungen zur Reformationsgeschichte, vols. 26 and 27, ed. M. Krebs and H. G. Rott (Gutersloh: C. Bertelsmann, 1959-60), vol. 26, pp. 22-23.

²⁹*Ibid.,* p. 148, lines 12-14: "h. ammeister acht uff die widertäuffer haben;

desgleichen die ratsherrn, wo sie die erfaren, eim rat anzeigen, domit sie gestraft werden."

[30] *Ibid.*, vol. 27, p. 3, lines 12-21.

[31] George Huntston Williams, *The Radical Reformation* (Philadelphia: The Westminster Press, 1962), pp. 237-298.

[32] Hofmann's accusation appears in *Quellen*, vol. 27, p. 19, lines 38-39. Marpeck and Scharnschlager collaborated on two extended criticisms of Schwenckfeld's spiritualism after all three left Strasbourg. The passage mentioned can be ascribed with but a small measure of uncertainty to Scharnschlager. *Pilgram Marpeck's Antwort auf Kaspar Schwenckfelds Beurteilung des Buches der Bundesbezeugung von 1542*, ed. J. Loserth (Vienna: Kommisionsverlag der Verlagsbuchhandlung Carl Fromme Gesellschaft, 1929), p. 544, line 31–p. 546, line 18. Scharnschlager's role has customarily been understated, although the discovery of the *Kunstbuch* has given him some greater notoriety. For example, see J. Seguy, *Les assemblées Anabaptistes—Mennonites de France* (Paris: Mouton, 1977), pp. 96-101, 231-233. Notwithstanding Littell's relatively infrequent reference to Marpeck, interest in his role in Strasbourg and thereafter in Augsburg has grown tremendously. In this connection, note the recent edition and English translation by William Klassen and Walter Klaassen of *The Writings of Pilgram Marpeck* (Scottdale, Pa.: Herald Press, 1978); and, on the the disputed nature and extent of Scharnschlager's collaboration in much of this work and therefore in the formulation of the moderate sectarian position, consult J. J. Kiwiet, *Pilgram Marpeck* (Kassel: Oncken, 1958), pp. 72-77; Harold S. Bender, "Pilgram Marpeck, Anabaptist Theologian and Civil Engineer," *The Mennonite Quarterly Review*, vol. 38, no. 3 (July, 1964), pp. 254-260; and William Klassen, *Covenant and Community* (Grand Rapids, Mich.: Wm. B. Eerdmans Publishing Co., 1968), pp. 50-56.

[33] *Quellen*, vol. 26, p. 299, lines 11-26.

[34] *Ibid.*, lines 14-16, 27-29.

[35] *Ibid.*, vol. 27, p. 29, lines 33-35; and vol. 27, p. 201, lines 23-32.

[36] *Ibid.*, vol. 26, p. 511, line 10; p. 512, line 4.

[37] *Ibid.*, p. 511, lines 32-33: "Es lebt aber in der welt, Darumb es warlich, was zu dissem leben von nötten, erfordert: under dem ist die oberkeit das fürnembst."

[38] *Ibid.*, vol. 27, p. 311, line 13.

[39] *Ibid.*, p. 346, line 34; p. 347, line 18.

[40] *Ibid.*, p. 351, lines 4-20.

[41] Scharnschlager, *Meldung*, p. 297.

[42] Scharnschlager, *Ein Frag: Ihr wollet nicht dass ein Christ möge ein Oberer werden*, *Kunstbuch*, pp. 285-286.

[43] *Quellen*, vol. 26, p. 69, lines 24-25, and p. 511, line 14.

[44] John H. Yoder, "Der Kristallisationspunkt des Täufertums," *Mennonitische Geschichtsblätter*, vol. 24 (1972), pp. 34-47.

[45] *Quellen*, vol. 26, p. 81, line 21; p. 82, line 4.

[46] *Ibid.*, p. 73, lines 14-16.

[47] K. Depperman, "Die Strassburger Reformatoren und die Krise des oberdeutschen Täufertums im Jahre 1527," *Mennonitische Geschichtsblätter*, vol. 30 (1973), p. 32.

[48] *Quellen*, vol. 26, p. 82, line 7.

[49] *Ibid.*, p. 69, line 33.

[50] John H. Yoder, *Täufertum und Reformation im Gespräch* (Zurich: EVZ-Verlag, 1968) and Berndt Moeller, *Reichsstadt und Reformation* (Gütersloh: G. Mohn, 1962), pp. 38-55.

[51] *Quellen*, vol. 27, p. 447, lines 3-4: "wir uns als ein christlich oberkait schuldig erkennen."

[52] *Ibid.*, vol. 26, p. 424, lines 32-34: "Der kindertauff zwinget niemand. So man dan auch gotteslesterung straffet und abschaffet, würt darumb auch noch nieman in die kirch gezwungenn."

[53] *Ibid.*, vol. 27, p. 202, lines 1-11.

[54] *Ibid.*, pp. 266-269 and 392, lines 11-16.

[55] *Ibid.*, p. 352, lines 13-20.

[56] Cf. Paul Peachy, "The Radical Reformation, Political Pluralism, and the *Corpus Christianum,*" *Origins and Characteristics of Anabaptism,* ed. M. Lienhard, pp. 10-26.

[57] A. D. Lindsay, *The Essentials of Democracy* (Oxford: Clarendon Press, 1929) pp. 37-38.

Were the Earliest
English Baptists Anabaptists?

Joseph D. Ban

Various historians have explored the possible connections between English Baptist beginnings and the Continental Anabaptist movements. Winthrop S. Hudson made a significant contribution to the discussion with two related articles. Hudson stated his argument succinctly: "Actually the Baptists and the Anabaptists represent two diverse and quite dissimilar Christian traditions."[1] He began the second article: "If the early Baptists were clear about any one thing, they were clear in their insistence that they were not to be confused with the Anabaptists."[2] Both the General Baptists in their confessions of 1611 and 1660 and the Particular Baptists in 1644 and 1646 insisted they were not Anabaptists.

Hudson presented five arguments to make his case that the "Baptists were not Anabaptists." First, he argued, the early Baptists firmly rejected "the distinctive features of Anabaptist life and thought." The unacceptable life aspects included "the Anabaptist opposition to civil magistracy, the holding of public office, military service, oaths, and going to court." The Baptists adopted the Westminster Confession as the base for their theological position. Secondly, the greater number of "early Baptists had been Congregationalists" before becoming Baptists. Hudson saw the Baptists as a distinct group in the lay movement in English Puritanism. Thirdly, the influence of Anabaptists is not necessary in order to account for the adoption of believer's baptism by the Baptists. Fourthly, there was John Smyth's own career. Smyth first baptized himself and then others in what Smyth called "true Christian Apostolic baptism." Smyth's contact with the Dutch Mennonites followed that decisive act. Hudson pointed out the sizable barrier language created between the Dutch and the English congregations. Fifth, the "more temperate and judicious" of the opponents of the early Baptists did recognize that the charges of being Anabaptist were unfounded.[3] Hudson claimed the English Baptists to be the "left-wing of the Puritan movement." The Baptists diverged from the Anabaptists on central theological issues. Baptists affirmed the doctrine of justification as in the Reformed tradition. The Anabaptists insisted that salvation came by "cognition" or "knowledge" derived from the Scriptures. While the Baptists affirmed the Calvinistic doctrine of original sin, the Anabaptists rejected the notion. The Baptist attitude toward state and society was positive and affirming, while the Anabaptists "emphasized separation from and indifference to the world." Hudson described the Anabaptists as biblical literalists prone to idolize the written Word "whereas the Helwys Confession of 1611 in good Reformed style spoke of the Bible as 'containing' the Word of God."[4]

The search for authentic roots is needed, contended Hudson, in order that Baptists might more clearly appreciate just who they are. Significant differences exist between the Reformed and the Anabaptist traditions. The way a community of believers expresses its Christian faith has an impact not only upon how it organizes its life and conducts its worship but also upon how it relates to the larger society around it in both political and economic matters.

Hudson's twin articles have served as a benchmark for discussions of the possible relationship of the Continental Anabaptist movements to English Baptist origins. The earliest reactor, Ernest Payne, insisted that Hudson had not done justice to the complex nature of the Anabaptist movement in Europe. Payne also drew attention to the question of geography. "Can it really have been accidental that the first gathered churches appeared in Kent and East Anglia where in the middle of the sixteenth century there were colonies of Dutch refugees, some of whom are known to have been Anabaptists?" Payne also took issue regarding the influence of the Dutch Mennonites upon Smyth and Helwys. Payne's article was weakened by statements such as "By implication Dr. Hudson appears to be denying all similarity or connection." Payne plainly argued that similarity implies connection, as in his statement that "what was *common* to almost all the left-wing groups was a belief in a gathered church of believers, a repudiation of infant baptism, and a claim for toleration and freedom of conscience."[5]

92 The Hudson articles represent the English separatist tradition among historians discussing the origins of English Baptists. Payne's arguments indicate an opposite tradition that finds a "spiritual kinship" between the Continental Anabaptists and Baptist roots in England. These two positions define the polarities of a controversy that has continued.

This chapter considers more recent developments in the ongoing discussion. Attention will be given to various books and scholarly articles that bear upon the Baptist-Anabaptist question. A recent scholarly attempt to replace Champlin Burrage's classic interpretation will be analyzed in some detail.

Lonnie Kliever has provided significant support for Hudson's thesis that the General Baptists arose as "a left-ward movement of Puritanism and a logical extension of Separatism." Kliever found the views of early Separatist Robert Browne on the church and society to be "significantly different from main-line Continental Anabaptism in any of its expressions." Kliever examined basic doctrines and found that Helwys and the General Baptists in England "stood in a completely different theological tradition from the Waterlanders."[6]

Using the confessions hammered out in the debates that led to the Smyth-Helwys split, Kliever concluded that the distinctives of the General Baptists, their rejection of infant baptism, their insistence that baptism was for believers only, their gathering of a "visible church on the basis of a believer's baptism," their Arminian modification of Calvinism and their concerns for religious liberty all grew out of "influences and resources" already present within their English Separatist roots.[7] The results of Kliever's researches led him to conclude:

> Every distinctive Mennonite doctrine which Smyth included in either of his confessions of 1609 or 1612 was countered by Helwys—the doctrines concerning rejection of original sin, freedom of will, analytic view of justification, Hofmannite Christology, the particular concept of the "gathered church," the ministry and its exclusive powers, the severity of discipline, the precedence of the New Testament over the Old, and the believer's relation to government, war and oathtaking.[8]

In order to compare theological doctrines of Baptists and Anabaptists, it is necessary to find comparable items. To date, no evidence of a theological statement from sixteenth-century English Baptists has been uncovered. In this regard, Kliever cautioned that the critical problem in making comparative judgment was "ascertaining just what the Anabaptist views in England were" at that time. He warns against reading back into that period concepts based upon a later, mature Anabaptism. He also noted the distortions that arose "from the opposition's then-current understanding of Anabaptism."[9]

Two independent Baptist traditions existed in seventeenth-century England. The earliest churches, founded by Helwys and his successors, were General Baptists. Arminian in theology (a modified Calvinism), they believed in "general election, universal atonement, and falling from grace; some of them denied original sin and upheld free will."[10] A later group developed out of the congregation led first by Henry Jacob, then John Lathrop, followed by Henry Jessey.[11] Because of their stricter Calvinist doctrine, these churches became known as Particular Baptists. Their beliefs included "personal or particular election, particular or limited atonement, bondage of the will, and perseverance of the saints." Hugh Wamble notes that the two groups differed chiefly over "their views of atonement."[12]

For the General Baptists we have key theological statements such as Helwys's *An Advertisement or Admonition unto the Congregation* that provides his theological views that arose from his controversy with Smyth. For the Particular Baptists we have the Confession of 1644 and its successors.[13] There is no comparable English Anabaptist theological statement.

The first of seven articles in the Swiss Mennonite "Schleitheim Confession," adopted in early 1527, deals with baptism ". . . which is to be given only to 'those who have learned repentance and amendment of life . . . and . . . who walk in the resurrection of Jesus Christ.'"[14] This statement discloses a significant difference in the Anabaptist and Baptist understanding of baptism. In the Particular Baptist Confession of 1644, baptism was to be administered after "profession of faith of the gospel." Such a requirement clearly lacks the Anabaptist emphasis upon "those who have learned repentance and amendment of life." The latter phrase communicates an important difference that emerged between the Continental Anabaptists and the earlier Reformers. Hans J. Hillerbrand describes the difference:

> In place of Luther's evangelical discovery that man is justified by faith in Christ's work of redemption, the Anabaptists suggested that God through Christ will forgive those who in humility and obedience imitate Christ's suffering. Man becomes aware of his sinful nature, repents of his sins, and is forgiven *through a commitment to be Christ's disciple*. It is the integral place of this additional commitment which marks the distinctive feature of the Anabaptist view.[15]

Similarly, while some have sought a connection between the way the Anabaptists employed excommunication and the way the Separatists and the early Baptists made use of discipline, the latter usage is traced directly to the Genevan Reformer. As François Wendel comments: "Now in Calvin's eyes the right to excommunicate was the cornerstone of his whole system of ecclesiastical discipline."[16] Nor is it reasonable to attempt to correlate English Baptist beliefs with such Schleitheim articles as these: (4) separation from the world, including participation in civic affairs; (6) the sword, its use in self-defense or in military affairs, was forbidden; (7) oaths were not to be taken.[17] With each such article, major differences appear between the practice of English Baptists and their Continental counterparts.

B. R. White is the leading contemporary Baptist historian researching and writing about early English Baptists. His work *The English Separatist Tradition* offers a careful analysis of the original sources. White demonstrates that Separatists arose independently of any Anabaptist influences. White concluded that "evidence of anything approaching direct influence from Anabaptism upon the English Separatists before John Smyth arrived in Amsterdam appears to be completely lacking."[18] Drawing upon primary sources, White shows that the English Separatists, while yet in England, "had normally refused baptism at the hands of the parochial clergy."[19] This contradicts Murray Tolmie's suggestion that Smyth and his congregation were convinced by the Waterlanders that "their baptism was false because [it was] administered to infants who were incapable of saving faith."[20] White dates Smyth's "unease about the baptism which he and others had received at the hands of the Church of England" in the autumn of 1607. Smyth had indicated such views in a section of *Parallels, Censures, Observations* written while Smyth was still in England. White further finds, in contrast to Tolmie, that Smyth's contact with the Mennonites at the time he published *Character of the Beast* was not very close.[21]

Two recent books, in contrast with Kliever and White, champion a historical connection between European Anabaptists and English Separatist beginnings. Michael R. Watts, in *The Dissenters: From the Reformation to the French Revolution*, presents a useful study of the Dissenting movements in England and Wales. Watts writes:

> . . . both Champlin Burrage and B. R. White have denied that there is any evidence that continental Anabaptism influenced English Dissent before the early seventeenth century, and Lonnie Kliever has argued that it made little impact even then. But while concrete literary evidence may be lacking, there is a good deal of circumstantial evidence to suggest a link between Lollardy, Anabaptism, and the General Baptists of the seventeenth century. Irvin Horst has drawn attention to the existence of an Anabaptist group in London in the 1530s and while his contention that they were 'old Lollards' cannot be regarded as proven, he does show that Anabaptist opinions were held and disseminated in England in the reign of Henry VIII not only by immigrants from the Low Countries, but also by native Englishmen.[22]

95

What constitutes that "circumstantial evidence"? On the basis of such evidence Watts proceeds with the assumption that the link connecting Lollardy, Anabaptism, and the General Baptists actually has been adequately demonstrated.

Watts's statement depends upon the study by Irvin B. Horst, *The*

Radical Brethren. Horst claims to have discovered a historical link between the Anabaptists of the Lowlands and English Lollardy. Horst wrote: "Early in the 1530's, probably in 1532, several English and Flemish persons were taken into custody because they had imported and distributed an anabaptist book."[23] While acknowledging that it was the arresting authorities who pinned the name Anabaptist upon the prisoners and the confiscated works, Horst added that "the details of the deposition support the correctness of this usage." He promised to provide the evidence to confirm this judgment.

The importance of this find, by Horst, of a book reputed to be an Anabaptist work is evident when it is recalled that Champlin Burrage wrote: "Before 1550, too, it appears that no Anabaptist books were printed in England, either in English or in any other language, and no English translations of the works of Continental Anabaptists are known to have been published before the time of the Civil Wars."[24] Horst's find, if substantiated, would mean that there was an English translation of an Anabaptist work published more than a hundred years earlier than any previously known book of its type.

Horst notes that while "the document is undated" it "has been calendared" under the year 1532 in the *Letters and Papers* of the reign of Henry VIII.[25] Then Horst suggests that 1532 "may be too early, but some evidence can be found, as we shall note, to support this date." Again, the critical reader will await such evidence. Next Horst reiterates that the cause of the arrest was a heretical book identified as an "Anabaptist confession." "As for the quantity," Horst states, "John Clark was suspected of having received 300 copies but had only 44 in his possession at the time of the search, while John Raulinges had distributed 40 copies. Two other members were known to have had copies. The total number of copies may have been in the neighborhood of 500."[26] The author of *The Radical Brethren* does not relate how he decided upon the figure of 500 books, but the Public Record Office copy does tell us how the arresting officer arrived at his figure of 300: "We conjecture," he wrote for the record. Note the progression toward certainty. The conjecture of the deposition becomes, in Horst's use of it, 300 actual books or even as many as 500. For, in his following paragraph, Horst contends that "John Clarke either had dispersed or hidden 256 copies."

The deposition identifies 44 confiscated books as an "Anabaptist Confession." Horst acknowledges that "we are left in the dark as to its further identification. As a confession it must have contained articles of religion. Its Anabaptist character is attested to by details about the persons and their views as recorded in the deposition."

The cautious reader, again, will await the supporting evidence. Now Horst makes a statement that is hard to challenge: "A copy of the actual book, however, is not known, or at least recorded. It may be considered a lost book."[27]

In this same paragraph Horst conjectures that it may have been such a copy of an Anabaptist confession received by John Calvin in Geneva "from far countries" and which occasioned Calvin's writing in 1544 *Briève instruction pour armer tous bon fidèles contre les erreurs de la secte des Anabaptistes* which, in turn, was published in English in 1548 as *A Short Instruction for to arme all good Christian people agaynst the pestiferous errors of the common secte of Anabaptistes.* Horst concludes: "It is possible that Calvin wrote this work to combat the 'Anabaptist Confession' circulated in England."[28] The incredulous reader again awaits substantiating proof.

The resourceful author of *The Radical Brethren* remedies the lack of a copy of the lost book with an ingenious identification. Horst writes: "The Confession was probably an English translation of the popular and widely-known *Brüderliche Vereinigung etzlicher Kinder Gottes, sieben Artikel betreffent* (Brotherly Union of a Number of Children of God Concerning Seven Articles). The earliest printed editions extant are from the 1530s, but the work was written in February, 1527. . . ."[29] Then follow two solid paragraphs describing the contents of the seven articles. Horst concludes: "'The booke of Anabaptist Confession' may well have been an English translation of the *Articles.*"[30] Here Horst omits to clarify a significant detail: nowhere does he suggest that there was an English translation of *Artikel* in the sixteenth or seventeenth centuries. His one footnote leaves the impression that an English translation appeared in print in 1545. The painstaking reader may find this acknowledgment buried in the middle of Appendix B at the back of the book: "We are at a considerable disadvantage by not having at hand a copy of the English confession, but to date a copy has not been found or at least recorded."[31]

Corroborating data is promised in the "details about the persons and their views as recorded in the deposition which reads "one Bastiane, a flemmying, which is said to be the byshop & reder to the Anabaptistes." Horst describes this reference as "one of the most helpful clues in the document." He interprets this to mean that English and Flemish members cooperated and that Lollard and Anabaptist traditions had been amalgamated. He bases this conclusion on his identification of "'reader' as typically Lollard, while 'byshop' was used for leaders among Dutch and Flemish anabaptists." Horst does not raise the question whether this Bastiane had identified himself as a bishop or whether that appellation had been given by the arresting officer, for "Bishop" was an English term as well. As to the merging of the Lollard and Anabaptist traditions, Horst found that "the refusal to 'beleue nothyng but the scripture' was common to both the Lollards and anabaptists, although the view 'that no man expounding scripture should be believed' had more of a Lollard than an anabaptist accent."[32] Horst found the clearest evidence of Anabaptist doctrine in the phrase "strange doctrines" linked with "touchyng the humanitie of Christe" which Horst identified with Melchior Hofmann's heretical notions. The deposition offers too little evidence to make the identification a certainty.[33]

Horst had promised to confirm the date of 1532, the year in which the deposition was calendared, as the correct date. This data is presented in a long paragraph that begins: "Who were the English and Flemish persons involved in this incident?" Then he inserts this gratuitous statement: "The name Baughton (Boughten) occurred frequently among the later Lollards in London." The four citations for this are from John Thomson, *The Later Lollards*. Thomson confirms two individuals named Boughton, one named Joan who was burned at the stake at 80 years of age and the other a Thomas "who was also an enthusiast for attending sermons, as long as they agreed with his ideas.[34] For whatever historical value there is in such information, there were at least two Boughtons among the later Lollards. The reader's critical vision should not be blurred by such facts of supererogation, for the discussion concerns concrete proof establishing the date for the deposition. Horst reminds the reader that the 'byshop' was a certain Bastiane. The author points out that there was a printer named Herman Bastian arrested in Hesse (Germany) during the spring of 1536. Horst concludes:

> Since the English deposition has to do with a 'Bastiane' who was a 'byshop & reder to the Anabaptistes,' and with the importation of an anabaptist book, it is possible that on this occasion Herman Bastian had visited England. It was quite typical for an anabaptist leader to be engaged in a trade.[35]

Noting that the question is that of dating the deposition, Horst argues that if his identification of "Bastiane, the anabaptist bishop of London, with Herman Bastian in Hesse" is correct, then a closing date was established by the arrest of Bastian in Hesse in the spring of 1536. Horst offers "a more precise date" by turning to the arrest of John Gough whose name appears on the same deposition, though as a separate item. Horst assumes that Gough was apprehended at the same time the Anabaptists were arrested. It was a possibility, although it cannot be proven exactly when Gough, or any of the others, were picked up. Horst continues his argument:

'The Confession of the citie of Geneva' cannot be identified, as a copy evidently is not recorded. . . . It is known that a work entitled *The Articles of Geneva* had been translated and published in 1532. . . . If the *Articles of Geneva* may be identified with the Confession of the City of Geneva, which is entirely plausible, we may with some confidence propose 1532 as the date of the deposition.[36]

Such legerdemain then is the "circumstantial evidence" from which Michael Watts drew his conclusion that Lollardy and Anabaptism and the English General Baptists were linked. Yes, a book that no one since has seen, identified as a work admittedly never translated into English, available in a quantity the greater part of which is conjecture, about people who may be Lollards or may be Anabaptists or just may be unconventional; with an invented voyage of a known German for whom there is no evidence that he spoke English or had ever been in England where supposedly he was arrested as a Flemish bishop—nor has evidence been produced that the real, the German Herman Bastian was ever considered a bishop among German Anabaptists—in a deposition whose date is documented by a printer who may or may not have been arrested the same day or even the same year as the three Englishmen and the one Scottish man, and who may or may not have been the printer of *The Articles of Geneva* (for which printing another man actually was charged and freed) and which may or may not have been the book cited in the deposition; such are the facts presented, not to mention Boughten—whom Watts has as Broughton—a name that ". . . occurred frequently among the later Lollards" and, as a fact, Thomson mentions both Joan and Thomas, not necessarily related. One unassailable fact emerges from these cited pages of *The Radical Brethren:* this demonstrably is "circumstantial evidence."

Early in his book, Horst made a point of emphasizing "the inductive method" which, he wrote, "requires a strict reckoning with the contemporary data; that is, we stay by historical events and ideas which can be identified as anabaptist." Horst stands judged by his own statement: ". . . the student of anabaptism has to face squarely the hiatuses and the dead-ends in the evidence without trying to read too much into or beyond them."[37]

Why try to untangle the ingenious scenarios that enliven the pages of *The Radical Brethren?* First, because Horst seriously claims: "An alternative to Burrage's interpretation of early anabaptism is tentatively offered in this book."[38] Second, because other respected historians working in this period of history have taken Horst seriously. Watts's linkage of Lollardy-Anabaptism-General Baptists depended upon Horst's research.[39] B. R. White identifies Horst's material, especially the article on "England" in the *Mennonite Encyclo-*

paedia, as the basis for George Huntston Williams's section on England to 1540 in *The Radical Reformation*.[40] A Southern Baptist historian, William R. Estep, has used Horst as the foundation for his presentation of *The Anabaptist Story*.[41] Third, at least two reviewers took *The Radical Brethren* seriously, though neither subjected it to extensive criticism. C. J. Dyck hailed it as the "long awaited . . . study of Anabaptism in England" in the *Mennonite Quarterly Review*. Dyck valued the work as "a most significant contribution to our in-depth understanding of events at the heart of early Reformation in England."[42] Eric Gritsch was more restrained in his review in *Church History*: "This is a preliminary study and does not yet warrant conclusions about English anabaptism."[43] No critic as yet has said that Dr. Horst "is a ruthless source-miner and a compulsive lumper" as J. H. Hexter once wrote about Christopher Hill.[44]

The consequences for the study of the radical and dissenting movements in sixteenth- and seventeenth-century England can be quite serious. Should Horst's awkward efforts replace the careful, painstakingly scientific researches of Champlin Burrage, the level of research in this period and field will have been eroded disastrously. Both B. R. White and Lonnie Kliever have called attention to the inconclusive character of Horst's findings.[45]

What may be learned from Horst's attempt at reconstructing history? To begin with, a careful definition is essential when one confronts the maze of facts, suppositions, claims, contending arguments, and beguiling documentation that hint at solutions but which, without corroborating evidence, remain useless. Champlin Burrage was well aware of the function of definition: ". . . the word Anabaptist . . . was evidently employed as a generic term to designate separatists, or indeed any persons of irregular or fanatical religious opinions."[46] Duncan Heriot noted that the State Papers are ". . . not too clear in the way they use the term 'Anabaptist.' This was due to the number of divisions that existed among the Anabaptists, but the authorities often designate anyone who differed from the State religion as an 'Anabaptist.'"[47] Heriot's last statement is significant. The historian who allows the representative of the absolute power of the Tudor monarchy to define terms is a researcher courting conclusions predetermined by others. Horst's broad definition of Anabaptism made him captive to the vagaries of the loose definitions of the accusing State officers. Horst wrote: "For working purpose in this study it is proposed to define 'anabaptism' in specific as well as in generic terms, that is, to allow that it may refer to rebaptism as a practice or teaching, or to a general nonconformity with one or more views characteristic of anabaptism."[48] In his conclusion Horst wrote: "Anabaptism in England may be described as a current of lay-nonconformity which took its inspiration chiefly from the Protestant Reformation."[49] Dyck described Horst's conclusion: "Anabaptism in England was a religious movement, but more broadly involved in socio-political terms than may have been true of continental Anabaptism."[50] Horst's heavy reliance upon official documents framed by the accusing State seriously distorted the picture. Nor did the English Anabaptist movement develop either the literature or the confessions that make it possible to write with certainty about the Anabaptists in Europe.[51] Dyck made a trenchant critique of *The Radical Brethren*. He concluded an enthusiastic first paragraph with this query: "Can non-separatist Anabaptism practice discipline, believers' baptism, and the other accepted elements of 'normative' Anabaptism; and, if not, is it really Anabaptism we are talking about?"[52] This is a serious and fair question.

In defining two movements that, at once, were so similar in some characteristics (i.e., nonconformity) yet so diverse in some essential beliefs and practices (i.e., pacifism for Anabaptists) as were Lollardy and Anabaptism, both Watts and Horst would have benefited from reflection upon a footnote. In it, A. G. Dickens warned: "But Canon Maynard Smith goes too far in saying that Anabaptists were 'indistinguishable from Lollards except in name.'"[53] Had Horst taken Dickens seriously, he would not have concluded that "there is truth no doubt in the claim that 'Anabaptists were indistinguishable from Lollards except in name.'"[54] Watts did recognize that Horst's contention that the London "Anabaptist' group in the 1530s were but "old Lollards" could not be proven. Yet Watts persisted in making a facile linkage between Lollardy and Anabaptism.[55] Maynard Smith had suggested that Lollardy was employed as a scare tactic to impel conformity. He wrote: "Just as now someone starts a scare about the subversive propaganda in Communist Sunday Schools, so before the Reformation someone worked up suspicion of the evil designs of the Lollards."[56] It was in the particular context of the Tudor state reacting to Anabaptism in much the same way it had earlier responded to Lollardy that Smith meant that the two were "indistinguishable . . . except in name."

<u>101</u>

Examining the presuppositions of any expositor is one of the marks of the historical-critical method. An example of an *a priori* assumption is found in a *Mennonite Quarterly Review* editorial. The editor wrote: "The undeniable similarity of views on such major articles as baptism, the nature of the church, and separation of church and state invite an almost automatic conclusion of the influence from the earlier Anabaptist movement on the later Baptist movement."[57] Ernest Payne employed a more sophisticated version of such assumptions, as noted earlier.[58]

Such a compulsion to lump together things because they look alike led Lonnie Kliever to caution:

> Too often commentators have seen believer's baptism, or the "gathered" church, or separation of church and state in both the Anabaptist and Baptist traditions and on this basis uncritically assumed theological and historical kinship. However, these doctrines are based on quite different assumptions and hence carry quite different implications for each group.[59]

An egregious example of the loose assemblage of superficial characteristics was A. J. D. Farrer's statement, in commenting on the Anabaptists, "Now this broad type of a simple, practical Christianity ruled by the individual's own devout study of the New Testament reappears on English soil in the Baptists. . . ."[60] Certain patterns of religious study and reflection, expressed in firmly held convictions and translated into how one lived within an increasingly alien and hostile society, were common enough to both Continental Anabaptists and English Baptists. But convictions born out of the concentrated study of the Bible and conditions born out of oppression do not necessarily mean that the two groups are directly related except by similarities of circumstances.

Another serious danger in such clustering of ideas is the unintended but no less real confusion that arises from associating ideas that had quite different meanings in different historic periods. For example, separation of church and state in the late eighteenth century in the United States cannot be equated with Helwys' appeal for toleration in seventeenth-century England. One was a mature political doctrine with consequences for the disestablishment of religion, while the other was an individual's passionate plea to a Christian monarch. Of course, the two are connected through a history of ideas, but they are not equivalents. It is misleading to suggest that disestablishment and the toleration of dissent are identical concepts or beliefs. Similarly, beliefs need not be the same, even if the same word is used. For example, baptism by immersion means different things depending upon whether one attends a Baptist or an Eastern Orthodox church.

102

The geography of England encourages another type of assumption. For instance, Watts argues that "the strongest evidence to support the thesis of a continuing radical tradition linking the Lollards and Anabaptists of the early sixteenth century with the General Baptists of the seventeenth is geographic."[61] Payne earlier had asked a similar question.[62] Geoffrey Nuttall demonstrates both the curiosity and discipline of a historian when he writes: "the Baptists' predominance in the county [Kent], which [is] . . . reflected in the 1672 licences, is certainly the most marked and remarkable feature of the situation. Almost all Kentish Baptists were theologically General [or Arminian] Baptists, not Particular [or Calvinist]. We may suspect some derivation from the Anabaptists reported in Kent during the reign of Elizabeth I, but no clear evidence is yet forthcoming."[63]

It is worth noting that Watts and Nuttall use the same word "evidence" but in quite different ways. Nuttall, unlike Watts, recognizes that while geographic coincidence arouses a historian's "suspicions," this by itself does not provide conclusive evidence. Until substantive evidence is found, the historian must remain content with curious questions and interesting hypotheses.

We may here cite White's rule that "when a plausible source of Separatist views is available in Elizabethan Puritanism and its natural developments, the onus of proof lies upon those who would affirm that the European Anabaptists had any measurable influence upon the shaping of English Separatism."[64] This rule applies to the discussion of early Baptist beginnings in England. For Smyth and Helwys first were Separatists, and out of their experience emerged the congregation which, under Helwys, returned to English soil as the first of the General Baptist congregations in England. White's contention may be buttressed by the so-called 'law of parsimony' that dictates that an elaborate argument need not be employed when a simple one that answers all of the same conditions is at hand.

Why, then, the seeming parallels and close similarities between Continental Anabaptist views and those of English Baptists, especially the early General Baptists? White's study of the English Separatists provides the practical suggestion that the relationship of viewpoints is derived from a common dependence upon the same source, the Bible. It was because they viewed the Bible in a way common to their century and, as well, because they functioned within a similar context—for both groups were nonconformists operating within a society where the nation's religious establishment held punitive power—that they arrived at apparently similar conclusions.[65] Yet, as White concludes, "given the original New Testament source material and the nature of the contemporary Protestant appeal to it, such developments need not imply, and without clear evidence ought not to be taken to imply, any direct borrowing."[66]

Winthrop Hudson's original contention, that Baptists and the Anabaptists represent diverse traditions which are not to be identified, still engages the support of critical historians. The few efforts

103

to refute the Hudson-White-Kliever position have floundered for lack of significant empirical evidence. The strongest case for the spiritual connections between European Anabaptists and early English Baptists depends upon apparent similarities. White's magnificent study of the rise of Separatism corroborates Hudson's claim that English Baptists are rooted in the Reformed tradition. One need not posit Anabaptist influence in order to account for the development of English Baptist convictions and congregations.

NOTES

[1]Winthrop S. Hudson, "Baptists Were Not Anabaptists," *The Chronicle*, vol. 16, no. 4 (1953), pp. 171-179.

[2]Winthrop S. Hudson, "Who Were the Baptists?" *The Baptist Quarterly*, vol. 16 (1956), pp. 303-312.

[3]*Ibid.*, pp. 304-308.

[4]*Ibid.*, pp. 311-312.

[5]Ernest A. Payne, "Who Were the Baptists?" *The Baptist Quarterly*, vol. 16, (1956), p. 340.

[6]Lonnie D. Kliever, "General Baptist Origins: The Questions of Anabaptist Influence," *The Mennonite Quarterly Review*, vol. 36 (October, 1962), pp. 294, 299, 313. (Cited as *M.Q.R.*)

[7]*Ibid.*, p. 316.

[8]*Ibid.*, p. 313.

[9]*Ibid.*, p. 296.

[10]Hugh Wamble, "Inter-Relations of Seventeenth Century English Baptists," *Review and Expositor*, vol. 54, no. 3 (July, 1957), p. 409.

[11]B. R. White, "The Doctrine of the Church in the Particular Baptist Confession of 1644," *Journal of Theological Studies*, New Series, vol. 19 (October, 1968), pp. 572-573.

[12]Wamble, p. 409.

[13]White, "The Doctrine of the Church," pp. 570-590.

[14]Ernest A. Payne, "The Anabaptists," *The New Cambridge Modern History*, ed. G. R. Elton (Cambridge: Cambridge University Press, 1958), vol. 2, p. 125; William L. Lumpkin, *Baptist Confessions of Faith* (Valley Forge: Judson Press, 1959), p. 25.

[15]Hans J. Hillerbrand, "Anabaptism and the Reformation: Another Look," *Church History*, vol. 29, no. 4 (December, 1960), p. 412. See also L. J. Trinterud, "The Origins of Puritanism," *Church History*, vol. 20 (1951), pp. 36-57; Jens G. Moller, "The Beginnings of Puritan Covenant Theology," *The Journal of Ecclesiastical History*, vol. 14 (1963), pp. 46-67.

[16]François Wendel, *Calvin*, trans. Philip Mairet (Glasgow: Wm. Collins Sons, Fontana edition, n.d.), p. 73.

[17]Payne, "The Anabaptists," p. 125.

[18]B. R. White, *The English Separatist Tradition* (Oxford: Oxford University Press, 1971), p. 162. (Cited as *E.S.T.*)

[19]*Ibid.*, p. 131.

[20]Murray Tolmie, *The Triumph of the Saints/The Separate Churches of London 1616-1649* (Cambridge: Cambridge University Press, 1977), p. 70.

[21] White, *E.S.T.*, pp. 131-134.

[22] Michael R. Watts, *The Dissenters: From the Reformation to the French Revolution* (Oxford: Clarendon Press, 1978), p. 8.

[23] Irvin B. Horst, *The Radical Brethren: Anabaptism and the English Reformation to 1558* (Nieuwkoop: B. DeGraaf, 1972), pp. 49-50. Reprinted with kind permission of DeGraaf Publishers, Nieuwkoop.

[24] Champlin Burrage, *The Early English Dissenters in the Light of Recent Research* (1550–1641) (Cambridge: Cambridge University Press, 1912), vol. 1, p. 42. (Cited as *E.E.D.*)

[25] Horst, *The Radical Brethren*, pp. 49-50.

[26] *Ibid.*, p. 50.

[27] *Ibid.*

[28] *Ibid.*

[29] *Ibid.*

[30] *Ibid.*, p. 51.

[31] *Ibid.*, p. 186, Appendix B.

[32] *Ibid.*, p. 51.

[33] *Ibid.*, pp. 51-52. Compare the description in the deposition with the more specifically Melchiorite content of the accusation against Joan Boucher: "That you believe that the worde was made fleshe in the virgyn's belly, but that Christe toke fleshe of the virgin you beleve not. . . ." George Huntston Williams, *The Radical Reformation* (London: Weidenfeld and Nicolson, 1962; also Philadelphia: The Westminster Press, 1962), p. 349.

[34] Horst, *The Radical Brethren*, p. 52; John A. F. Thomson, *The Later Lollards, 1414–1520* (Oxford: Oxford University Press, 1965), pp. 81, 156, 159, 240, 247, 252.

[35] Horst, *The Radical Brethren*, p. 53.

[36] *Ibid.*

[37] *Ibid.*, pp. 33, 177.

[38] *Ibid.*, p. 7.

[39] Watts, *Dissenters*, pp. 6-14.

[40] Williams, *Radical Reformation*, pp. 401-403; White, *E.S.T.*, p. 162, footnote 1.

[41] William R. Estep, *The Anabaptist Story*, rev. ed. (Grand Rapids: Wm. B. Eerdman Publishing Co., 1975), pp. 202-203. See also J. K. Zeman, *Baptist Roots and Identity* (Toronto: Baptist Convention of Ontario and Quebec, 1978), pp. 4-6.

[42] C. J. Dyck, "Book Review of *The Radical Brethren* by Irvin B. Horst," *M.Q.R.*, vol. 47, no. 3 (July, 1973), pp. 248-250.

[43] Eric W. Gritsch, "Book Review of *The Radical Brethren* by Irvin B. Horst," *Church History*, vol. 42 (1973), pp. 134-135.

[44] J. H. Hexter, "The Burden of Proof," a review of Christopher Hill's *Change and Continuity in Seventeenth-Century England* in *Times Literary Supplement*, October 24, 1975. See Hill's reply, November 7, 1975, as well as letters of November 14, 28, and December 12, 1975.

[45] White, *E.S.T.*, p. 162; Kliever, "General Baptist Origins," p. 294.

[46] Burrage, *E.E.D.*, p. 41.

[47] Duncan B. Heriot, "Anabaptism in England During the 16th and 17th Centuries," *Transactions of the Congregational Historical Society, 1933-36*, pp. 256-271, 312-320. Cited page is p. 256.

[48] Horst, *The Radical Brethren*, p. 32.

[49] *Ibid.*, p. 177.

[50] Dyck, "Book Review," p. 249.

[51] Williams, *passim*; Franklin Hamlin Littell, *The Anabaptist View of the Church* (n.p.: American Society of Church History, 1952); consult *M.Q.R.*, *The Mennonite*

Encyclopedia, and Angel M. Mergal and George H. Williams, eds., *Spiritual and Anabaptists Writers,* Library of Christian Classics, vol. 25 (Philadelphia: The Westminster Press, 1957).

[52]Dyck, "Book Review," p. 248.

[53]A. G. Dickens, *Lollards and Protestants in the Diocese of York, 1509–1558* (London: Oxford University Press, 1959), p. 11.

[54]Horst, *The Radical Brethren,* p. 31.

[55]Watts, *Dissenters,* pp. 8-9.

[56]H. Maynard Smith, *Pre-Reformation England* (London: Macmillan and Co., Ltd., 1938; reissued 1963), p. 292.

[57]Kliever, "General Baptist Origins" p. 290.

[58]Payne, "Who Were the Baptists?" p. 340.

[59]Kliever, "General Baptist Origins," p. 313.

[60]A. J. D. Farrer, "The Relation Between English Baptists and the Anabaptists of the Continent," *Baptist Quarterly,* vol. 2 (1924–1925), p. 341.

[61]Watts, *Dissenters,* p. 13; see also pp. 283-284.

[62]Payne, "Who Were the Baptists?" p. 340.

[63]Geoffrey F. Nuttall, "Dissenting Churches in Kent Before 1700," *The Journal of Ecclesiastical History,* vol. 14 (1963), p. 181.

[64]White, *E.S.T.,* p. 164.

[65]*Ibid.,* p. 163.

[66]*Ibid.,* p. xiii.

Lockian Liberalism: A Radical Shift from the Biblical Economic Ethic

Prentiss Pemberton

W inthrop S. Hudson did his homework with painstaking thoroughness before publishing his first scholarly work. Indeed, what began as his doctoral dissertation flowered into a major assessment not only of John Ponet's thought but also of his influence in shifting Calvinism toward a more limited theory of monarchy. This initial study of Hudson was entitled *John Ponet (1516-1556), Advocate of Limited Monarchy* (Chicago: The University of Chicago Press, 1942). It contains the full, original text of Ponet's *A Shorte Treatise of Politike Power* (Strassburg, 1556).

I wish also to call attention to an additional, significant Hudson essay. It appears as chapter 6 in *Calvinism and the Political Order.*[1] One primary value of this *Shorte Treatise* is its analysis of why John Locke became the public voice for a number of the Puritan controversialists. Too often Locke is seen today as a spokesperson for the secular rationalist camp of natural law, not theologically and philosophically as the "heir of Puritan rationalism."[2]

The concern dominating my own article on Locke and Classical Liberalism stems from the political economy of which Locke was unquestionably a leader. My conclusion is that C. B. Macpherson's *The Political Theory of Possessive Individualism* has sharpened the criticism of Locke's economic stance. His two kinds of property (body-hands and object-thing) and his inadequate justification for what Macpherson terms "possessive individualism" and "possessive markets" raise serious difficulties for Lockian Liberalism.

This second period of modernization following the commercial revolution accelerated the tempo and scope of political and economic change. This was particularly true in England and in its North American colonies. Such terms as Classical Liberalism or the Enlightenment denoted new philosophical, ethical, and cultural forces. Constitutional or parliamentary democracy characterized the

107

Anglo-American political scene, capitalism the economic one in its early stages.

Since our primary concern is economic, it is pertinent to note that no vocational economists made their appearance until the last part of the eighteenth century. There was as yet no such academic discipline as economics. Two philosophers, however, became significant "bridge" thinkers as political economists who conjoined politics and the incipient field of economics. These two were Thomas Hobbes (died in 1679) and John Locke (died in 1704). For our economic purposes, we shall do well to concentrate upon John Locke and the Liberalism to which he contributed much.

Locke developed original insights into the nature of the moral self, into how such selves relate in political experience and how they can legitimately acquire and use the material goods of nature and society. He was a leader in shifting Western political economy from its roots in the biblical tradition of economic obligation into the new soil of sensate pleasure and possessive individualism.

Locke's Theory of God's Natural Order and How Private Property and Government Came into Being

John Locke, in his Second Treatise on Government,[3] conceptualized his fanciful picture of what economic experience was like in the original state of nature. Note that in what follows, his doctrine of God's creation presupposes neither the biblical perfect order prior to sin and the "fall" nor a seriously corrupted order after sin and the "fall." Indeed, Locke largely ignores traditional orthodox theology. Instead, he improvises his novel doctrine of a deistic God, of a problematic, self-centered human nature, and of an idealistic natural law within which privileged, middle, and upper classes are to govern.

We can quickly summarize his vision of the state of "freedom" and "equality" in which rational humans were created (*Second Treatise,* chapter 2, sections 4-5). The problem is that as industrious, rational individuals acquire their own property, they must protect it against encroachments by covetous, irrational rivals. Locke then devises his "remedy for the inconvenience of the state of Nature" (*ibid.,* chapter 2, section 13). In that natural state each responsible, rational citizen has to become police and judge in order to protect his own property. He concludes that upright citizens have the good sense to contract together to establish civil government. Hence, individuals "however free" in their natural, precontractual state, "unite for the mutual preservation of their lives, liberties, and estates, which I call by the general name—property."[4]

We need next to summarize Locke's famous chapter five on property and how individuals can rightfully possess property.

"God, who hath given the world to men in common, hath also given them reason to make use of it to the best advantage of life and convenience. Nobody has originally a private dominion exclusive of the rest of mankind" (chapter 5, section 25). Yet alongside this natural property belonging to people in common, there is one form of property which from the beginning is *exclusively* each person's private possession.

> Though the earth and all inferior creatures be common to all men, yet every man has a "property" in his own "person." This nobody has any right to but himself. The "labour" of his body and the "work" of his hands, we may say, are properly his. Whatsoever, then, he removes out of the state that Nature hath provided . . . , he hath mixed his labour with it, and joined to it something that is his own, and thereby makes it his property (chapter 5, section 26).

Thence, persons have a basic property in themselves, in their body and hands. It is this foundational property that empowers and authorizes them to appropriate from nature their private property in things, in land, fruits, animals, and other goods.

Locke starts off, in other words, with a radical communalism where each person has individual access to the common bounties of nature. Thence, each individual can convert the private property one has in one's own self into the appropriating power which issues from the "labour" of one's body and the "work" of one's hands. From this absolutely private self-possession, Locke proceeds to explain and justify the right to preempt the bounties of nature exclusively for oneself. What at one moment presupposes equality and mutuality in appropriating everyone's property from the common riches of nature quickly becomes a property belonging only to excluding individuals. In one fell swoop Locke challenges the very foundations of the biblical economic ethic and its inclusive structure of property obligations to those lacking property. No longer do we read anything about the duties of stewards; no longer do the poor have any claim on the superfluous wealth of the rich. Here is an entirely self-centered theme which legitimizes possessive individualism within its context of a dawning capitalism.

Immediately a troublesome question needs to be raised. What if an inventive and energetic individual acquires more from nature's storehouse than he or she really needs? This, concedes Locke forthrightly, could become exploitive. Indeed, he is ready with a relevant moral principle. Each procurer can acquire ethically only as much from nature as ". . . one can make use of to any advantage of life *before it spoils*. [Italics not in the original.] Whatever is beyond this is more than his share, and belongs to others. Nothing is made by

God for man to spoil or destroy" (chapter 5, section 30). Natural spoilage, then, seems to place a definite limit upon the quantity which acquisitive individuals can retain for themselves.

Again, however, no sooner does Locke seem to affirm an equalitarian justice for property holders than he promptly clouts this equality and justice. He repudiates his own vision of persons peacefully laboring according to the natural law, wherein each can acquire only enough to fulfill one's needs. He concludes that humans invent a new mechanism—one which makes it not only legitimate but also highly beneficial and just for some individuals to accumulate wealth. Let Locke introduce his potent new mechanism.

> . . . I dare boldly affirm, . . . that the same rule of propriety—viz. that every man should have as much as he could make use of, would hold still in the world . . . had not the invention of money, and the tacit agreement of men to put a value on it, introduced (by consent) larger possessions and a right to them . . . (chapter 5, section 36).

Locke concluded that if a person

> would give his nuts for a piece of metal . . . , he invades not the right of others; he might heap up as much of these durable things as he pleases; the exceeding of the bounds of his just property not lying in the largeness of his possessions, but the perishing of anything uselessly in it (chapter 5, section 49).

> Find out something that hath the use and value of money amongst his neighbors [by mutual consent], you shall see the same man will begin presently to enlarge his possessions (chapter 5, section 49).

Why do people voluntarily leave the freedom they enjoy in the state of Nature? Because each, alone, encounters "inconveniences" in having to defend one's property. Hence, people unite in forming commonwealths for the "mutual preservation of their lives, liberties and estates, which [Locke calls] by the general name—property." Then the invention of money justifies individuals in accumulating wealth in this durable form of money, since they are no longer guilty of allowing their excess possessions to spoil.

110 Locke's Politico-Economic Revolution Is Built upon His Possessively Individualistic Ethic

A major watershed can be dated from the last part of the seventeenth and all through the eighteenth and nineteenth centuries. No longer will the biblical economic ethic furnish moral foundations for the emerging secular ethos. Instead, Hobbes, Locke particularly, and the first laissez-faire economists appeared during the waning years of the Commercial Revolution. These thinkers legitimized the emerging Industrial (capitalistic) Revolution. Modernization in the West was to leap forward at a dramatic new pace.

Let us pinpoint the dynamic change which Locke's possessive individualism wrought. To do this we turn to the wisdom of C. B. Macpherson, who, to my knowledge, is the creator of this "possessive individualism" phrase. He used it in his reinterpretation of the work of both Hobbes and Locke. His book is *The Political Theory of Possessive Individualism.*[5]

Passages from Macpherson can take us to the heart of his assessment of Locke:

> The individual in market society *is* human [in his capacity] as proprietor of his own person . . . his humanity does depend on his freedom from any but self-interested contractual relations with others. His society [i.e., his one area of relatedness to others] does consist of a series of market relations.[6]

In the Preface of his volume, Macpherson acquaints us with his development of the phrase "possessive individualism": "Some time ago I suggested that English political thought from the seventeenth to the nineteenth centuries had an underlying unity which deserved notice. I called the unifying assumption 'possessive individualism'. . . ."[7]

He finds the roots of this acquisitive individualism in the Levellers, particularly John Lilburne and Richard Overton. Macpherson also traces how seventeenth-century individualism was plagued with the consequences of the notion of possessing property in one's own person.

The possessive quality in liberal-democratic theory

> is found in its conception of the individual as essentially the proprietor of his own person or capacities, owing nothing to society for them. The individual was seen neither as a moral whole, nor as part of a larger social whole, but as an owner of himself. . . . Society becomes a lot of free equal individuals related to each other as proprietors of their own capacities and of what they have acquired by their exercise. Society consists of relations of exchange between proprietors. Political society becomes a calculated device for the protection of this property and for the maintenance of an orderly relation of exchange.[8]

Let us next interpret three developments which constitute major negative consequences that flow from Locke's impact upon Classical Liberalism.

1. Locke almost totally reversed the long biblical tradition which warned against evils in covetousness and the love of money.

Money becomes, for Locke, the positive factor which obliterated the original equalitarian society which he had fantasized. Money was the mechanism which set people loose to acquire as much wealth as possible. It did this by eliminating almost all ethical constraints arising from the spoilage factor. Durable money solves this problem. Locke's only social accountability, as individuals appropriate wealth, centers in the minimal taxes required to finance small, laissez-faire governments. Certainly taxes could remain insignificant as long as the "best government is the one that governs least." Recall that the U.S. government could impose no federal income taxes until the constitutional amendment was adopted in February, 1913.

2. Locke largely undermined the biblical economic ethic.[9]

Locke recognized no role for stewards as that role is set forth in the Bible, and he certainly never paid heed to consideration of the poor.

He mentions no limit on the right of individual acquisition nor any obligation in the use of property . . . . The great purpose of the political order designed to fulfil the natural law is, therefore, to protect life and property, not to secure its just distribution and use.[10]

Locke was confident that his historical basis for the approval of wealth seeking eliminated personal and institutional obligations to the poor. After all, Locke assumed that humankind as a whole had at least tacitly "consented" to the exchange of perishable commodities for money, with its assurance of hoarding without spoilage. He conjectures that all wealth at least originally has been earned by the labor of people's bodies or the work of their hands. Did not this clearly imply that the impoverished were definitely responsible for their precarious station? They had failed in the race to appropriate money. Here we can clearly discern the fateful seeds which were to mushroom into modern vocational "success" or "failure."

We need to ask at this point, however, Is not this indifference to the plight of the poor dangerous? Might not they, in times of economic scarcity, use their ballots to elect a government more committed to their needs? Locke had good reason, however, not to worry about that threat!

112

3. Locke designed a "democracy" which denied the right-to-vote to both the idle and the working poor.

The simple fact was that Locke had nothing to fear from the vote of the indigent and all laborers because they were virtually disfranchised. He developed an "inherent differential in rationality," (Macpherson) which excluded the laboring classes, along with beggars, alms-takers, and vagrants, from casting the ballot. Indeed, this exclusion of laborers meant a so-called democracy which needed their work but which denied their political rights. "Not merely the idle poor, who had been treated as outcasts from Tudor times, but the labouring poor as well, were now treated almost as a race apart, though within the state."[11]

All of this meant a shift from feudal *status* to *contract* society. Land, resources, and labor would be owned by individuals and would become alienable or salable. Salability meant that landowners, merchants, and workers could offer their land, goods, or labor for sale in a competitive market. Countless new contracts would have to become ratified day-in and day-out between landowners, manufacturers, merchants, enterpreneurs, and laborers.

It is within the context of this emerging contractual market economy that we can perceive the far-reaching, injurious import of Locke's emphasis upon the workers' natural property right in their own bodies. What seems to be a profound right to the labor of one's body and the work of one's hands becomes a useless possession— *if one cannot find an employer who will contract for this labor at a living wage*. Macpherson probes to the subtle hoax which Locke introduced:

> Once the land is all taken up . . . those without property are . . . dependent for their very livelihood on those with property, and are unable to alter their own circumstances. The initial equality of natural rights, which consisted in no man having jurisdiction over another cannot last after the differentiation of property. To put it another way, the man without property in things loses that full proprietorship of his own person which was the basis of his equal natural rights. . . . Civil society is established to protect unequal possessions [after the invention of money], which have already in the state of nature given rise to unequal rights.[12]

Only the possession of object property "things" could secure people their right to become full-fledged, voting citizens.

Within a century Adam Smith and other new-breed economists were to build this possessive individualism into the emerging injustice of capitalism's Industrial Revolution.

113

Limitations in Locke's Social Ethic of Freedom and Equality

We should now be in a position to appreciate the extent of the economic revolution which Locke's acquisitive ethic initiated in England. This second revolution meant a zest for possessive, not traditional, markets. Everything seemed to be open to contractual bargaining. Everything and every person seemed to be up for sale or hire. Let the buyer beware!

It was precisely in the face of the lasting impact of Locke's possessive individualism and its possessive market society that we do well to probe the basic socio-ethical values upon which Locke rested his Liberalism. As we read the *Second Treatise*, two value-terms frequently meet our eyes: *Freedom* and *Equality*. Both are central to Locke's state of nature and the law of nature which govern this state. Thus, he starts from the estate in which all persons would naturally be, "that is, a state of perfect freedom to order their actions and dispose of their possessions and persons as they think fit . . . without asking leave or depending upon the will of any other man."[13] Immediately he adds that this natural state is also one of "equality, wherein all the power and jurisdiction is reciprocal, no one having more than another. . . ."[14] Freedom and equality Locke finds most fundamental in his hypothetical state of nature.

We have earlier seen, however, that when we attempted to follow his train of reasoning which moved from a mythic nature to the hard realities of English politico-economic history, we had to be on guard against subtle enticements in both his logic and his interpretation of facts.

Freedom, or liberty, became the password for all who entered the ranks of Liberalism. Locke's particular version of freedom became, however, tightly linked with persons' concern for property and the liberty to share in profitable exchanges in the new contractual marketplace. This meant that the possessive aspect of his individualism surfaced in both economics and the monadic, isolated nature of each independent self. This further "freed" all potential employees to contract for a job in Locke's new possessive market *only when the employer freely decided it would be profitable to offer such a contract*. This contractualism of the early Industrial Revolution became "free" to enact laws which refused labor the right to meet and organize unions. In sum: workers were now free to be proprietors of their bodies and hands, but it was the employers who had a more decisive freedom—that to make such bodies and hands *marketable or unmarketable* within possessive contractualism.

Lockian freedom, on the more positive side, upheld key civil liberties—personal, political, religious—and assured greater toleration for minorities. Locke should be credited with these advances in personal and social freedom, as far as they went. But these commitments could not go far enough, given Locke's espousal of an economic "freedom" which could not assure increasing numbers of persons the primal power to translate their labor into a decent livelihood.

It is when we move to Locke's second ethico-political value, *equality*, that we encounter even more serious tension in his Lib-

114

eralism. Here Locke's possessive individualism seemed to make everyone equal in the original state of nature, by dint of designating everyone's body and hands to constitute their innate and inalienable property. Yet what did this really mean? Actually, it meant nothing more than an elemental biological equality, which empowered everyone to supply all basic physical needs in a bountiful but purely imaginary nature.

We note, next, that in Locke's mythical natural order there existed another type of equality—the never ceasing equal "inconvenience" where all proprietors had to protect their two kinds of property, that is, (1) their body-hands property and (2) their object or "thing" property acquired by means of the labor and work of their body-hands property. Throughout our remaining consideration of Locke, we need to keep clearly in mind these two properties and what happens because of them.

Finally, persons freely chose to shift from the "inconvenience" of their natural, individualistic arrangement to a new political order that protected everyone's property. They did this, presumably to provide a new dimension of equal property protection.

Precisely at this point, however, the equal-protection aspect of the new politico-property system backfired in the faces of those who found themselves possessing a body-hands property, *and nothing more!* If no one offered them employment in this contractual, employer-employee economy, there was no other way by which they could utilize their so-called innate and inalienable body-hands property to procure the "thing" property they had to have to live decently. To assure that there was absolutely no other way, recall that Lockians and others worked to disfranchise the idle and working poor. Thus, ironically, the ballot became the supreme symbol of inequality.

To cap all of this inequity, Locke now reasoned that the invention of durable money legitimized successful employers in piling up ever greater wealth. The earlier natural spoilage limits no longer applied to durable money. Wealth could be acquired with no worries about becoming covetous.

The Practical Problem of Democratizing Governments and People   115

We have now assessed Locke's politico-economic revolution based upon possessive individualism and upon inadequate theories of freedom and equality. We propose next to inquire into manifest and latent flaws which have periodically undermined the democratizing endeavor in the United States. These weaknesses have not been expunged during more than two hundred years of statehood.

The democratizing "blood count" in the United States is ominously low when compared with other political democracies.

We note at the outset that fifty-five delegates (many of them Lockians), participated in the Constitutional Convention in May, 1787. We sense the high vision which they affirmed in their Preamble to the Constitution. Still these highly conscientious and competent Founding Fathers were guilty of structuring three irreparable flaws into their newborn democracy.

First was their acceptance and indirect approval of one of the cruelist systems of slavery ever concocted by humans who had come under at least some influence of Christianity. Some 460,000 blacks were slaves (20 percent of the nation's population, as of 1770), who were denied utterly the "blessings of liberty" that the Fathers had fought so heroically to secure for themselves and their posterity.

From the very inception of the nation, the "half-free, half-slave" impasse was to haunt and tear asunder the "grand experiment." Recurring tragedies have borne witness that the fallout from the democracy-slavery contrariety was to bear its evil fruit right down to today's white racism.

The *second* of these three weaknesses is termed the Lockian syndrome, or what Macpherson interprets as Locke's possessive individualism. One result of this syndrome is the contradiction Macpherson finds between economic Liberalism and political democracy. In this strained situation democracy is requiring *direct* and *full* equality ever more relentlessly.

Direct equality means that indirect factors, such as money, social status, race, or other extraneous elements cannot deprive the poor of their fair share of political and economic resources. Decent incomes, adequate educational facilities, and competent health care are three assets, in other words, without which persons cannot confirm their dignity as human beings in modern democracies. *Full equality* means that the poor and disadvantaged must be able to join with the advantaged in generating new forms of socio-political power.

Until both direct and full equality are achieved, the United States is flawed by fractional democracy—only a fraction of the potential power for justice and equality is being marshaled. And obviously, the very phrase "fractional democracy" is a contradiction in terms.

Along with its agonies resulting from the failures of a half-free, half-slave impasse and the Lockian syndrome, we find also embedded in the patriotic mood of this nation a *third* basic weakness— political extremism.

Put most succinctly, extremism is patriotism run amuck! It is a superpatriotism which splinters a society in the process of exalting its "good Americans" and castigating its "unAmericans." This patriotism of extremists is contrived by persons who cannot comprehend the "state of mind" which undergirds authentic democracy. This democratic "state of mind" is obviously a staunch commitment to pluralism[15] which "remains commonly accepted as the fixed spiritual center of the democratic political process. . . ."[16]

Eduard Lindeman makes clear that there is one thing people must do if they are to enact authentic democratizing: they must discipline themselves to a unity which can be achieved only through the "creative use of diversity."[17] Extremism undermines the safety and order required to maintain a creative diversity. Lipset and Taab have penetrated to the precise limits which the democratic political process must always impose upon extremism, because "extremism means going beyond the limits of the normative procedures which define the democratic political process."[18]

The Deepening Conflict Between Economic Liberalism and Political Democracy

Our next task is to let Macpherson and others who have contributed to the theme thrust upon us an awareness of the clash between Liberalism and democracy. Unfortunately, the nature of economic Liberalism and political democracy and the deeply rooted encounters between them have not been clearly interpreted. Let us seek clarity.

We note first that this political Liberalism has little to do with full democratizing, little to do with the liberties of the propertyless, little to do with full equality. Indeed, Alan Wolfe insists that the very words "liberal democracy" are a contradiction in terms. He finds Classical Liberalism—as formulated by Locke, Jeremy Bentham, and John Stuart Mill during the seventeenth into the nineteenth centuries—always tilted toward the economic rights and freedoms of property holders. It was free men, writes Wolfe, who "would buy and sell land, commodities, and each other's ability to work in an atmosphere unencumbered by . . . obstructive regulations. Liberalism was the ideal political philosophy for an emerging powerful capitalist revolution."[19]

Alongside economic Liberalism, another set of revolutionary forces were to emerge during the nineteenth century. They were cited by Macpherson and Wolfe as democracy and full equality. Democracy, in contrast to an economically oriented Liberalism, arose in opposition to the "very conditions that Liberalism tried to create." It was not until the nineteenth century that the rising working class demanded universal suffrage, rights of women and minorities, and control over the market in labor. Democracy em-

117

phasized two themes that Liberalism did not: direct equality (in opposition to the indirect equality of the market), and participation of all "in the affairs of the human community." [20]

Wolf then points out that in spite of the differences between (economic) Liberalism and (political) democracy, they could live in relative harmony, *as long as Western societies engaged in a continuous process of economic growth!* Liberal societies could acquire their property and profits alongside democratic provision for more equality and more participation of workers in the industrial process.

Then in the 1970s came a collapse in continuous economic growth, or, as Wolfe puts it, the end of "expanding expansion." Liberal capitalisms are now barely holding their own economically. Thence, Wolfe concludes that Liberal democracy's crisis is very real. "Its roots lie in the fact that in Western societies the economic system is liberal and capitalist while the political system is formally democratic and therefore potentially socialist." [21]

Signals from this strain by the 1980s were becoming louder and clearer in this nation—a surge of political-economic pressures from the Right and Left; a weakening of the Center; more extremism, less consensus.

It is at this point that we draw upon Amitai Etzioni, as the originator, and Warren Breed, as Etzioni's synoptic interpreter, to help us assess this deepening struggle between Right, Left, and Center. This is especially the case since the emergence of ever more sophisticated mass media. Watergate should have taught us much. In this connection David Halberstam's *The Powers That Be* [22] should be required reading for everyone concerned about a more responsible and effective political process or democratizing.

For the condensed model of democratizing which we are developing, let Breed introduce us to Etzioni's formulation of three forces operative in all political-economic activity. These forces become ever more significant in the politico-economic pressures activated by the mass media. These forces can be indicated by the words and phrase *alienation, inauthenticity,* and the *"appearance of responsiveness."*

Breed uses alienation largely in the Marxist sense to refer to persons who experience both a "feeling of resentment" and an "expression of objective conditions which expose a person to forces beyond his understanding and control." [23] Breed next brings in Etzioni's crucial bond between alienation and inauthenticity. "A relationship, institution, or society is inauthentic if it provides the appearance of responsiveness while the underlying condition is alienation." [24] Breed then initiates us to a crucial factor: the insidious manner in which inauthentic structures "devote a higher ration of their efforts than do alienating ones to concealing their contours

118

and to building the appearance of responsiveness."[25] Here is a sharpening of Marx's classic work on alienation. Here inauthenticity, by building an appearance of responsiveness, becomes more deceptive than does alienation.

Conclusion and a Brief Summary

We have completed our inquiry into Lockian Economic Liberalism and its stance with respect to the self, nature, society, government, property, and economics. We have seen how Locke largely ignored Luther, Calvin, and the Reformation's attempt to shift the biblical economic ethics of stewards into the economic ethos of the Commercial Revolution. Locke became a case in point of sixteenth-century Reformers failing to create politico-economic contexts that could be turned into latent values of Liberalism.

Within the larger context of the ethics and economics, let us stress that Locke's Liberalism failed to develop a *sound and adequate moral structure*. His seventeenth-eighteenth-century economic Liberalism failed to develop freedom for the propertyless, allowing freedom only for the propertied. It remained for a new dimension of democracy to emerge in the nineteenth century—political democracy which emphasized direct equality and the participation of everyone "in the affairs of the human community."

The inherent conflict between economic Liberalism and political democracy was significantly submerged through the process of economic growth, beginning especially in World War II. Then, in the mid-seventies and on into the eighties "expanding expansion" in most of the capitalist nations has been slowly weakening.

This slowdown has sharpened the conflict between the surging Right (which endeavors to resuscitate Lockian Liberalism under today's banner of supply economics and conservative politics) and the wavering Left (which is groping for new ways to coordinate more planned, demand-side economics and more egalitarian politics). In such a time, it becomes ever more urgent for those committed to full democratizing to probe the dynamics of alienation, inauthenticity, and the appearance of responsiveness. There is particular need for a disciplined new Center–Left to expose how mass-media politics and economics may develop new ways to manipulate electorates.

NOTES

[1] Winthrop S. Hudson, "John Locke: Heir of Puritan Political Theorists," *Calvinism and the Political Order*, ed. George L. Hunt (Philadelphia: The Westminster Press, 1965), pp. 108-129.

[2] *Ibid.*, p. 110.

[3] John Locke, *Of Civil Government*, Everyman's Library edition (London: Dent & Sons, 1943). Additional citations to this source identified by parenthetical references in the text.

[4] Even before we ascertain precisely what Locke means by property and how he sees people justly acquiring it, we should emphasize his repeated avowals that the chief end of government is to safeguard citizens' properties. I quote only some of the many affirmations of this notion. Citizens unite for peaceable living in a political state "in secure enjoyment of their properties" (chapter 8, section 95). People come under the laws of government and "therein seek the preservation of their property" (chapter 9, section 127). They would not "tie themselves up under" government, "were it not to preserve their lives, liberties, and fortunes" (chapter 9, section 137). "For the preservation of property being the end of government and that for which men enter into society . . ." (chapter 9, section 138). If any governor levies taxes without the consent of the people, "he thereby invades the fundamental law of property, and subverts the end of government" (chapter 9, section 140).

[5] C. B. Macpherson, *The Political Theory of Possessive Individualism* (London: Oxford University Press, 1962). Used by permission of Oxford University Press.

[6] *Ibid.*, p. 275.

[7] *Ibid.*, p. v.

[8] *Ibid.*, p. 3.

[9] In this study two major principles are designated as the Christian or biblical economic ethic: (1) the self-denying or proportional inclusiveness of forgoers or stewards; (2) the just entitlement to surplus wealth of the rich in behalf of the very poor.

[10] W. T. Bluhm, *Theories of the Political System* (Englewood Cliffs, N.J.: Prentice-Hall, Inc., 1965), p. 321.

[11] Macpherson, *The Political Theory*, p. 228.

[12] *Ibid.*, p. 231.

[13] Locke, *Of Civil Government*, chapter 2, section 4.

[14] *Ibid.*

[15] T. V. Smith and Eduard C. Lindeman, *The Democratic Way of Life* (New York: The New American Library, A Mentor Book, 1951), p. 9.

[16] Seymour Martin Lipset and Earl Raab, *The Politics of Unreason* (New York: Harper & Row, Publishers, Inc., 1970), p. 5.

[17] Smith and Lindeman, *Democratic Way*, p. 91.

[18] Lipset and Raab, *Politics*, p. 5.

[19] *The New York Times*, (March 18, 1978), C. 23.

[20] *Ibid.*

[21] *Ibid.*

[22] David Halberstam, *The Powers That Be* (New York: Alfred A. Knopf, Inc., 1979).

[23] Warren Breed, *The Self-Guiding Society* (New York: The Free Press, 1971), p. 198.

[24] *Ibid.*, p. 199.

[25] *Ibid.*

III

Themes on the History of Christianity in the United States

Beyond the Protestant Era in American Religious Historiography

Eldon G. Ernst

During the past quarter century it has become increasingly apparent that the Protestant era in American religious historiography is ending. Not surprisingly, this change in the scholarly endeavor roughly coincides with a large-scale alteration in the configuration of American religious life. A decline in Protestant influence since World War I has accompanied the coming-of-age of Roman Catholicism and Judaism, the growth of formerly marginal sects and cults, the rise of new religious movements, and the increasing secularization of major sectors of American culture. The emerging scholarly interpretations of what has been taking place have commonly referred to the notions of post-Protestant, post-Christian, and post-Christendom America. These "post" labels naturally presuppose an earlier Protestant-Christian-Christendom identity of American civilization that no longer exists as it once did, despite the fact that Christianity remains vigorously alive in the nation.[1]

One primary source for documenting the premodern Protestant-Christian-Christendom perception of America's fundamental religious identity is a century-long Protestant tradition of American religious historiography. Its major historians included Robert Baird, who published *Religion in America* in 1843 in Scotland (reprinted the following year in America); Philip Schaff, whose lectures in Germany on *America* were translated and published in the United States in 1855; Daniel Dorchester, whose massive survey of *Christianity in the United States from the First Settlement Down to the Present Time* first appeared in 1888; Leonard Woolsey Bacon, who published *A History of American Christianity* in 1897; and William Warren Sweet, whose first edition of *The Story of Religions in America* was published first in 1930 and revised in 1939 and 1950.[2]

I

From a Reformation Protestant heritage perspective, this succession of historians interpreted the American nation as a frontier of Western civilization and the unfolding of purified Christendom in a new age. American Christendom, unlike the Christian tradition in the European nations, traced roots not directly to medieval Catholicism but to sixteenth- through eighteenth-century Protestantism primarily through the Reformed tradition. Bacon thus associated Columbus's "timely discovery of the western hemisphere, in its relation to church history," to the closing of the fifteenth-century "dense darkness that goes before the dawn" of sixteenth-century Reformation—both Catholic and Protestant. Then as the Reformation and counter-Reformation drama unfolded in the Americas, wrote Schaff, "the ecclesiastical life of North America [struck] its deepest roots in those mighty religious and civil contests, which shook England in the seventeenth century."[3] Protestant England won major victories and made the dominant religious imprint in those Atlantic coastal regions of North America that eventually were to become the United States of America.

The emergence of Protestant New England in a territory surrounded by Spanish and French Catholic entrenchments thus began American religious history proper. New Spain and New France fit into this conceptual framework, if at all, as the vanquished front line of Roman Catholic crusading forces whose subsequent influence in American religious history would be nil. Their grandiose historic presence in North America (something of a romantic antiquarian curiosity) accentuated the fact that in the face of this seemingly insurmountable obstacle, Anglo-Saxon Protestantism nevertheless was destined to win the battle for religious foundation and identity of the new nation. "New England bore the brunt of the struggle," wrote Sweet, and, of course, gained the final victory.[4]

The odds against this victory appeared so great to the nineteenth-century historians that only their theological sense of providence provided an idiom through which they could make their historic accounts credible to readers of their day. Although Schaff, Dorchester, and Bacon agreed with Baird's belief in "that superintending Providence which rules in all things," they found in America's religious beginnings an extraordinary example of God's mysterious control of human history. New Spain and New France thus prefaced American religious history through their "providential preparations" of the New World for the coming migration of the settlers of destiny. That this later migration did not begin until England had become a Protestant nation secured the Protestant destiny of America; for "in the pangs of the Reformation a new people was

124

begotten," explained Dorchester, "with new ideas, invested with loftier prerogatives and aims, and intended by Providence to found in the New World a great Christian Republic, one of the mightiest agencies in human progress."

> While thirst for gold, lust for power and love of daring adventure served the Providential purpose of opening the New World to papal Europe, and Roman Catholic colonies were successfully planted in some portions, the territory originally comprised within the United States was mysteriously guarded and reserved for another—a prepared people.

This "prepared people" who comprised, in Bacon's words, "a series of disconnected [British Protestant] plantations along the Atlantic seaboard, established as if at haphazard, without plan or mutual preconcert . . . unsustained by government arms or treasurers . . ." miraculously overcame the Spanish and French contenders for the control of Christendom.[5] Henceforth the original Anglo-Saxon Protestant carriers of European religion to the New World would permeate the historical accounts of America's religious life and thought.

Dorchester considered it "one of the marvels of the age that the United States [did not become] a Roman Catholic country" because until the end of the eighteenth century "scarcely a Protestant existed within those extensive domains" of North America occupied and controlled by Spain and France.[6] Yet across those extensive domains the American churches, developing from primarily Anglo-Saxon Protestant rootage, expanded westward from the Atlantic to the Pacific as an aggressive missionary and benevolent force, combating "infidelity," "barbarism," and "Romanism" every step of the way. In a nation rescued from Roman Catholicism, little more need be said about the French and Spanish cultural accretions along westward trails. As the midnineteenth century approached, Baird was prepared to call the United States "the most powerful of all Protestant Kingdoms . . . a great Protestant Empire."

> The religion of the overwhelming majority, and which may therefore be called national, is, in all essential points, what was taught by the great Protestant Reformers of the sixteenth century. . . . Our national character is that of the Anglo-Saxon race, which still predominates among us in consequence of its original preponderancy in the colonization of the country, and of the energy which forms its characteristic distinction.

125

Likewise, Schaff described America as "a land thoroughly Protestant, almost to an extreme,"

> since Protestantism embraces not merely the large majority of the

population, but is the source, at the same time, of all its social and political principles; in fine, is interwoven most intimately with the entire national life, and goes hand in hand with all the nobler struggles after freedom and ideas of progress.[7]

Within this "great Protestant Empire" the Roman Catholic church of English ancestry, quite distinct from the once-feared colonial French and Spanish powers, began to thrive with the accession of Irish and German Catholic immigrants arriving in large numbers during the antebellum period. American-born Anglo-Saxon Catholics could be accepted as innocent enough, but immigrant Catholics introduced foreign political and religious "elements." In a fundamentally Protestant land American Catholics might be viewed as a challenging minority current within a religious mainstream or even as a separate stream running alongside a rushing river. By midcentury it had become clear to Baird "that the Roman Catholic Church [had] gained a firm and extensive footing in the United States," that all Protestant denominations were concerned about its influence, and that one could not predict how well the immigrant Catholics would fit into the American political environment. Many Protestants, even those not involved in the unfortunate anti-Catholic nativist movement, wondered if their republic thereby was endangered by a foreign-based power structure. According to Schaff,

> The public opinion, formed under the influence of Puritanism, regards Romanism, whether justly or unjustly, as the veritable Antichrist, Intolerance and Persecution personified, a system of the most terrible spiritual despotism, which, if successfully established, would also annihilate all political freedom and arrest the progress of history. Hence the more this church grows . . . the more do national jealousy and hatred, which have already found vent in manifold riotous proceedings, increase also.

Dorchester recorded that "the Pope divided the United States into six ecclesiastical provinces, with suffragen dioceses, thus inaugurating among the simple republican institutions of the United States a hierarchical organization of bishops and archbishops, with miters and pompous forms." Bacon pointed to the conservative adherence to Roman papal power by the American Catholic church which, unlike some European state church traditions that "give an effective check to the absolute power of Rome," could not identify with the United States government. Ironically, therefore, Protestant fears of a Roman power in their midst plus their anti-Catholic attitudes helped to strengthen American Catholic loyalty to Rome. "The conditions were favorable for the development of a race prejudice aggravated by religious antipathy." In Bacon's judgment, moreover,

126

"the presence of a great foreign vote, easily manipulated and cast in block, was proving a copious source of political corruption. . . . The conditions provoked, we [Bacon] might say necessitated, a political reform movement, which took the name and character of 'Native American.'" Sweet labeled the anti-Catholic Know-Nothing movement "unjust and ill-timed"; and "in spite of such attempts to resist the growth and influence of Catholicism in the United States, their numbers were increasing by leaps and bounds."[8]

The real danger, however, was home based and homebred, though originally imported: Slavery qualified national Christian pretensions and divided the republic on bloody battlefields. Slavery superceded nativist concerns and received the historians' most virulent comments, each writing from a Northern perspective. Baird thought of slavery as "an accursed inheritance which the Old World bequeathed to the New." Schaff referred to slavery as "the political and social canker, the *tendo-Achilles*, in the otherwise vigorous system of the United States [that] contradicts alike its own republican symbol and the spirit of Christianity and philanthropy." Looking back, Bacon recognized "that horrible and inhuman form of slavery which had drawn upon itself the condemnation of the civilized world." In the Civil War, concluded Dorchester, "the main arteries [of slavery] were opened and the monster at last succumbed."[9]

Once through the valley of the shadow of death leading to Appomattox, during which time the nation was tested for its integrity and endurance, the Protestant Empire North and South resumed its expansion to the Pacific and into new urban, industrial, and intellectual frontiers. The religious foundation had been laid, sturdy walls and roof built, and the mighty storm weathered. "The discipline of the war proved a tonic to languid moral nature," thought Dorchester; "conscience was quickened and moral perceptions became clearer." Equally certain though more sober, Bacon concluded that "the war was a rude school of theology, but it taught some things well. The church had need of all that it could learn, in preparation for the tasks and trials that were before it."[10]

It now remained to insulate the Protestant establishment from new, challenging elements both outside and within. Prospering American Protestantism during its late nineteenth-century "halcyon years" met foes through crusading missions at home and abroad, optimistic that it stood at the precipice of a glorious though mysterious new era destined to reach global proportions. "To high Christian faith," extolled Dorchester, "our Country is the ridge of destiny, where Christianity has already won some of its greatest triumphs, and is destined to achieve still grander victories." For Bacon the future appeared more mysterious but no less hopeful, due to "the great providential preparations as for some 'divine event' still hidden behind the curtain that is about to rise on the new century." Even for Sweet, writing thirty years later during "the age of big business," after World War I and on the eve of the Great Depression, closed his story of religions in America with a note celebrating the splendid vision of Protestant unity: "There is every indication among all the Protestant churches, great and small, that the day of contented separation is fully passed and there is undoubtedly a growing will to, as well as an enlarging expectation of, union."[11]

Religion in America never has been limited to Protestant Christianity, of course, and each of the historians under consideration took account of the varieties of religious life and thought that flourished under conditions of religious freedom and voluntarism. While celebrating these conditions as the best possible environment for the growth of evangelical denominations, the historians rather grudgingly accepted concomitant success of "unevangelical denominations" and "heresies" (Baird), "divergent currents" and "convergent currents" (Dorchester), major and minor sects (Bacon), and "the strange and unusual religious movements," the "extravagances" and "fads" and, by implication, insane Christians (Sweet). Schaff and Bacon, with a broad understanding and deep appreciation of the larger contours of church history, were less inclined than were Baird, Dorchester, and Sweet to criticize any particular Christian expression, including established church traditions as well as extreme sectarianism, because all contained some essential expression of the total historical body of Christ. This conviction, however, somewhat qualified their enthusiasm for complete religious freedom, with its scandal of disunity, without equal anticipation of the reunion of Christendom.[12]

Baird and Sweet, whose interests went beyond Christianity, treated Jews briefly with polite respect. But harsh judgments were delivered to Mormonism, Adventism, Spiritualism, and Christian Science. Of these the Mormons received the most scathing attacks. Baird called them "a body of ignorant creatures" deluded by the "cunning" of their leaders who were "atrocious imposters" whose "hope of founding a vast empire in the Western hemisphere soon [would] vanish away." Schaff pleaded that America not be judged "in any way by this irregular growth." Dorchester had seen Mormonism grow into "an ecclesiastical despotism of immense strength," but concluded that it was "only a local ulcer" with "no sure lease of the future." Bacon, describing Mormonism as "a system of gross, palpable imposture contrived by a disreputable adventurer, Joe Smith," who "drew a number of honest dupes into the train of the knavish leaders," took the Utah empire seriously, yet judged it "only incidentally that the strange story of the Mormons" (whom he did not classify as Christians) "is connected with the history of American Christianity."[13]

Roman Catholicism demanded more serious attention. Even in 1843 it had become apparent that the Roman Catholic church was becoming more than incidental to American religious history. Baird placed Roman Catholics in the highest class of "unevangelical denominations," above the Unitarians and Universalists whom he castigated as dangerous heretics. Roman Catholics, who held true doctrines but "buried" them "amid the rubbish of multiplied human traditions," had increased enough in number to arouse Protestant fears of "Romanism" by the midnineteenth century. Schaff felt that "on the free Republican and Puritanic soil of North America, the Roman Catholic Church with its medieval traditions, centralized priestly government, and extreme conservatism [was] almost an anomaly." For Catholicism to succeed in America, therefore, it would have to "assume a more liberal character" and "more or less approach evangelical Protestantism." Later in the century, Dorchester perceived the large growth of Roman Catholicism to be "one of the striking religious phenomena of this century" and something of a threat to free institutions. Bacon, appreciative of the virtues in each historic Christian body, found some in "the Roman system" of order and stability; and in Protestant American environment he expected the Roman Catholic Church to be "modified for the better." Yet he found "the Catholic advance in America" not especially successful, for the nation remained solidly Protestant. Whereas Sweet noted that in 1890 "all the great cities throughout the country had become centers of Catholic influence and power," he all but omitted reference to Roman Catholicism as the story of religions moved through the first quarter of the twentieth century.[14]

The great tradition of religion in America, to these its historians, was Protestant to the core. Regardless of the remarkable growth of other Christian traditions, as well as the growing presence of Judaism, Protestantism remained the constant point of reference and primary subject of discussion from beginning to end. Other religions were considered marginal, with no significant place in the overall scheme of American religious history.[15] Protestantism, in fact, seemed to provide the clue to the nature and destiny of the nation itself.

129

II

The notion that there should be an evolving national story with historical direction and meaning has been a peculiarly Judeo-Christian notion, even more a Western European Christendom notion, and most of all a Reformed Protestant and even British Puritan notion. The Anglo-Saxon Protestant creation of an American epic endured partly because these people represented the majority and the power during the time of national pregnancy, birth, and early nurture. The *meaning* of America thus developed according to their own sense of identity including heritage and destiny. Distinctive to this identity was a nationalistic modification of the Augustinian *(The City of God)* theological foundation of medieval Christendom expressed in British millennial eschatology. To Americans of this heritage, England's sacred covenant to be the New Israel had aborted, whereupon the mission transferred to the New World.

In fact, the New World transcended the Puritan vision of its meaning, despite the permeating force of Puritanism in colonial America. The First Amendment to the Constitution both reflected and encouraged a free-developing religious diversity. The Enlightenment atmosphere facilitated an emerging democratic ideology that defined the new nation as a social experiment grounded in the free play of natural law and human reason. Various kinds of Americans could embrace this national ideology as divinely ordained. Nevertheless, British-rooted Protestantism and its appropriation of this civil religious ideology weighed heavily on the developing nineteenth-century American mind and institutions.[16] Protestants influenced public schools, political forces, popular media, and literature. Protestants wrote American history in their own image and their religious history in a national image.

It seems clear that, in fact, Protestantism dominated the early decades of nineteenth-century American religious life and thought and that it penetrated the developing culture and ethos of the new nation. Near the end of the century Dorchester and Bacon recognized new challenges to Protestant dominance, but the churches expressed enough vigor and optimism to convince these historians that Protestantism would maintain itself. Writing after World War I, however, Sweet could see the widening cracks in the Protestant empire, and he expressed the defensive Protestant posture common during the mid-1920s through the 1950s. Historically he viewed the quarter century preceding the Civil War as an "era of religious chaos," during which time popular alternatives to the "sane" Protestant churches ran rampant. Yet Sweet could not quite recognize the profound and long-range implications of new religious currents that appeared later in the nineteenth century and that by World War I had contributed to the virtual demise of Protestant American Christendom.[17]

Nevertheless, with good reason and credibility did Protestants express optimistic enthusiasm during the post-Civil War half-century, for they prospered from the prominent position they had gained in American society and had reason to believe that new challenges to their position could be overcome with sufficient commitment and organization. American Protestant national identity entered the twentieth century with nearly unchecked self-confidence. During World War I, public Protestant rhetoric most fervently tended to confuse American civil ideology with Christianity in a crusading fashion that approached sheer nationalistic cultism. But these public displays during World War I do not mean that Protestants controlled the national religious mind, mood, or culture. Other religious traditions long had been coming of age. True, Protestants continued to own the nation in their own minds and according to their public affirmation and actions until well into the twentieth century. Some even identified themselves as the "Moral Majority" during the 1980 presidential election. But the historiographical question that has accompanied Protestantism's "drift and indecision" asks if that which Protestants have thought and said about themselves with regard to the nation should any longer command inherent primacy among the variety of religious data available to historians concerned about the whole unfolding story of religion in America.[18]

Even as William Warren Sweet's Protestant-oriented interpretation of American religious history enjoyed the "standard account" status for some thirty years, younger historians with a mid twentieth century perspective were laying groundwork for a new interpretation of the story.[19] Not only did they challenge Sweet's frontier orientation by rejuvenating attention to European influence in American religion, but they also developed a theme of the decline of Protestant influence in the twentieth century, and this insight began to alter the whole sense of American religious history. As major new histories began to appear during the 1960s, the end of Protestant America was virtually announced by authors tracing the period of Protestant "sickness unto death" roughly through their own lifetimes.

If the Protestant era in American religious historiography has ended, however, the new era remains in its dawning stage. A Protestant hegemony persists. All of the new comprehensive histories of religion in America are the products of Protestant interpreters, including Clifton E. Olmstead, Winthrop S. Hudson, Edwin S. Gaustad, Sydney E. Ahlstrom, and Robert T. Handy.[20] Furthermore, specialized interpretations of religion in America by such scholars as Sidney E. Mead, William A. Clebsch, and William G. McLoughlin concentrate almost exclusively on Protestantism.[21] Winthrop S. Hudson, Martin E. Marty, and Robert T. Handy have written creative new historical interpretations of American Protestantism.[22] Yet it is striking that this plethora of Protestant-oriented scholarship has contributed heavily to our growing awareness of the larger than Protestant meaning of American religious history. Quite simply, it no longer will be historically satisfying to mold the whole interpretative framework of American religious history on the changing fortunes of popular main-line Protestant denominations and evangelical movements. Long ago these ceased to represent the normative religion of the American people. Surely the rise and decline of Protestant America is a true story; but it is not the whole story or the only way to interpret the history of religion in America.

III

From an international as well as domestic or even indigenous perspective, religion in America offers a variety that seriously challenges the great tradition of Anglo-Saxon Protestant-oriented historiography. Those who fought for their rights as Englishmen must always remain central to the story, but other characters deserve a large share of the spotlight.

The historiographical problem is not simply the fact of American religious pluralism. Pluralism *per se* is not unique to America. Rather, the problem is how pluralism fits into the whole historical interpretation. Winthrop S. Hudson, for example, sees pluralism primarily as a post-Civil War development in American religion but not becoming a significant factor until after World War I. He weighs heavily the size and public influence of a religion in gauging its historical significance as well as its entrance into the narrative. "Late-blooming" religious groups, such as Judaism, therefore, are "deferred to the period when they began to loom large on the American scene." At some points, however, Hudson pays special attention to *origins* in interpreting a religion. The Mormons, for example, are discussed only in terms of the origin and early development of the church (until 1870), even though not until well into the twentieth century did Mormonism begin to loom large on the American scene.[23]

In one important respect *origins* dominate the story as a whole. Hudson refers to the period of American origins for the touchstone of the nation's religious history. He understands those origins to have been fundamentally Protestant-rooted, including the Enlightenment.[24] American religious history thus primarily traces the rise and decline of this identifiable Protestantism. Consequently, Protestant development away from its Reformation orientation in theology and practice marks the emergence of American (versus European) culture-religion. This is Protestantism on the decline, losing its true identity amid the growing strength of other religious identities.[25]

The appearance of Hudson's *Religion in America* in 1965 successfully replaced Sweet's interpretation of "the story" and set forth a new framework upon which others have built. Pluralism has demanded increasing attention. If the nature of religious origins does not remain central to the entire historical interpretation, the rising pluralism of religious life and thought rather than the declining traditions may assume a greater share of the historian's attention. The essential nature of religion in America as well as the nation's "soul" may be discovered not in what was being lost so much as what was emerging. In his preface to *A Religious History of America*, Edwin S. Gaustad seems to imply an interpretative framework based on emerging religion by disclaiming "the decline and fall of archaic forms" as a guide to the story. Although some rising religious forms receive little sustained attention in his account (Mormons, Jehovah's Witnesses, Dispensationalists, for example), Gaustad covers a wide religious territory and presents a stimulating panoramic view of religious life in twentieth-century America. In *A Religious History of the American People*, Sydney E. Ahlstrom intended to balance the Anglo-Saxon Protestant "mainstream" with "the radical diversity of American religious movements." Yet the destiny of Protestantism remains even in this book the primary framework for tracing American religious history to its post-Protestant era, which does not finally blossom until after 1960. Consequently twentieth-century Judaism, Roman Catholicism, Eastern Orthodoxy, harmonial religions, and black religions are discussed in separate chapters following twelve chapters in which the historical context is presented in terms of Protestant life and thought. Nevertheless, Ahlstrom's masterful narrative has greatly advanced the historiographical enterprise beyond its Protestant era by incorporating a wide variety of significant actors in the drama of pluralistic religious Americana.[26]

ROMAN CATHOLIC AMERICANS. Another tradition of American religious historiography has developed alongside the one dominated by Protestant identity. Its great historian is John Tracy Ellis, who succeeds such scholars as John Gilmary Shea, Thomas O'Gorman, and Theodore Maynard.[27] Until recently, American Catholic historiography has concentrated on its church as persecuted and alienated within a Protestant-dominated nation. Almost by necessity this has been a denominational history responding to the neglect of Roman Catholicism in the general survey histories of religion in the United States. Protestantism appears, especially in the earlier Catholic studies, usually as an oppressive foe in the struggle for Christendom. Much Catholic historiography thus ex-

133

presses the defensive posture of its church in America throughout most of its history. Against Protestant historians' fears, insinuations, and accusations, Catholic historians have defended the compatibility of their church with their nation, the primacy of their church vis-a-vis Protestant claims, and the amazing growth of their church against great odds into an aggressive, national, religious force.

By the end of the nineteenth century the Roman Catholic Church had become, in O'Gorman's words, "a huge fact in the life of the republic." He concluded his study confident "that the Catholic Church is in accord with Christ's revelation, with American liberty, and is the strongest moral power for the preservation of the republic from the new social dangers that threaten the United States as well as the whole civilized World." As the twentieth century progressed, Catholic triumphalism gained confidence. In 1941 Theodore Maynard wrote with conviction that "except for isolated 'fundamentalists'—and these are pretty thoroughly discredited and without intellectual leadership—Catholicism could cut through Protestantism as through so much butter."[28] Protestants and Catholics frequently have been at each other's throats during their American experience, which has affected their historical memories. The twentieth-century Catholic search for unity, identity, and power in America finally gave way to an upheaval during the 1960s leaving the church in a state of confusion similar to much of Protestantism.[29] The American Christendom mentality thus has been Catholic as well as Protestant, even though the demise of Protestant America did not result in the establishment of Catholic America.

The post-Vatican II atmosphere is opening American Catholic history to new scholarly interpretation. From the Enlightenment to nineteenth-century missions and popular revivalism through twentieth-century progressive reform and intellectual renaissance, the American religious "mainstream" is being traced through its emerging Catholic expression.[30] Even more significant than new histories of American Catholicism, however, would be the appearance of a history of religion in America written by a Roman Catholic historian. Such an account would be especially enlightening if the Spanish and French presence in the North American territories surrounding the British Colonies were woven into the fabric of subsequent religious life in the nation in appropriate fashion.

The old Spanish culture from Florida westward through Texas, New Mexico, and California never evaporated. It haunts the Southwest and is reborn in modern Hispanic Catholicism, which represents a rapidly increasing proportion of all American Roman Catholics.[31] Moreover, the Spanish presence remained not only as a

134

factor in American manifest destiny ideology and emotion at least through the Spanish American War of 1898, but also as a point of heritage contact for the diverse Roman Catholic Church struggling for its place in the new nation. Likewise French Catholicism left its permanent mark in territories north, west, and south of New England; and very early in the nineteenth century new French immigrant priests and laity became important links with the former New France as well as assets to the British-rooted Catholic Church in America. Meanwhile, whereas Spanish Catholicism mixed with American Indian spirituality in the Southwest, French Catholicism mixed with African spirituality of Haitian émigrés in the Louisiana Territory by the end of the eighteenth century. When all is considered, in the long run, these Spanish and French Catholic plantings in North America are significant ingredients of American religious history. John Tracy Ellis cautiously suggests the connection:

> The favored position of Catholics in Spanish and French colonies was not the source from which the main stream of American Catholic life took its rise. Rather it was the minority group along the Atlantic coastline that set the pattern for future Catholic development, a development destined to reach out to the West and South in the early nineteenth century and there be joined by the descendants of the Spaniards and French where Catholic elements fused on the distant frontiers.[32]

To take "the distant frontiers" seriously is to recognize that beyond the relative attention given to Protestant or Catholic ingredients *per se* in American religious history loom more far-reaching historiographical considerations. Historians have debated the degree to which religion in America has its antecedents in Europe, thus qualifying its truly innovative expressions. Preoccupation with European-rooted Christianity has limited this debate to an unfortunate provincialism. In fact, both the distinctive quality of American religion and its international dimensions demand attention beyond exclusively European antecedents. The fact that contemporary South American liberation theologians are providing a major source and inspiration for creative theological construction in the United States and the fact that Asian and South African theologians likewise are influencing North American theologians stimulate the historiographical imagination. If one visualizes American religious history from a far Western perspective, for example, one discovers that the rich and varied culture of the Californios left a permanent Spanish-Mexican-Indian legacy. Hispanic Catholicism rather than British Puritanism permeated the historic atmosphere of California. After midnineteenth century not only European-rooted settlers but also Afro-American pioneers and Asian immigrants added tremen-

135

dous complexity to the religious culture of the nation from its Pacific basin side.

AFRO-AMERICANS. African antecedents to American religious life first arrived through channels of the Atlantic community. Black religious identity in America cannot be understood apart from the African heritage of black people who came to the New World unwillingly as slaves in chains. Unlike Europeans, Africans did not come to America for social, political, economic, or religious freedom. To the contrary, Africans lost their freedom in America. Not only did their American religious sensibility assume a liberation orientation from the beginning, but it also blended African spirituality with European-rooted Christianity. This unique religious identity and formation thus originated in America under slave conditions. Whereas European-rooted Christianity permeated the dominant cultural traditions and social institutions of the nation, African-rooted religion in America had to exist more as an underground movement in a minority subculture almost invisible to white society. Accordingly, black religious culture barely received notice during the Protestant era of American religious historiography.[33]

The entire spectrum of black religious expression, if allowed to extend beyond the status of sidelights off center stage, might have far-reaching effects in the whole story of religion in American history.[34] Historically developing adaptations of African religiosity to American environment interacted, for example, with traditional white Protestant and Roman Catholic Christianity, in some ways distinct from these two traditions while expressing possible linkages between them. Black church traditions do not look to the sixteenth-century European Reformation–Counter-Reformation heritage for their vital roots in the same manner that white Protestants and Roman Catholics experience their historic identities. Essentially, black churches are eighteenth- and nineteenth-century Christian traditions in origin whose previous heritage leads to Africa more profoundly than to Europe. Although naturally learning Protestant or Catholic biases from their white brothers and sisters, black American Christians escaped the deeply ingrained European origins of this extreme rift within Christendom. In addition, while manifesting much of the traditional Protestant emphasis on "sacramental preaching" and congregational hymn-singing, black churches also have expressed the wholeness of a parish ethos that characterized much of American immigrant Catholic church life. Generalizations about the breakdown of parish structures in American environment or about old world characteristics preserved in immigrant church ghettos, therefore, must be qualified by the phenomenon of Afro-American Christianity.

Another generalization that requires qualification to the extent that Afro-Americans are considered part of the story is the homogeneity of American civil religion prior to the 1960s.[35] At almost every point those people subjected to racist prejudice and discrimination, whose roots pass through slavery, have not shared the American dream heritage in the manner common to most voluntary immigrants to America. Neither the enlightened philosophy of natural rights nor the Puritan version of God's new Israel had included black people. To them manifest destiny, Christian Americanization, and the symbols of American democratic faith included oppression—the object of extreme prophetic judgment.

ASIAN-AMERICANS. Not all voluntary immigrants escaped the plague of racism. Asians arrived much later in America than did Africans, and most of them first touched western rather than eastern shores. In the middle of the nineteenth century Philip Schaff noted that "all Christian denominations and sects, except the Oriental, have settled in the United States."[36] Shortly thereafter this exception would not hold, for Chinese immigrants began arriving, followed later by Japanese and by other Asian peoples still later. "Hitherto Christian civilization has had all the disadvantages of contact with paganism on its own soil by a few missionaries and merchants," wrote a Presbyterian missionary in the 1880s, "but here, for the first time, paganism comes as a visitor upon Christian soil, and sojourns for awhile amid the genius and spirit of our Gospel institutions."[37] Thus was expressed a common American Christian perception of the newly arrived Asians, whose "non-Christian" religious and cultural patterns added a fundamentally new ingredient to the American "melting pot." Most American denominations evangelized the Asian immigrants, thinking that they eventually would return to whence they came perhaps as Christian missionaries; they usually did not escape the racist attitudes of white Americans generally.

Asian immigration into the United States has continued to make an impact on American religious life, despite immigration laws of the 1920s. The Second World War ushered in a new era of mobility and migration of peoples from Asia and the Pacific Islands. Following the Korean War, Korean immigration to America has increased in number, many bringing their Christian ties with them—ties rooted originally in European and American missions of an earlier time yet distinctively Korean in identity. A recent religious phenomenon of wide notice combining Buddhism, Confucianism, and Shamanism with Christianity in America, arriving from Korea first in Eugene, Oregon, in 1959 via the missionary Young On Kim, is the Unification Church. Having developed a primary base in the San

Francisco Bay Area during the 1960s, the Unification Church has gained solid footing in major cities throughout the nation and now exists in 120 countries around the globe.[38]

Asian-Americans do not appear in the general accounts of American religious history. No subject deserves the American religious historian's attention more than does the Asian presence, for no subject has been so ignored. Buddhism in America, a century-long history, has attracted some scholarly attention.[39] But the rich story of developing Asian Christian life and thought will have to be researched nearly from scratch.[40] From their Pacific Coast centers, spreading throughout the nation, the variety of Asian-American communities has manifested significant exceptions to the European nature of American culture. Their religious history, too, is part of the larger story.

AMERICAN INDIANS. The most thorough exceptions to American religious antecedents abroad are those whose roots lead to the tribal peoples of the New World who greeted newcomers from lands across the seas. American Indians did not share the heritage or the destiny—surely not the rights—of Englishmen. Nor have American Indians received their share of attention from American religious historians. William Warren Sweet and his predecessors referred to them periodically as objects of Christian missions. Although often remarkably resistant to Christian evangelism, American Indians did eventually become at least nominally Christian in fairly large numbers. Their expression of Christianity usually related to tribal ceremonial practices and beliefs, a phenomenon generally ignored by American religious historians.[41] Yet the North American Indians always have represented an indomitable alternative to all forms of Judeo-Christian imports. Given the nature of their encounter with aggressive immigrant cultural forces, it is remarkable that American Indians—their cultures and their religions—have persisted. Religion in America properly begins with tribal religions of the native peoples; and these never should be lost sight of throughout the story to the present.

American Indians have offered a cultural-religious alternative to Western Judeo-Christian modes of thought and action. The difference has not been primarily a theological conception of divinity as much as it has pertained to cultural world views. This difference in world views has been described in terms of the Western Judeo-Christian historical orientation as over against the American Indian aloofness from historical thought: "time is regarded as all-important by Christians, and it has a casual importance, if any, among the tribal peoples." More significant to the latter is space: "American

Indians hold their lands—places—as having the highest possible meaning."[42]

Space has been an important reality to both cultures; the difference is what space has meant and how it has been utilized. Confronting the predominant religious belief in dominion and destiny that "built this nation" through a passionate ethic of work and technology is the American Indian belief in the sacredness of space that might help stimulate a passion for preserving the nation in its natural as well as technological wholeness. As land and natural resources begin to run out, the new Americans who once enjoyed too much space and too little time to integrate tribal peoples into a nation-building program now may begin to consider how those pushed-aside "teachings from the American earth" offer insights for programs of humanization and ecological health. That nature itself may be historical, with humanity a responsible natural agent of change, is a concept not central to Western Christendom or to American Indian heritage, but one that the two traditions in dialogue or dialectic might entertain.[43] One thing is certain: American Indian cultures at the very least offer the historian an authentic alternative to any definition of main-line religion in America—an alternative of contemporary value that was here first and remained.

IV

Roman Catholics, Afro-Americans, Asian-Americans, and American Indians are but four important actors on the stage of American religious history who play alongside and in interaction with the white main-line Protestant majority. Others, such as Jews, Mormons, and Eastern Orthodox Christians, extend the dimensions of the field further. And then, simply to notice the feminine participants in all aspects of the story, even more to take their roles seriously, would extend the field into hitherto unmapped territories. English women as well as English men fought for their rights two centuries past, and the women's struggle has not ceased. "A surprising feature," writes Winthrop S. Hudson about his *Religion in America*, "is the recurring frequency of women's names in the narrative. They appear as founders of religious groups, as leaders of humanitarian enterprises, as troublers of the established political and ecclesiastical order, as influential literary figures, and as agitators for woman's rights. It is surprising because it was unintentional, and it serves to emphasize how much more needs to be done to illumine the role of women in the religious life of the United States."[44]

So much more needs to be done, indeed! The emerging new era in American religious historiography will have to be intentional about integrating women into the story.[45] The varying and devel-

139

oping roles of women as well as men of all ethnic, racial, and religious identities and from all regions of the nation must be illumined if the distinctive qualities of American religious life and thought are to be recognized.[46]

NOTES

The present essay utilizes material found in *Foundations*, vol. 23, no. 2 (April-June, 1980).

[1] For a critical analysis of "Postmanship" applied to American religious history, see Sidney E. Mead, "The Post-Protestant Concept and America's Two Religions," in *Religion in Life*, vol. 33, no. 2 (Spring, 1964), pp. 191-204. See also Franklin H. Littell, "Is America 'Post-Christian'?" in his book *The Church and the Body Politic* (New York: The Seabury Press, Inc., 1969), pp. 19-25. Throughout the essay America refers to the United States.

[2] Robert Baird, *Religion in America, Or an Account of the Origin, Progress, Relation to the State, and Present Condition of the Evangelical Churches in the United States, with Notices of the Unevangelical Denominations* (New York: Harper & Row, Publishers, Inc., 1844). Philip Schaff, *America: A Sketch of Its Political, Social, and Religious Character*, ed. Perry Miller (Cambridge, Mass.: Harvard University Press, 1961). Though not intended to be a full history of the subject, Schaff's published lectures contained much history and interpretation and became quite influential in the work of later historians. Daniel Dorchester, *Christianity in the United States from the First Settlement Down to the Present Time* (New York: Phillips & Hunt, 1888). Leonard Woolsey Bacon, *A History of American Christianity* (New York: The Christian Literature Co., 1897). William Warren Sweet, *The Story of Religions in America* (New York: Harper & Row, Publishers, Inc., 1930).

[3] Bacon, *American Christianity*, pp. 3, 32; Schaff, *America: A Sketch*, p. 89.

[4] Sweet, p. 184. Sweet followed Schaff's account in omitting discussion of Spanish and French Catholicism in colonial America except for a brief tracing of Indian missions (pp. 239-241).

[5] Baird, *Religion in America*, book 1, chapter 3; Dorchester, *Christianity in the U.S.*, pp. 24-25; Bacon, *American Christianity*, pp. 30-31, 185.

[6] Dorchester, *Christianity in the U.S.*, p. 753.

[7] Baird, *Religion in America*, book 1, chapters 3, 4; Schaff, *America: A Sketch*, p. 214.

[8] Baird, *Religion in America*, book 7, chapter 3; Schaff, *America: A Sketch*, p. 214; Dorchester, *Christianity in the U.S.*, p. 556; Bacon, *American Christianity*, pp. 311-313; Sweet, *The Story of Religions*, p. 395.

[9] Baird, *Religion in America*, book 8, chapter 12; Schaff, *America: A Sketch*, p. 6; Bacon, *American Christianity*, p. 346; Dorchester, *Christianity in the U.S.*, p. 562.

[10] Dorchester, *Christianity in the U.S.*, p. 570; Bacon, *American Christianity*, p. 350.

[11] Dorchester, *Christianity in the U.S.*, p. 765; Bacon, *American Christianity*, p. 419; Sweet, *The Story of Religions*, p. 523.

[12] Dorchester, *Christianity in the U.S.*, pp. 194-211, 300-324, 492, 651-674; Sweet, *The Story of Religions*, pp. 395-411. Bacon thus entitled his concluding chapter, chapter 22, "Tendencies Toward a Manifestation of the Unity of the American

Church." Schaff's understanding of church history appeared in his *What Is Church History? A Vindication of the Idea of Historical Development* (1846) and his address on "The Reunion of Christendom" at the 1893 World's Parliament of Religions in Chicago; but his love-hate attitude toward the vigor of sectarian Christianity plus his vision of ultimate Christian unity permeated his lectures on *America: A Sketch* as well. See also Sweet, *The Story of Religions*, pp. 395-411; Dorchester, *Christianity in the U.S.*, pp. 194-211, 300-324, 492, 651-674; and Baird, *Religion in America*, book 7.

[13] Sweet, *The Story of Religions*, pp. 489-490, 501-503; Baird, *Religion in America*, book 7, chapter 8; Schaff, *America: A Sketch*, p. 203; Dorchester, *Christianity in the U.S.*, pp. 538-542, 646-649, 780; Bacon, *American Christianity*, p. 335.

[14] Baird, *Religion in America*, book 7, chapter 1; Schaff, *America: A Sketch*, p. 181; Dorchester, *Christianity in the U.S.*, p. 614; Bacon, *American Christianity*, pp. 323, 330-332; Sweet, *The Story of Religions*, p. 488.

[15] See John F. Wilson, "The Historical Study of Marginal American Religious Movements," in *Religious Movements in Contemporary America*, ed. Irving I. Zaretsky and Mark P. Leone (Princeton, N.J.: Princeton University Press, 1974), pp. 596-611.

[16] For critical scholarly discussion of the idea of American civil religion see especially Elwyn A. Smith, ed., *The Religion of the Republic* (Philadelphia: Fortress Press, 1971); Russell E. Richey and Donald G. Jones, eds., *American Civil Religion* (New York: Harper & Row, Publishers, Inc. 1974); and John F. Wilson, *Public Religion in American Culture* (Philadelphia: Temple University Press, 1979). Important positive yet divergent interpretations of the general phenomenon are Robert N. Bellah, *The Broken Covenant: American Civil Religion in Time of Trial* (New York: The Seabury Press, Inc., 1975); and Sidney E. Mead, *The Nation with the Soul of a Church* (New York: Harper & Row, Publishers, Inc., 1975).

[17] In the 1950 edition of Sweet's volume, the final added and revised chapters discuss Roman Catholicism in America in a frankly Protestant polemical tone, betraying the author's fear and hostility toward Catholic power (see especially pp. 441-448). On the antebellum period see pages 404, 411.

[18] The historiographical discussion surged forward after the publication of Henry F. May, "The Recovery of American Religious History," *American Historical Review*, vol. 70 (October, 1964). Some of the many essays on the subject published since 1964 are cited in Edwin S. Gaustad, *Religion in America: History and Historiography* (Washington, D.C.: American Historical Association, 1973).

[19] A major critique of Sweet's interpretation was made by Sidney E. Mead, "Professor Sweet's Religion and Culture in America," *Church History*, vol. 22 (March, 1953), pp. 33-49.

[20] Clifton E. Olmstead, *History of Religion in the United States* (Englewood Cliffs, N.J.; Prentice-Hall, Inc., 1960); Winthrop S. Hudson, *Religion in America* (New York: Charles Scribner's Sons, 1965); Edwin S. Gaustad, *A Religious History of America* (New York: Harper & Row, Publishers, Inc., 1966); Sydney E. Ahlstrom, *A Religious History of the American People* (New Haven, Conn.: Yale University Press, 1972). Two additional major works are limited to Christianity: H. S. Smith, R. T. Handy, and L. A. Loetscher, eds., *American Christianity: An Historical Interpretation with Representative Documents*, 2 vols. (New York: Charles Scribner's Sons, 1960); and Robert T. Handy, *A History of the Churches in the United States and Canada* (New York: Oxford University Press, 1977).

141

[21] Sidney E. Mead, *The Lively Experiment: The Shaping of Christianity in America* (New York: Harper & Row, Publishers, Inc., 1963); William A. Clebsch, *From Sacred to Profane America: The Role of Religion in American History* (New York: Harper & Row, Publishers, Inc., 1968); William G. McLoughlin, *Revivals, Awakenings, and Reform: An Essay on Religion and Social Change in America, 1607-1977*

(Chicago: University of Chicago Press, 1978). For interpretations with a larger than Protestant scope see, for example, Edwin S. Gaustad, *Dissent in American Religion* (Chicago: University of Chicago Press, 1973); Martin E. Marty, *A Nation of Behavers* (Chicago: University of Chicago Press, 1976); Eldon G. Ernst, *Without Help or Hindrance: Religous Identity in American Culture* (Philadelphia: The Westminster Press, 1977); and Peter W. Williams, *Popular Religion in America* (Englewood Cliffs, N.J.: Prentice-Hall, Inc., 1980).

[22] Winthrop S. Hudson, *American Protestantism* (Chicago: University of Chicago Press, 1961); Martin E. Marty, *Righteous Empire: The Protestant Experience in America* (New York: The Dial Press, 1970); and Robert T. Handy, *A Christian America: Protestant Hopes and Historical Realities* (New York: Oxford University Press, 1971).

[23] Hudson, *Religion in America*, pp. viii-ix. Mormonism curiously has been neglected in its twentieth-century development by historians, who have been concerned mainly with the spectacular origins and early westward migration of the movement. Jan Shipps, in "The Mormons: Looking Forward and Outward," *The Christian Century*, vol. 95, no. 26 (August 16-23, 1978), p. 761, notes that "while the Mormons are definitely not moving toward the American religious mainstream, that mainstream could well be moving toward them." The twentieth-century growth of Mormonism is no less spectacular than were its origins. Two recent books do cover the modern period: Leonard J. Arrington and Davis Bitton, *The Mormon Experience: A History of the Latter-Day Saints* (New York: Alfred A. Knopf, Inc., 1979); and Marcus Hansen, *Mormonism and the American Experience* (Chicago: University of Chicago Press, 1980).

[24] Hudson, *Religion in America*, pp. 92-95, emphasizes the Puritan and Calvinist origins of much Enlightenment political thought, such as that of John Locke's and the American founding fathers Adams's and Jefferson's. He distinguishes their political ideas from their unorthodox deist religious views that exerted little influence except among some intellectuals, compared to the orthodox churches' influence that rallied support among the masses during the American Revolution. In contrast, Sidney E. Mead, especially in *The Nation with the Soul of a Church*, places great emphasis on the primacy of the Enlightenment as the theoretical foundation of American religious freedom and pluralism transcending Protestant or any other particular religious monopoly of national meaning and experience. That he might have expanded this vision is suggested by LeRoy Moore in "Sidney E. Mead's Understanding of America," *Journal of the American Academy of Religion*, vol. 44 (March, 1976), pp. 133-153. The most thorough analysis of the Enlightenment is Henry F. May's *The Enlightenment in America* (New York: Oxford University Press, 1976).

[25] A remarkable number of religious personalities and groups outside the major Protestant denominations and Roman Catholicism appear in Hudson's *Religion in America* with no polemical tone whatsoever from the author, thus expressing the new tone of books of its kind. Hudson saves his criticism for wayward Protestant developments, for example, p. 413. In 1981 the third edition of Hudson's book appeared with a new insightful concluding chapter covering the past decade of diverse religious life throughout the nation.

[26] For an historiographical analysis of Ahlstrom's book see John F. Wilson, "A Review of Some Reviews of *A Religious History of the American People*, by Sydney E. Ahlstrom," in *Religious Studies Review* (September, 1975). Robert T. Handy's *A History of the Churches in the United States and Canada* sets forth a new synthetic interpretation that widens the scope of the field of American religious history. See C. C. Goen, "A Handy Chronicle of Religion in America: An Essay Review," in *Foundations*, vol. 21, no. 1, (January-March, 1978).

[27] Two of John Tracy Ellis's many works are *American Catholicism*, 2nd rev. ed.

(Chicago: University of Chicago Press, 1956) and *Documents of American Catholic History* (Milwaukee: Bruce, 1962); John Gilmary Shea, *History of the Catholic Church in the United States*, 4 vols. (New York: J. G. Shea, 1886-1892); Thomas O'Gorman, *A History of the Roman Catholic Church in the United States* (New York: Christian Literature, 1895); and Theodore Maynard, *The Story of American Catholicism* (New York: Macmillan, Inc., 1941).

[28] Maynard, *American Catholicism*, p. 224; O'Gorman, *Roman Catholic Church in the U.S.*, p. 1.

[29] See David J. O'Brien, *The Renewal of American Catholicism* (N.Y.: Oxford University Press, 1972); George Devine, *American Catholicism: Where Do We Go from Here?*" (Englewood Cliffs, N.J.: Prentice-Hall, Inc., 1975); and Philip Gleason, "In Search of Unity: American Catholic Thought, 1920-1960," *Catholic Historical Review*, vol. 65, no. 2 (April, 1979), pp. 185-205.

[30] On the Enlightenment see Joseph P. Chinnici, "American Catholics and Religious Pluralism, 1775-1820," *Journal of Ecumenical Studies*, vol. 16, no. 4 (Fall, 1979), pp. 727-746. On parish missions see Jay P. Dolan, *Catholic Revivalism: The American Experience 1830-1900* (Notre Dame: University of Notre Dame Press, 1978). On the progressive era see Alfred J. Ede, "The Lay Crusade for a Christian America: A Study of the American Federation of Catholic Societies 1900-1920," unpublished Ph.D. dissertation, Graduate Theological Union, 1979. On intellectual renaissance see William Halsey, *The Survival of American Innocence: Catholicism in an Era of Disillusionment 1920–1940* (Notre Dame: University of Notre Dame Press, 1980). But the most exciting new work is James Hennesey, S. J., *American Catholics: A History of the Roman Catholic Community in the United States* (New York: Oxford University Press, 1981).

[31] Today more than 25 percent of the Catholic population of the United States are Spanish-speaking—over fifteen million *chicanos* (Mexican Americans) plus *latinos* from Puerto Rico, the Dominican Republic, Cuba, and other Latin American countries; moveover, "demographic projections based on birth rate and immigration indicate that by the year 2000, 50 percent of U.S. Catholics will be of Latin American origin." From Enrique Dussel, *History and the Theology of Liberation: A Latin American Perspective*, trans. John Drury (Maryknoll, N.Y.: Orbis Books, 1976), p. 171.

[32] Ellis, *American Catholicism*, p. 40.

[33] The nineteenth-century historians ignored black religion. Sweet's four-page treatment in *The Story of Religions* betrays ignorance of black religion and a condescending attitude toward black people (pp. 473-476).

[34] A significant recent study of religion among Afro-American slaves is Albert J. Raboteau, *Slave Religion: The "Invisible Institution" in the Antebellum South* (New York: Oxford University Press, 1978). On nineteenth-century American black religious life outside of slave conditions, see Larry G. Murphy, "Equality Before the Law: The Struggle of Nineteenth-Century Black Californians for Social and Political Justice," Ph.D. dissertation, Graduate Theological Union, 1973. On the historiographical state of black church studies prior to 1968 see Robert T. Handy, "Negro Christianity and American Church History," in Jerald C. Brauer, ed., *Reinterpretation in American Church History* (Chicago: University of Chicago Press, 1968). Important works published since 1968 are included in Gayraud S. Wilmore and James H. Cone, eds., *Black Theology: A Documentary History 1966–1979* (New York: Orbis Books, 1979).

[35] See J. Earl Thompson, Jr., "The Reform of the Racist Religion of the Republic," in *The Religion of the Republic*, ed. Smith.

[36] Schaff, *America: A Sketch*, p. 80.

[37] Ira. M. Condit, *Chinese in America: Questions and Answers for Mission Circles*

and Boards (Philadelphia: Woman's Foreign Missionary Society of the Presbyterian Church, 1886), p. 107.

[38] See Michael L. Mickler, "A History of the Unification Church in the Bay Area: 1960–1974," unpublished M.A. thesis, Graduate Theological Union, 1980.

[39] Three recent studies are Emma McCloy Layman, Buddhism in America (Chicago: Nelson-Hall, 1976); Tetsuden Kashima, Buddhism in America (Westport, Conn.: Greenwood, 1977); and Charles Prebish, "Reflections on the Transmission of Buddhism to America," in Jacob Needleman and George Baker, eds., Understanding the New Religions (New York: The Seabury Press, Inc., A Crossroad Book, 1978), pp. 153-172.

[40] Groundwork is being done by Wesley Woo in his unpublished doctoral research papers in the Graduate Theological Union, such as "Chinese Churches in America, 1880–1920" (Fall, 1977) and "American Catholicism and Chinese Americans, 1850–1890" (Spring, 1977). See also Sumio Koga, comp., A Centennial Legacy—History of the Japanese Christian Missions in North America 1877–1977 (Chicago: Nobart, 1977); and Grant John Hagiya, "Japanese Americans and the Christian Church: The Struggle for Identity and Existence," unpublished D.Min. Thesis, Claremont School of Theology, 1978.

[41] Baird's account of "the Aborigines of North America," which begins his history in Religion in America (book 1, chapter 2), is especially noteworthy for its description (albeit critical) of Indian culture, including religious beliefs and practices. His successors, however, did not retain this interest. Sam D. Gill correctly notes that by omitting Indian religions, "the history of religious studies in America has shared in the moods and prejudices of that history," in "Native American Religions," The Council on the Study of Religion Bulletin, vol. 9 (December, 1978), p. 128. An important new contribution is Henry Warner Bowden, American Indians and Christian Missions (Chicago: The University of Chicago Press, 1981).

[42] Vine Deloria, Jr., God Is Red (New York: Dell Publishing Co., Inc., A Delta Book, 1973), pp. 111, 75. On the conception of deity see Paul Radin, "Monotheism Among American Indians," in Teachings from the American Earth: Indian Religion and Philosophy, ed. Dennis Tedlock and Barbara Tedlock (New York: W. W. Norton & Co., Inc., Liveright, 1975). See also Joseph Epes Brown, The Spirituality of the American Indian (Wallingford, Pa.: Pendle Hill Publications, 1964). In 1844 Baird noted that Indians had "some notions of a Supreme Power which governs the world, and of an Evil Spirit who is the enemy of mankind." He also noted the difference between Indian and European sense of the historical: "Even of their origin they have nothing but a confused tradition, not extending back beyond three or four generations. As they have no calendars, and reckon their years only by the return of certain seasons, so they have no record of their past," Religion in America, book 1, chapter 2. However, that Amerindian religion in its own terms may be understood as universal, theistic, historical, and moral is argued by Dale Stover, "The Amerindian Liberation of European Religious Consciousness," The Council on the Study of Religion Bulletin, vol. 12 (June, 1981).

[43] Tedlock, The American Earth. On the historicity of nature concept see Rosemary Radford Ruether, "The Biblical Vision of the Ecological Crisis," Christian Century, vol. 95, no. 38 (November 22, 1978), pp. 1129-1132. The space-time categories framed the first chapter of Sidney Mead's The Lively Experiment. The American mind has been influenced by Indian culture and has been concerned about natural resources. For example, see Roderick Nash, Wilderness and the American Mind, rev. ed. (New Haven, Conn.: Yale University Press, 1973); and Eileen Trudeau, "A Sense of Place: Changing Symbols of the Land-Person Relationship in America," unpublished M.A. thesis, Graduate Theological Union, 1977.

[44] Hudson, *Religion in America*, p. ix.

[45] Two recently published volumes have significantly advanced our knowledge and understanding of the roles of women in American religious life and thought: Janet Wilson James, ed., *Women in American Religion* (Philadelphia: University of Pennsylvania Press, 1980); and Rosemary Radford Ruether and Rosemary Skinner Keller, eds., *Women and Religion in America, Volume 1: The Nineteenth Century* (New York: Harper & Row, Publishers, Inc., 1981).

[46] A major contribution to the expanding field of American religious history has been made by Edwin S. Gausted, ed., *A Documentary History of Religion in America to the Civil War* (Grand Rapids, Mich.: William B. Eerdmans Publishing Company, 1982).

Revivalism and Millenarianism in America

Jerald C. Brauer

Any historian who surveys the development and spread of Christianity from the seventeenth to the twentieth centuries in Europe and North America is struck by the fact of the massive presence of revivalism and millenarianism in the United States. Not that it is absent from the European and English scene; millenarianism was probably more prevalent in seventeenth-century England than in the American colonies. Rather revivalism and millenarianism combined at the time of the Great Awakening in the colonies and proceeded to dominate the religious scene in the United States in a way unmatched either in England or on the Continent. Why do revivalism and millenarianism usually go hand in hand? Does one precede the other, or does one actually give birth to the other? Is it possible to be a serious millenarian and not be a revivalist, or is it possible to be a revivalist and not be a millenarian?

Before addressing these questions, it is necessary to make clear in a very brief way how revivalism and millenarianism are understood for the purpose of this discussion. Revivalism as a distinct movement does not come into being in Christian history until the eighteenth century. It begins in the American colonies of New Jersey and Massachusetts at approximately the same time the Evangelical Awakening in England is triggered by the field preaching of George Whitefield and John Wesley. Revivalism draws deeply from Puritanism and Pietism but develops into a distinct movement of its own which comes to have a profound impact on the British scene and virtually dominates American Protestantism throughout its history.[1]

Revivalism, a particular way of becoming, being, and remaining Christian, is distinguished from other forms and types of Christianity. The absolute necessity of a personal, highly self-conscious, individual conversion experience is the bedrock on which revivalism is built. Without such an experience, without being born again, one cannot be a Christian and certainly one cannot minister to others. So profound and central is the conversion experience that the whole of one's individual and communal life is utterly determined by it. One can clearly mark the day and even the moment that one was born again.[2]

The whole of the Christian faith is determined by that experience. It gives both form and substance to the cult and ritual of Christianity—the nature, the content, and the style of the sermon, the hymns that are sung,[3] the form and the delivery of prayers, and the structure of the worship service itself. All are conditioned by the necessity of converting sinners from death to life in Jesus Christ. The way Scripture is understood, employed, and handled is determined by the centrality of conversion. The very form of the associational life of the Christian community is posited on the assumption of conversion. No institutional arrangement of the religious community, be it Presbyterian, Congregational, or Episcopal, will suffice unless it becomes an instrument and bulwark for the conversion experience.

Though Scripture alone is the source of authority for revivalism, only the truly converted are in a position to interpret Scripture properly; therefore, in a very profound sense, authority itself is grounded in the conversion experience. It also provides the dynamic for Christian behavior. Revivalism is marked by an oversimplification of ethical problems. Everything is black or white, right or wrong, godly or godless, and converted people know exactly which is which. The attitude itself is grounded in the conversion experience which clearly divides the saved from the damned.

Beginning with the Great Awakening in the mideighteenth century, revivalism spread through the American scene until it became the predominant way of building and sustaining church life in the United States. Conversion itself was not the only way one could become and remain a Christian. Particularly in Roman Catholicism,[4] Lutheranism, Anglicanism, and some Reformed traditions, one was baptized into the Christian community as an infant and was nurtured in the faith throughout one's life. One might or might not have a conversion experience, but that was never determinative of becoming or remaining Christian. The legitimacy of ministry was in no sense determined by the fact of whether or not the priest or minister had had a personal conversion experience. But revivalism was present in almost all religious communities in America, and it totally dominated the Methodist, Baptist, Disciples of Christ, Pentecostal, Holiness, and black denominations. It made considerable inroads into Presbyterianism, Congregationalism, and some progress even within Lutheranism. It provided the "great names" for

Protestantism, such as Jonathan Edwards, George Whitefield, Lyman Beecher, Charles Finney, Dwight Moody, all the way up to a contemporary such as Billy Graham.

Millenarianism, a particular form of Christian eschatology, is grounded especially in the books of Daniel and Revelation. It is one of the oldest and most pervasive traditions in Christian history, and it stretches from Montanists to present-day dispensationalists.[5] Though there was never a time that it was not present in Christian history, there were certain periods when it dominated the Christian ethos. Only in the past twenty years have historians taken seriously the millenarian tradition and recognized its appeal not just for the dispossessed or emotionally unbalanced, but also for vast numbers of Christians from all walks of life, including the most educated and intelligent as well as the unlettered and ignorant. From the mid-seventeenth through the early eighteenth century in Britain and the United States it grasped the imagination and the commitment of such outstanding figures as John Milton, Richard Baxter, Isaac Newton, John Cotton, and Jonathan Edwards.[6] Few movements could claim such distinguished devotees.

Though millenarians differed profoundly in their interpretation of prophecies and in their view of the nature and time of Christ's appearance, they were united in two fundamental beliefs. All of them believed that the prophecies in Scripture, particularly those in Daniel and the book of Revelation, were directly applicable to history—past, present, and/or future. They might disagree in exactly *how* these prophecies were to be interpreted and brought to bear, but all were engaged equally in an effort to decipher and understand them. Also, they were agreed on the reality of a thousand years' reign of Christ and its imminent inception. They argued over whether Christ would appear prior to the millennium or after the conclusion of the millennium, but all agreed that there would be a millennium and that it marked the last stage of history prior to the creation of a new heaven and a new earth and a final judgment.

At what point a clear distinction is made between premillennialists (those who believed that Christ would come in judgment and inaugurate the final thousand years' reign) and the postmillennialists (those who believed history had already entered the millennium and was slowly moving toward the ultimate triumph of Christianity which would culminate in the ultimate appearance of the Christ at the end of that period) is still open to considerable discussion.[7] Likewise, the variety of possible interpretations of millennialism elicits continuing research.[8] Though none of these differ-

149

ences are to be ignored or taken lightly, they are not of central importance for this particular paper.

As one surveys the prevalence of both revivalism and millennialism in the American scene, one is struck by the fact that they appear almost coterminous. So closely have they been intertwined that it is probably impossible to unravel them in order to determine which might have caused which. Jonathan Edwards stood in a long English and New England Puritan tradition when he started to speculate about the millennium a good decade prior to the outbreak of the revival in his Northhampton parish.[9] But it was neither his preaching on the millennium nor his views of the millennium that triggered the outburst of conversions in his parish. Rather, when Edwards came to interpret the significance and the meaning of the revivals, millennialism provided him with the framework in terms of which he could understand the history of redemption both personal and cosmic. From Edwards to Graham and even to Jerry Falwell, revivalism and the vast majority of revivalists have been millenarians. Why?

Historically, the millenarian tradition precedes the occurrence of revivalism as an ongoing movement in Christian history, but that does not mean that millenarianism caused or created revivalism. When revivalism first appeared on the American scene, it did not have to turn to millenarianism to make sense of itself or to appeal to the population, but revivalism did so in the beginning. The nature and the structure of each are almost identical, or at least sufficiently similar so that it is all but inevitable that they go together. The dynamic of each as a form of religious experience is such that one almost demands the other so that the two together provide a full-orbed religious experience that embraces the individual and the entire cosmos. Together revivalism and millenarianism provide religious orientation both for the self as individual self and for the self in relation to the entire cosmos and its history.

A careful analysis of the dynamics of individual conversion in revivalism demonstrates an exact parallel with the dynamics of judgment and salvation of the cosmos as envisioned by millennialism. Revivalism's first stage in conversion involves judgment—both the judgment of God on the self and subsequent self-judgment in light of that.[10] In earlier revivalism this was usually a prolonged struggle with peaks and valleys, tension and resolution, a struggle between the forces of good and the forces of evil at work in the soul of the sinner. This was no gradual growth in grace or a maturing of the Christian faith. It was a struggle to the death in which the forces of the devil were pitted against the forces of God. The object was to make known to the individual the extent, depth, and pervasiveness of one's sin.

The potential convert had to be brought to a knowledge of the utter enormity of the power and the hold of the devil and his minions of evil. An individual was called upon to look at every facet of one's life and, finally, even at the very core of life itself. Step by step, one had to unravel the mystery of sin as it was encountered in countless particular sins and finally in the very root of sin itself which pervaded the heart of every human being. Such a perception did not come easily. Human beings fought it every step of the way. The primary purpose of preaching, Bible readings, prayer, and consultation was to convict the individual concerning the power and the enormity of that sin. Its purpose was clear—to make precise and particular the judgment of God against oneself.

The purpose of the conflict was to lead one to utter despair at the sense of one's total inability to cope with the problem. All the individual's pride, assurance, and ability had to die. The object of the struggle and conflict was to bring one to the point of death of the self, the death of the old Adam. Death of the old self was not merely a metaphor; it was to be an existential experience. In extreme forms revivalism was marked by people who groaned, wept, shook, cried out, or even fell unconscious on the ground as they died to the old self.[11] Without death to sin and self, there could be no new life. Nobody could measure the length of time the conflict would endure. For most, it was a matter of days or even months, but for some it was a matter of years and for others a matter of hours. In all cases nobody knew in advance how long the struggle would endure, though all knew it was inevitable and that it would end only in the death and judgment of the old self.

Judgmental death of the old self was followed by resurrection and the triumph of the spirit. The self was now dead to the old Adam and raised anew in Christ. One was reborn, converted from death to life. Old things were passed away and all things became new; one was a new creature in Christ living a new life. For the revivalist this was a peak experience that occurred at a specified time and in a particular place. The life, sufferings, death, and resurrection of Jesus the Christ were brought to bear personally and existentially in the life of the converted one. One no longer lived in oneself; one now lived in Christ. This was the center of the dynamic of the conversion experience. Everything led up to that point, and everything flowed out of that point. This was the judgment and the resurrection. Previously, one was confused, lost, damned, at enmity with oneself and with one's neighbors. Now one was reconciled to God and thus reconciled to self and to neigh-

151

bors. One was born again, with a fresh life to be lived in obedience and in gratitude.

The believer now entered a third stage in the dynamic of conversion, the stage of the new life in Christ, a life which exhibited either a steady growth in grace or even a life of perfection as a result of the indwelling Spirit. Either one was moving step by step toward a greater fulfillment of the will and law of God, or one had already achieved a state of holiness that was virtually if not actually perfection.[12] In one case, the moral life was closer to what one might call the afflictive model. That is, one lived the new life of a converted believer, and the difference was as great as that of black and white, but the struggle still went on. One was beset with temptations; occasionally one fell; but the grace of God prevailed so that even the bad and the evil could have good emerge out of it, for all things ultimately worked for good to those who loved God. Life remained a pilgrimage and a struggle, but its end was clearly marked for the true believer. In the other case, the moral life was already a totally different life of triumph piled upon triumph as one lived in ever higher stages of perfection. One lived in the Spirit and so in true holiness, obeying the will and the law of God with a relative ease unknown before one's conversion. In all cases, a converted life meant a new life of obedience and joy in fulfilling the will and law of God. This was the dynamic of the conversion experience.

One does not have to look closely to note an exact parallel with the dynamics of the millenarian religious experience.[13] The scenario for an individual's conversion in revivalism is identical with that of the scenario for cosmic salvation in millennialism. Millennialism is but the individual's conversion writ large. Perhaps it could be turned around and argued that millennialism's scenario of salvation is the macrocosm of which revivalism's picture of conversion is the microcosm. It is not necessary to argue which is prevenient because such cannot be demonstrated. The point is that the dynamics of salvation are parallel, if not identical, and that is the basic reason why revivalism and millenarianism go hand in hand through history once revivalism has appeared on the scene.

At the center of millennialism is belief in the rebirth of the cosmos, carried out purely through divine agency just as is the salvation of the individual in revivalism. The first stage is identical. There is a prolonged conflict in which the forces of good fight the forces of evil. It is an ongoing battle in which there are ups and downs, peaks and valleys, an unrelenting struggle as judgment is brought to bear on the entire process of history and even on the cosmos itself—the whole of nature groans in travail waiting for the redemption of the sons of man. The unrelenting pressure of judgment as the forces of good and evil struggle is brought to a point of culmination in which there is a final great battle in which the Divine Will ultimately triumphs. This leads to the total annihilation, death, and destruction of the devil and the forces of evil.

Just as the individual soul is reborn in revivalism, so in millennialism old history is ended and there is a totally new beginning— a new heaven and a new earth. For both pre- and postmillennialists, the new heaven and the new earth do not appear until after the fulfillment of the millennium and the utter triumph of Jesus as the Christ. So it is in revivalism that the converted, whether living in the millennium or awaiting the beginning of the millennium, whether struggling through the growth of grace or participating in degrees of perfection, await their death or their rapture so that they will finally and ultimately be fully translated or reborn as totally new creatures in Christ.

In both cases, the initiative is from God, and in both cases judgment is brought to bear through the process of struggle which culminates in divine victory and the reconstitution of life, both personal and cosmic. In revivalism and in millennialism there can be no salvation without personally experienced conversion; and however long the process, it ends in a cataclysm which destroys the past and recreates all that is for a new future. The experience is particular and it is decisive. Salvation is not something vague, general, or gradual. It is a process, but it is not a rational process whose stages are measured and reasonable. In fact, there is no reason why things ought to be the way they will be, and there is profound mystery as to how they will get that way. Even where divine hints are supposedly given in prophecy, it works better in hindsight and is never certain as to the future. The only thing certain is the ultimate outcome, and only the reborn can sense that possibility. Why some should be saved and some damned can never be explained, even by those of an Arminian bent; so one can never finally explain why history and cosmos will be summed up the way divine wisdom prophesies. Only the saved know in part, and they, too, see only dimly. As it is with personal salvation, so it is with cosmic salvation.

Both revivalists and millenarians use a similar Scripture hermeneutic. Each tends to view all of Scripture from a very specific focus or center. For revivalism the centrality and absolute necessity of conversion becomes a basic principle in terms of which all of Scripture, both Old Testament and New Testament, is interpreted. On the surface it appears as if Christology is the fundamental principle through which all Scripture is to be understood. A closer scrutiny reveals that it is Christological in a very special sense. Everything

153

points toward the function and the role of Jesus as the Christ in converting individual sinners and bringing them to salvation. The problem is not the Son in relation to the Trinity, nor the relation of Christ to the founding of his church, nor the foundation of morality and ethics in the divine reality. Soteriology, and that measured by personal conversion, is the ground of a hermeneutic for all Scripture.

Similarly, in millenarianism there is a single principle that tends to dominate all interpretations of Scripture. In this case it is the millennium and the salvation of history and the cosmos. Extraordinary effort is given to unraveling the mystery of prophecies in Daniel, Isaiah, and the book of Revelation. In dispensationalism, as in earlier forms of millenarianism, the whole of history and Scripture is divided into special dispensations, all of which prepare for and point toward the millennium.[14] There is no question of *sola scriptura*, but there *is* a question of where the weight of authority falls. Where inordinate attention is given to one aspect of revelation, as it is in millenarianism, other dimensions of Scripture and of the Christian faith are diminished. In this sense both revivalism and millenarianism represent particular kinds of reductionism in relation to Scripture, to the Christian faith, and to history. It is this pressure toward a reductionism that drives millenarianism and revivalism into the same camp. The fact that one centers on personal conversion and the other on personal conversion writ large helps to explain why the two always appear together.

It would be interesting and instructive to do an analysis of the way Scripture is employed by both movements. Suffice it to say at this point that both make extensive use of crisis texts. One of the favorite texts of almost all revivalists who are also millenarians is the parable of the wise and the foolish virgins. Countless revivalistic sermons have been delivered based on that text because the imminence of the last judgment provides an extraordinary pressure in the effort to convert.[15] For both revivalism and millenarianism the battle cry remains, "Now is the time!" People were interested in millenarianism because they believed they were living at a moment in history which was an immediate prelude to the end or on the very edge of the end itself. Revivalists had to bring individuals to believe that they were at the very end of their lives and that this may be their last possible opportunity to be saved. The sense of impending doom and the possibility of a glorious and totally new future pervades both movements. Thus, both employ Scripture in an almost identical way.

Two additional similarities with regard to Scripture are evident. Both movements require a high degree of biblical literalism, if not inerrancy. Just as they can brook no ambiguity nor tolerate a dialectic in soteriology or ethics, so they cannot permit any deviation from a very rigid view of scriptural authority. Before the era of biblical criticism and the impact of Darwin, there was no problem. All Christians looked upon Scripture from within the same framework, though they might have disagreed as to the method of interpretation.

Biblical criticism posed a major threat both to revivalism and to millenarianism. Text and higher criticism undercut the basic assumption of millenarianism that Scripture was the Word of God concerning both individual and cosmic salvation. In Scripture God provided a series of prophecies that were actually and literally true, and a believer had the responsibility to decipher those prophecies and apply them to history—past, present, and future. To accept the possibility of biblical criticism or evaluation was to destroy the entire millenarian enterprise.

Revivalism had the same problem in a somewhat different way. Conversion brooks no uncertainty. The problem of the nature of biblical authority did not become acute for the general American public until the 1880s. It cut through the ranks of evangelical revivalists and divided them asunder into nascent liberals and conservative revivalists headed by Dwight L. Moody.[16] From Moody to Billy Graham's chant "The Bible says . . .," revivalism has required an infallible Bible for absolute conviction.

A further point of identity and mutual support for millenarianism and revivalism is to be found in their preference for the same symbols in Scripture. Though, to my knowledge, no serious study has been made of this preference, it provides interesting possibilities for exploration. On the surface it appears that both movements gave undue emphasis to those biblical symbols that embodied radical decision, cataclysmic judgment, the actual content of heaven and hell, and the figure of Jesus.

Another emphasis shared by revivalism and millenarianism is a radical distinction between nature and grace. In revivalism, there can be no salvation except through a radical divine intervention. One does not grow toward salvation nor does one improve the quality and the level of one's life until one reaches the point where one is capable of salvation. Even for Wesley and subsequent Arminian revivalists, God alone saves. The human will can make an effort to respond to God's offer of salvation, but even that would not be possible unless God had first wrought and offered, through Christ, salvation to humanity. Grace is not the culmination of nature but is purely from divine love and activity. Revivalism and millenarianism always press for the radical distinction between God and

155

humanity, between evil and righteousness, and between salvation and damnation.

Nowhere is this seen more clearly than in the ethics, both public and private, which develop in revivalism. For the converted believer, there is only right or wrong and there is nothing in between. There is no such thing as a situational ethic or the possibility that one might have to do evil in order to accomplish good. Either one is for God or one is against God. One converted to the Lord Jesus Christ has turned one's back on evil, and now seeks only to do the will of the Lord. If one slips, and it is possible, one will soon be brought up short, repent, and seek again to do only the good. Nobody can do good except those who are converted to Jesus Christ. All others are lost in sin and stumble in unrighteousness, though they may from time to time do something that appears good.

There is no question of what is right for the converted. They are prepared to tell each other and the entire world exactly what the right is at each point. Whether the world is told this by Gilbert Tennent in the eighteenth century, by Charles Finney in the nineteenth century, by Dwight Moody in the late nineteenth century, or by Jerry Falwell today—all are acting out of the same conviction. The world is divided into the saved and the damned, and there is nothing in between. There is the kingdom of grace, and there is the kingdom of nature, and they have nothing to do with each other except to have enmity and opposition between them.

Millenarianism operates in an identical spirit. Whether the world is moving inexorably toward the triumph of the Gospel and the dawn of the millennium, or whether the world is lost in evil as the saints struggle to prepare for the coming of the millennium, there is a radical distinction between the good and the evil, between grace and nature. Though the evil may triumph temporarily, it is clearly distinguished from the good. Just as God has no difficulty telling his saints apart from sinners, so do those committed to a belief in the millennium have no difficulty in sorting out the true believers from the false. Millenarianism also makes radical distinction between nature and grace. With the coming of Christ, a radical break is made in human history and in the entire universe. From his coming to his coming again in glory to judge the world, there are only two forces at work. One includes those saints who have already been saved by the Lord and have the task of calling others to be saved, and the remainder are those under the power of the devil and slaves of evil.

The task of the faithful is to interpret Scripture so that they can discern the signs of the time, mark evil for what it is, and play their role in the coming of the millennium. They are empowered to do this by the Holy Spirit, and so they can make exact judgments as to the will of God. They can pronounce doom and they can point to the embodiment of evil. Thus they are enabled, if needs be, to suffer and even to die, knowing that they are part of the divine process. They live now in the realm of grace and not in the realm of nature. They bear a special burden, but they are recipients of special gifts. Theirs is the high and holy calling to decipher the prophecies, to proclaim the coming of the Lord Jesus Christ, and to save as many human souls as is possible in these last days. Little wonder that revivalists are millenarians and millenarians are revivalists!

Both are possessed by the conviction that they reach out in behalf of Christ and save others before it is too late. Already the night is far spent, and they have been given a rare opportunity to participate in bringing in the kingdom of God or to witness its imminent revival. The dynamics of the personal salvation are recapitulated in the revealed plan of the world's salvation. There is no discrepancy between the way an individual is saved and the way history is summarized, condemned, and ultimately saved. Scripture, their source of authority, is read from a single, clear center which sweeps aside ambiguity and elevates rebirth to the point of preeminence in revelation.

This is true both for the individual and for the cosmos. Whether this sets one free to recreate the cosmos and help destroy the forces of evil before that blessed day, or whether this impels one to bear the sufferings and torments of a disintegrating world prior to the final conflagration, the motivation and the faith are the same. God rules, it is God's universe, and the saints can rest assured as to their place in the cosmos, both now and forever after. It is this vision of both the individual and the cosmos that marks revivalism and millenarianism. Little wonder that since the advent of revivalism the vast majority of revivalists have been millenarians and that millenarians have been revivalists!

157

NOTES

[1] There is a massive bibliography on revivalism in America and England. The best works remain those of William G. McLoughlin, Jr., *Modern Revivalism: Charles G. Finney to Billy Graham* (New York: The Ronald Press Company, 1959), and *Revivals, Awakenings, and Reforms* (Chicago: University of Chicago Press, 1978). An excellent analysis of revivalism in relation to millenarianism and fundamentalism is in George M. Marsden, *Fundamentals and American Culture*

(New York: Oxford University Press, 1980). Of special help on revivalism in England and America is the recent study by Richard Carwardine, *Transatlantic Revivalism* (Westport, Conn.: Greenwood Press, 1978). In spite of the flood of books, monographs, and articles on revivalism, it is surprising how few, if any, have attempted a serious study of the nature of revivalism as a religious phenomenon.

[2]Lewis R. Rambo, "Psychological Perspectives on Conversion," *Pacific Theological Review*, vol. 13 (Spring, 1980), pp. 21-26; Jerald C. Brauer, "Conversion: From Puritanism to Revivalism, "*The Journal of Religion*, vol. 58, no. 3 (July, 1978), pp. 227-243.

[3]D. Dickson Bruce, *And They All Sang Hallelujah* (Knoxville: University of Tennessee Press, 1974); Sandra J. Sizer, *Gospel Hymns and Social Religion: The Rhetoric of Nineteenth Century Revivalism* (Philadelphia: Temple University Press, 1978).

[4]Jay P. Dolan, in his *Catholic Revivalism: The American Experience, 1830-1900* (Notre Dame: University of Notre Dame Press, 1978), argues that the Roman Catholic parish "mission" movement in America reflects aspects of revivalism in America.

[5]See Marjorie Reeves, *The Influence of Prophecy in the Later Middle Ages: A Study in Joachimism* (Oxford: Clarendon Press, 1969).

[6]See especially Bryan W. Ball, *A Great Expectation: Eschatological Thought in English Protestantism to 1660* (Leiden: E. J. Brill, 1975), pp. 1-15; and William M. Lamont, *Richard Baxter and the Millennium* (London: Croom Helm, 1979), pp. 9-26.

[7]Marsden, *Fundamentals*, pp. 48-55.

[8]Hillel Schwartz, in "The End of the Beginning: Millenarian Studies, 1961-1975," *Religious Studies Review*, vol. 2, no. 3 (July, 1976), pp. 1-15, offers an excellent critical analysis of recent millenarian studies with a helpful bibliography. Some of the major issues in millenarianism as addressed by recent scholarship are admirably surveyed by Leonard I. Sweet in "Millennialism in America: Recent Studies," *Theological Studies*, vol. 40, no. 3 (September, 1979), pp. 510-531. Not to be overlooked is a brief but penetrating chapter on historiography in Clarke Garrett, *Respectable Folly: Millenarians and the French Revolution in France and England* (Baltimore: The Johns Hopkins University Press, 1957), pp. 1-15.

[9]Stephen J. Stein, ed., *The Works of Jonathan Edwards, Apocalyptic Writings* (New Haven: Yale University Press, 1977), vol. 5.

[10]Cf. J. C. Brauer, "Conversion," pp. 233-236.

[11]Catherine C. Cleveland, *The Great Revival in the West* (Chicago: University of Chicago Press, 1916).

[12]Donald Dayton, *The American Holiness Movement: A Bibliographic Introduction* (Wilmore, Ky.: B. L. Fisher Library, Asbury Theological Seminary, 1971); Timothy S. Smith, *Called unto Holiness* (Kansas City, Mo.: Nazarene Publishing House, 1962), pp. 11-26.

158   [13]"Is not salvation, regeneration, an instantaneous work of God's grace, a crisis in the life of an individual? Now, if regeneration in the individual is a sudden work, wrought by power divine, what will it be in the earth?" from L. L. Pickett, *The Blessed Hope of His Glorious Appearing* (Louisville, Ky.: Pickett Publishing House, 1901), p. 267. I am indebted for this quotation to Phyllis Airhart from an unpublished University of Chicago seminar paper, "Millenarianism in the Holiness Movement" (Spring, 1981), p. 25. In it she also establishes that a number of holiness revivalists were not millenarian in any respect, but they were fought bitterly by many of their premillenarian colleagues. In a splendid study, *The Logic of Millennial Thought: Eighteenth-Century New England*

(New Haven, Conn.: Yale University Press, 1977), p. 129, James West Davidson points out, "The pattern behind the grand history of the Revelation, when examined more closely, was in fact the same pattern which shaped the new birth of every believer."

[14]C. Norman Kraus, *Dispensationalism in America: Its Rise and Development* (Richmond, Va.: The John Knox Press, 1958). Especially helpful on many issues touched upon in this paper is Ernest Sandeen, *The Roots of Fundamentalism, British and American Millenarianism, 1800–1900* (Chicago: University of Chicago Press, 1970).

[15]Countless sermons were preached by revivalists on the wise and foolish virgins in an effort to link conversion with the coming in glory of the Christ. George Whitefield was typical when he cried, "So now the decree is gone forth, and the trump of God has given its last sound; all tongues, people, nations, and languages, both wise and foolish virgins, must come into his presence, and bow beneath his footstool; even Pontius Pilate, Annas, and Caiphas; even the proud persecuting high priests and Pharisees of this generation, must appear before him: for says our Lord, 'then,' (when a cry was made, Behold, the bridegroom cometh!) in a moment, in the twinkling of an eye, the graves were opened, the sea gave up its dead, and 'all those virgins, both wise and foolish, arose and trimmed their lamps,' or endeavored to put themselves in a proper posture to meet the bridegroom." See *Seventy-Five Sermons on Various Important Subjects* (London: W. Baynes, 1812), p. 372.

[16]James F. Findlay, Jr., *Dwight L. Moody: American Evangelist, 1837–1899* (Chicago: University of Chicago Press, 1969), pp. 259-260.

The Great Tradition and
"The Coercion of Voluntarism"

Edwin S. Gaustad

Since so much of American religion has been proclaimed by way of the text, it is appropriate here to employ one. And since this volume honors Winthrop Still Hudson, it is even more appropriate that the text come from him. In his 1953 monograph, *The Great Tradition of the American Churches,* Hudson wrote: "It is only when the coercion of voluntarism is translated into a compulsion to fulfill a distinctive and specific vocation in society that the churches are enabled to kindle the urgent enthusiasm and wholehearted commitment which constitute the bedrock of vigorous institutional life."[1] The "coercion of voluntarism," like Saint Augustine's "Love God, and do as you please," is wonderfully paradoxical. For it does not readily appear that what is coercive can also be voluntary, any more than it is immediately obvious just how self-pleasing can be yoked with God-loving. This apparent contradiction in terms deserves closer examination.

As with all paradoxes—intrinsically uncomfortable—they can be resolved or domesticated by altering the balance between the poles or by simply ignoring one of the poles. Augustine's dictum, by a reverse alchemy, changes gold to dross as it now simply reads: "Do as you please." And Hudson's "great tradition" is reduced to mere "voluntarism" without any taint of coercion or compulsion, duty or discipline, being retained. Religion in the United States may still find it romantic to speak of its "errand into the wilderness," but more often than not the errand runner carries no urgent message, or he has forgotten by whom he was sent, or for what specific purpose he runs. Hudson's paradox has been tamed. Perhaps it is worth returning to the original uncomfortable tension—"coercive voluntarism"—to inquire into its persisting force some three decades after that text was first set down. And, as befits a text, it shall have both explication and application through the discussion which follows in this essay.

161

I. "Compulsion to Fulfill a Distinctive and Specific Vocation"

The earlier use of the word "coercion" was clearly no accident, for here again voluntarism carries with it a severe modifier: compulsion. The paradox remains, if not an intolerable contradiction in terms. Is voluntarism that is compelled no voluntarism at all, but a delusion and a playing with words? Or is it a voluntarism that has content, direction, and meaning? Is it a voluntarism that responds to a call, discharges an obligation, and truly runs an errand? Once one sees the power of the paradox, it is difficult to settle for a shorthand of mere voluntarism subject to one's whim.

In the United States the balance between church and state has shifted so sharply in favor of the latter as to make voluntarism seem much less compelled or even possible. The state has grown even larger and more provident, the church ever narrower and less relevant. Churches look around them to see need after need met by an all-encompassing government; or, if not by government, then by science or education or credit cards or hot tubs. Religious voluntarism has some difficulty in locating its "compulsion to fulfill a distinctive and specific vocation."

Despite this gigantification of government along with the expansion of other agencies and institutions to meet—or create—human needs, it would nonetheless be difficult to argue that the churches' distinctive vocation has been supplanted or canceled. A society without direction or center, a population without purpose or self-esteem, calls out from desperate need and unnerved despair. In a recent novel one character plaintively inquires: "Liberated means you don't feel anything?"[2] And so it has appeared to much of a generation grown insensitive through sensitivity sessions, grown melancholy in the pursuit of pleasure. Hedonism is no fun. To a bewildered and empty people, to lives devoid of meaning, the churches' vocation remains as distinctive and specific as ever. To add some notion of compulsion to the incomplete concept of voluntarism results not so much in heavier burden as in clarified direction.

Sidney Mead located the notion of "denomination" somewhere between the all-inclusive "church" on the one hand and the escapist, withdrawn "sect" on the other. The denomination in America in its disestablished mode could not, like the national churches, assume responsibility for all of society; nor did it, confronted with the challenges of a new land and a new nation, flee from all of society. Rather, the major church groups accepted a kind of limited liability.[3] In the nineteenth century, however, the limits permitted much: the building of schools, hospitals, orphanages, along with

162

the launching of public crusades and the proclaiming of social reforms. In the twentieth century the nature of the liability and the extent of the limits have shifted but in differing ways.

Moral Majorities and Christian Voices see their liability as requiring a call for national repentance, for a turning toward God and away from "wicked ways" (2 Chronicles 7:14). Only then will the nation be healed and set back on its true course. A Deuteronomic view of history prevails—the populace has gone off after other gods, God has let loose plagues and calamities upon the land, men and women must repent, God will then bless. That the nation has many ills few persons in the 1980s would doubt. But many fear from the new religious right a cavalier disdain of First Amendment guarantees and even Article Six assurances concerning the illegality of religious tests. The American past is idealized into a Christian hegemony that never was; the American future is envisioned in terms of a Christian establishment that cannot constitutionally be.

The religious left, on the other hand, no longer calling the tune and no longer bolstered by abundant coffers and crowded pews, retreats from the larger and costlier commitments. "Liability" is understood more in terms of mortgages and utility bills, less with respect to schools, crusades, and public concerns. Keeping the ecclesiastical ship afloat is the issue; taking it out of the harbor into deeper waters is not. So "limited liability" is in danger of becoming no liability at all, as the jealously guarded right of free exercise gets exercised less and less.

In the great religious middle, churches continue to do what for generations they have done, often sustained more by inertia and tradition than by compelling call and energizing vision. The notion that they are history's allies in the great cosmic drama fades from view as they see other and more powerful forces determining the shape of the community, the economic and psychological health of their congregations, the very rhythms of life. Of course, good work is done, but sustenance and the discipline of the long-range and steady compulsion are often absent.

Voluntarism without vocation—is this not an anomaly, a nullity, and possibly even a calamity? It was Hudson's anxiety a generation ago; it is a pervading anxiety now. Part of the difficulty lies in an increased temptation to see religion as something which must be carefully watched, guarded, and kept under control. Religion at a certain temperature is socially acceptable, but raised a few degrees it strikes many as fearful, if not antidemocratic. Constitutional expert Mark DeWolfe Howe observed that the courts "have been compelled by the very structure of the First Amendment's prohibitions to acknowledge that it sought to do something more than

163

secure the people from ecclesiastical depredations." The free exercise guarantee demonstrates that the policy of separation was never intended "to frustrate or inhibit the religious experience." Of the Supreme Court itself Howe remarks that it has failed to take adequately into account "that the rule of separation was no less a postulate of faith than it was an axiom of doubt."[4] It is always possible, of course, that the courts have been deficient in their perception because the churches have been dilatory in their vocation.

When Lyman Beecher was fighting so valiantly against the disestablishment of Congregationalism in Connecticut, he recited his "Toleration Dream" in which he foresaw all the unhappy results which toleration would bring: licentiousness and indifference, social chaos and ecclesiastical impotence.[5] Beecher later gladly confessed that he had been quite wrong. From the perspective of a century and a half later, it may be that he confessed too soon. For Hudson is also haunted by that dream or nightmare in which "the churches remain content to say only what everyone [else] is saying and exhibit in the quality of their corporate life nothing that serves to distinguish their members from the generality of the community."[6] Freely exercising religion has become a matter of selling to the highest bidder or playing games with the tax collector or disguising a club as a church.

II. "Urgent Enthusiasm"

First, the specific vocation; then, and only then, the urgent enthusiasm. Religion in America's history has manifested too often a reversal of those priorities, becoming like Churchill's fanatic: one who redoubles his effort having lost sight of his goal. But enthusiasm is not easy to maintain, sometimes not even easy to justify. The world has become too complex, problems too unyielding, flesh—and budgets—too weak. And it is not surprising that an ever-receding kingdom of God in America results in failure of nerve. As Norman Maring has pointed out, Hudson's writing of *The Great Tradition* "brought painful inner struggle" for it "embodied a critique of the theological liberalism in which he had been reared. . . ."[7] The pain came first in recognizing, then in accepting, the obligation to declare that "the critical spirit . . . could be embraced not for the sake of releasing the rigorous demands of prophetic religion, but simply because the conventional demands of orthodoxy were irksome and resented."[8] Compulsion of any sort was avoided, enthusiasm to any degree was denied. And the religious fires were so thoroughly banked that sometimes the flame went out. This did not trouble the "cultured and the comfortable," but the "humble and the distressed" did suffer or often turned elsewhere for warmth.

164

"Enthusiasm" was a terrifying word to colonial Americans, calling forth the spectre of private revelation, of cool disdain for Scripture, clergy, and formal church. In the nineteenth century the word no longer meant private voices but a kind of public vision—a hearty voluntarism that accepted all challenges and discharged all responsibilities with vigor and effect. When Robert Baird wrote of the voluntary principle in 1856, it was impossible for him to do so without implying the necessity for a deep draft of enthusiasm in his very description of its characteristics.

The very activity, energy, and self-reliance [that voluntarism] calls forth are great blessings to the individual who exercises these qualities, as well as to those for whose sake they are put forth, and to the community at large. Men are so constituted as to derive happiness from the cultivation of an independent, energetic, and benevolent spirit, in being co-workers with God in promoting His glory, and the true welfare of their fellow-men.[9]

With energy and activity as the ingredients of enthusiasm, both the word and the deed won respectability in an enlarging, muscle-flexing America. Congregational voices urged their souls to awake, "stretch every nerve,/And press with vigor on!/A heavenly race demands thy zeal. . . ." Throughout much of the nineteenth century it seemed no hyperbole to argue that churches no less than people "are so constituted as to derive happiness from the cultivation of an independent, energetic, and benevolent spirit. . . ." For much main-line religion a century later, attaining happiness was seen as a more passive, less ebullient enterprise. Sometimes one saw urgency, but it was the urgency associated with survival more than with conquest.

All of this may be looking through the wrong end of the telescope: seeing the twentieth century as dilution of the nineteenth century's heroism and seeing that, in turn, a crumbling of stern colonial resolve. In analyzing Winthrop Hudson's place in religious historiography in America, Eldon Ernst observes that the notion of *"origins* dominates the story" of religion in the United States. We may be looking for the national "soul" in the wrong place, worrying about "what was being lost" and not concerning ourselves sufficiently with "what was emerging."[10] It is manifest that the new religions possess urgent and even explosive enthusiasms; indeed, without broad cultural support or sympathy, they survive only by virtue of intense and exuberant activity. It can be argued, therefore, that it is not in the Great Tradition of the American past that one will find the positive qualities that Hudson identifies; but on the fringes, in the subcultures, as an aspect of what Peter Williams calls the Little Tradition[11] will one find these qualities.

165

At the moment, however, much in the novel enthusiasms appears to be insular, limited, and peripheral. The new religions attract a disproportionate share of attention in the media, but that coverage bears little resemblance to the numbers directly involved or the influence widely felt. Many modern enthusiasts are tribalists, to use Martin Marty's word, exhibiting exclusivism and belligerence and talking "in a language they alone can understand because it takes rise from thought that cannot belong to any other group than theirs." Modern society can ill afford this further insularity and condescension toward the rest of the world. What is required, rather, is for "Christians not only to interact among themselves but also to build on common appeals to reason and humaneness for the ordering of the human city."[12] Marty makes a helpful distinction between "saving faith" and "ordering faith," the former being particular, ingrown, and private while the latter looks toward the universal, communal, and public. In *The Public Church* Marty would urge that equal time be given to the ordering faith, to the Great Tradition that refuses to turn from all liability to the culture that nourishes and protects—and occasionally cries for help. Both "saving faith" and "ordering faith" have roles to play.

One widespread expression of enthusiasm in the modern world, the charismatic movement, has rushed across denominational boundaries with astonishing disdain. Breathing new life into impersonal bureaucracies and passive assemblies, pentecostalism has been, if nothing else, notable for its enthusiasm. But it has not been notable for its ability to build a broad base for humane and rational discourse. Speaking in tongues does more for saving faith than for ordering faith; it does more to foster tribalism than to rise above it. Semantic problems are real problems precisely because the common ground on which we might stand, while conversing, sinks beneath us. To quote Marty once more:

> Theology, the interpretation of the life and language of a people, breaks down because there is no communion of people, there are only private strivers. To whom is the act of preaching to be directed, if the audience is made up of the people each of whom has already established a trajectory of life, and who present themselves in a congregation only so long as the message conveniently reaches an individual on that particular course?[13]

"Enthusiasm" can still be a frightening word, not because it suggests for us, as it did for those of an earlier time, that one is filled with the gods. The modern anxiety is that the enthusiast may be emptied of all civility and restraint, of all desire for discourse and persuasion, and may be filled only with a passion to castigate and divide. As Hudson reminded us, first the specific vocation, then the urgent enthusiasm.

III. "Wholehearted Commitment"

As several commentators on the current scene have noted, ours is an age of the halfhearted, the uncommitted, the hesitant, the "I'd rather not get involved." All is to be modulated carefully, tuned finely, tempered, compromised, and often shelved. If the temptation to commitment comes too close, one can resort to ridicule or scorn. The novelist John Gardner sees most modern literature as avoiding all commitment to anything except its own forms and structures. No longer does one ask or seek answers to the great humanistic questions; rather, artist, poet, and novelist content themselves with a concentration on technique and literary or artistic mode of expression.

Nothing could be more obvious, it seems to me, than that art should be moral and that the first business of criticism, at least some of the time, should be to judge works of literature (or painting or even music) on the grounds of the production's moral worth. [Any art is good] only when it has a clear positive moral effect, presenting valid models for imitation, eternal verities worth keeping in mind, and a benevolent vision of the possible which can inspire and incite human beings toward virtue, toward life affirmation as opposed to destruction or indifference.[14]

As a culture, Gardner adds, we allow ourselves to become fascinated with the superficial and the trivial because "we tend to feel we have nothing to say—or nothing to offer but well-intentioned propaganda—so we keep ourselves occupied with surfaces. . . . Texture is our refuge, the one thing we know we're good at."[15]

When one transfers that critique from the realm of the arts to that of religion, the aptness remains. There, too, the moral message is muted and trivia often triumph. The care of the physical plant, the elaborate planning for annual membership drives, the perpetuation and enlargement of full-time staff—these are the surfaces too readily mistaken for depths. A self-seeking, self-serving ecclesiasticism reaches into no profound depths of the human soul, inspires no bold stretch of the human spirit. ". . . America can do trivia exceedingly well."[16]

Christopher Lasch's much discussed *Culture of Narcissism*, addressing itself to similar themes, could almost have carried as its subtitle, "The Trivialization of America." For Lasch also saw a society determined to dodge hard truth and to escape anything which began to resemble Hudson's "wholehearted commitment." Once every inhibition is discarded and every impulse gratified, it is readily assumed that happiness flows in and peace of mind or soul prevails. Of course it is absurd, in the midst of such a societal climate, to talk of commitment—or of coercion, duty, discipline, urgency. For the narcissist the past offers no guidance and the future no challenge; one lives only for self and the moment, thereby debasing the self and robbing the moment of all meaning.[17]

If enthusiasm is currently out of fashion, commitment sounds permanently archaic. The sixteenth-century Reformation began in a quarrel about one sort of indulgence; a twenty-first-century Reformation may arise in reaction against another sort. In our own time no one worries about the purchase of forgiveness or plenary pardon—it is self-supplied. "Damn, I'm good," reads the bumper sticker. Fault, if such there be, does indeed lie in the stars or in the system or in the injustices of history—anywhere but within ourselves. Given such a world view, it makes little sense to reflect on the object of commitment when the very fact of commitment cannot be granted. Acculturated Protestantism—Hudson's provenance and his profound concern—saw itself as society's ally more than its critic, saw social forces moving inexorably toward a kingdom of God on earth, with only an occasional churchly nudge now and then required. And if the culture has become indulgent and uncommitted, those religious forces most closely tied to it are pulled into the same vortex of self-satisfaction and worldly ease.

The New Testament remains unambiguous about the fatal finality of that whirlpool—he that seeks to save his own soul shall lose it. That same authoritative source speaks in the imperative mood and unhesitant tone. Lukewarmness, along with equivocation and a noncommittal aloofness, receive no endorsement. Refusing even to look back, to say nothing of turning back, becomes the first law of discipleship. Churches of the Great Tradition falter not because they demand so much but because they demand so little. No rich young ruler is ever turned away.

IV. "Vigorous Institutional Life"

As the "text" introduced in the beginning makes clear, the fourth feature of coercive voluntarism is not so much an additional desideratum as it is the inevitable consequence of loyalty to the first three. Vocation followed by enthusiasm and commitment do, in fact, "constitute the bedrock of vigorous institutional life." When Hudson wrote these words a generation ago, he must have sounded like a peevish spoilsport. For America's institutional religion in the 1950s was pink-cheeked, confident, and strong. Membership was up, piety was in, building programs boomed. Anti-institutionalism was out of fashion, cults were quiescent, and cold-war politics identified the enemy without difficulty or ambiguity. Billy Graham revivalism flourished and Herbergian pluralism was good for America, better even than General Motors. Church mergers were both contemplated and consummated, as ecumenicity reached such a peak by the end of the fifties as to permit the presidency to be held by a Roman Catholic. This decade of goodwill (McCarthyism aside) collapsed into a decade of religious decline, a decade of assassinations with a theology that attempted to add God to the list of victims. Vatican II, the top religious story of the decade, added to the furies in an aftermath of controversy over liturgy, episcopacy, celibacy, and birth control. In 1962 and 1963, the Supreme Court, in its ruling on Bible reading and public school prayers, ignited fires of resentment still not extinguished two decades later. And that old-time, main-line religion which had seemed invincible only a few years before now grew querulous and unsure, now found itself confronted by stiff competition from unfamiliar, exotic, nonnormative religious quarters.

In the 1970s, a whole culture seemed to go awry, pulled belatedly from the political and moral abyss of Vietnam only to fall into the political and moral abyss of Watergate. Churches spoke in divided voice, if with any voice at all, as they found themselves thrown on the defensive for complicity with the culture, for exploitation of the black, for domination of the female, for WASPish superiority and contentment. Being born again was the media's message about certain evangelicals in the late 1970s, but being born again was what America's churches needed for themselves. Some sought such rebirth in the charismatic movement, some in the newly discovered power of television, some in an apocalytic mood that seemed to say that if the world wasn't coming to an end, it wasn't because it did not deserve to.

The 1980s opened on a note of realistic concern. Where had all the magic gone? Who now spoke for a religious America? Denominational leaders more accustomed to explaining how their churches grew now probed for the reasons for decline. A few found it timely to question the all-American fetish with statistics, with ecclesiastical GNP's, with membership rolls and cement mixers as the ultimate verification of a pastor's worth and a religion's truth. In our social scientific sophistication, 'let us take some notice of the "nonsociological work of the Holy Spirit," argued Peter Wagner. What God requires is "not growth but faithfulness," declared Robert Evans.[18] Meanwhile, those groups farther from the culture's center or even hostile to the culture found themselves less the objects of derision, less the unpopular or unacceptable alternative to "America's ways of being religious." The heavyweights of American religion were on the ropes, perhaps on the mat; now the lightweights could move freely about the ring, finding the crowd sometimes on their side.

Long before the numbers began to fall for the older denomina-

tions, Hudson called for a "thoroughgoing reconstruction of contemporary church life." His concern, however, was not with the
membership's quantity but with its quality. Historically in America,
qualitative reconstruction has come about through pervasive awakenings and revivals. In *The Great Tradition* Hudson pays much attention to revivalism's role: in Charles G. Finney, Dwight L. Moody,
and even Walter Rauschenbusch. Rauschenbusch saw the necessity
for something like revival's warmth and call to commitment necessary even in the midst of liberal Protestantism. While he acclaimed
the intellectual emancipation achieved through the newer historical
and biblical studies (men no longer need "believe with all their
hearts what they could not possibly understand with all their
heads"), Rauschenbusch recognized that "the rational subtractions
of liberalism do not necessarily make religion more religious."
Therefore, while the techniques of a Finney and a Moody had
become stylized, unthinking, and superficial (now concerned more
with quantity than quality), the classic message of sin, repentance,
and salvation was still in vogue. ". . . power in religion comes only
through the consciousness of a great elementary need which com-
pels men to lay hold of God anew."[19]

In a recent interpretive essay on revivalism in the life of America,
William McLoughlin also sees the continuing necessity for revivals.
For from these individual responses come awakenings—"periods
of cultural revitalization that begin in a general crisis of beliefs and
values and extend over a period of a generation or so, during which
time a profound reorientation in beliefs and values takes place."
McLoughlin sees the present generation as in the midst of just such
an awakening: a new beginning which is also a return to "a common
core of beliefs that has provided continuity and shape to American
culture. . . ." Those core beliefs include a sense of chosenness
respecting the "first new nation," a loyalty to the social ideal of a
free and morally responsible citizenry, and the conviction "that
freedom and responsibility will perfect not only the individual and
the nation but the world. . . ." Indeed, McLoughlin concludes,
American history is "best understood as a millenarian movement."[20]

By whatever means and however achieved, Hudson's "thoroughgoing reconstruction" appears the essential antidote to mere
nostalgia, to vestigial patterns of behavior, to lingering if ever-fading
loyalties. If not by becoming larger, then perhaps by choosing to
be smaller (genuinely communal and insistently voluntary), the
church can find a path to reconstruction. If not by revival, then
perhaps by restructure (a fellowship of believers and doers, a lev-
eling of laity and clergy, of male and female), the faithful church
can become a fruitful one. And if not by being concerned about the

170

nation's soul but only its own (not conforming to the world, but transforming it), the faithful and fruitful church can be the radically monotheistic church that H. Richard Niebuhr called for long ago.[21]

Once the nation's chief channel of compassion and charity, the churches have ceded that role to others. Why not make the local church the major collection agency from its own membership for Community Chest, personal rescue, and public weal? By giving *through* the local church (as well as *to* that institution), some vigor and authority are restored. Once the chief advocate for life's meaning and destiny, the churches find themselves competing against sex therapists, est seminars, and pop psychology. Why not regain the initiative in vocational and marriage counseling, in healing and restoring, in making life truly abundant? Once the chief arbiter between good and evil, between the heartless and the generous, the churches have found themselves bystanders in many of society's critical struggles. Why not, with resources fifty times greater than those of the National Rifle Association, again speak with a force that can be decisive in a culture's direction and a culture's quality?

When James Madison wrote in the Federalist Papers of the role of factions in a democracy, he saw a vitality and richness in the interaction and competition among groups that had a genuine interest, a ready involvement. The danger of the churchly faction is that it may retire too soon from the bruising fray. If Madison were to use the language of Hudson, he would today call for a "vigorous institutional life." Not laid back, not defeatist, not dug in behind stout theological or sociological walls, not mindless or heartless— but open, active, committed, enthusiastic, compelled. All this in the name of voluntarism, of course, but a voluntarism that is coercive. And that is exactly what the Sage of Rochester prescribed.

NOTES

[1]Winthrop S. Hudson, *The Great Tradition of the American Churches* (New York: Harper & Row, Publishers, Inc. 1953), p. 10.

[2]Leonard Michaels, *The Men's Club* (New York: Farrar, Strauss & Giroux, 1981), quoted in *The New York Times Book Review* (April 12, 1981), p. 28.

[3]Sidney E. Mead, *The Lively Experiment: The Shaping of Christianity in America* (New York: Harper & Row, Publishers, Inc., 1963), pp. 36-37.

[4]Mark DeWolfe Howe, *The Garden and the Wilderness: Religion and Government in American Constitutional History* (Chicago: University of Chicago Press, 1965), p. 10.

[5]Lyman Beecher, *Autobiography, Correspondence, Etc.* (New York: Harper & Row, Publishers Inc., 1864), ed. Charles Beecher, vol. 1, pp. 392-406.

[6]Hudson, *The Great Tradition*, p. 25.

[7]Norman H. Maring, "Winthrop S. Hudson: Church Historian," *Foundations*, vol. 23, no. 2 (April-June, 1980), p. 133.

[8]Hudson, *The Great Tradition*, p. 232.

[9]Robert Baird, *Religion in America*, rev. ed. (New York: Harper & Row, Publishers, Inc., 1856), pp. 366-367.

[10]Eldon G. Ernst, "Winthrop S. Hudson and the Great Tradition of American Religious Historiography," *Foundations*, vol. 23, no. 2 (April-June 1980), pp. 114-115.

[11]See Peter W. Williams, *Popular Religion in America: Symbolic Change and the Modernization Process in Historical Perspective* (Englewood Cliffs, N. J.: Prentice-Hall, Inc., 1980).

[12]Martin E. Marty, *The Public Church* (New York: The Crossroad Publishing Co., 1981), pp. 123, 129.

[13]*Ibid.*, p. 26.

[14]John Gardner, *On Moral Fiction* (New York: Basic Books, 1978), p. 18. © 1978 by John Gardner. By permission of Basic Books, Inc., Publishers, New York.

[15]*Ibid.*, pp. 60, 61.

[16]*Ibid.*, p. 56.

[17]Christopher Lasch, *The Culture of Narcissism* (New York: W. W. Norton & Co., Inc., 1978), pp. 13-14, 27.

[18]See the several sophisticated analyses in Dean R. Hoge and David A. Roozen, eds., *Understanding Church Growth and Decline: 1950–1978* (New York: The Pilgrim Press, 1979). Wagner's comment is on p. 276 and Evans's on p. 296.

[19]Hudson, *The Great Tradition*, pp. 231-233.

[20]William G. McLoughlin, *Revivals, Awakenings, and Reform* (Chicago: University of Chicago Press, 1978), pp. xiii-xiv.

[21]H. Richard Niebuhr, *Radical Monotheism and Western Culture* (New York: Harper & Row, Publishers, Inc., 1960).

Religious Freedom and Popular Sovereignty: A Change in the Flow of God's Power, 1730–1830

William G. McLoughlin

Efforts to explain the great transformation in the concept of religious freedom which took place in America between 1730 and 1830 are conflicting. Some historians hold that religion scarcely ranks as a cause of the Revolution because there is no significant correlation between the religious persuasions of those who became Tories and those who became Patriots.[1] Others hold that "civil millennialism," the concept of God's covenanted nation, the fear of an Anglican episcopate in the colonies, and the Quebec Act were major religious causes of the Revolution.[2] Some historians maintain that those who had imbibed Enlightenment rationalism (like Jefferson and Madison) were the principal architects of disestablishment;[3] others find that evangelical dissenters, especially the Baptists, were the driving force behind it.[4] Winthrop Hudson has traced religious freedom to "left-wing Puritanism."[5] Perry Miller claimed that an almost fortuitous combination of Enlightenment and evangelical ideas and interests held the key to the development of religious freedom in America.[6] The most popular interpretation, until recently, held that the simple fact of diversity among denominations forced a pragmatic solution—no one persuasion could dominate the nation; so all had to be equal.[7]

In the past decade a great deal of stress has been laid upon the first Great Awakening as the source of the religious ferment which climaxed in independence and disestablishment. This view, pressed initially by Alan Heimert, emphasizes the "enthusiasm" of the New Light movement, the rise of dissenting separatists, the postmillennial doctrine of neo-Edwardsians, the new sense of intercolonial identity, optimism, and activism fomented by religion as the dynamic factors behind the spread of democratic fervor and religious freedom. According to Heimert, the Arminians and rationalists were less enthusiastic rebels than the Pietists, and religious freedom owes comparatively little to them.[8] A modified version of this interpretation holds that "apocalyptic Whiggism" is a more likely source of revolutionary enthusiasm than the apolitical millennialism of Jonathan Edwards. In this view, as Nathan Hatch explains it, Americans first had to go through a process of identifying the development of religious and civil liberty with the development of the British constitution before they made the leap to their own defense of these ideals. It became possible for Americans to stand as the true defenders of freedom only after 1765 when Parliament and the king threatened *our* civil and religious liberty.[9]

In addition to this cornucopia of options regarding the origins of religious liberty, today's student has an almost equal variety of options as to the final culmination of the process. He can point to the adoption of various statements in the bills of rights of the first state constitutions, to the adoption of Jefferson's Bill for Establishing Religious Freedom in Virginia in 1785, to the First Amendment of the Constitution in 1791, to the final demise of Massachusetts's establishment in 1833, or to the trial of Abner Kneeland in 1838, the last man imprisoned in America for blasphemy. Even then he must cope with the claims of de Tocqueville and Lord Bryce that there emerged a "second establishment" soon after 1830 which wedded nationalism to Protestantism and denied effective equality to Mormons, Roman Catholics, American Indians, nonbelievers, Jews, and Orientals. It can even be argued that because of tax exemption for church property, the use of chaplains in the military and legislatures, and the bias of the public school system (still struggling to maintain daily prayers in the classrooms), there has never been a complete separation of church and state in America. Many leaders in our churches, the Congress, and the courts can be quoted to the effect that America is a religious nation and that it is, in fact, "a Christian nation." Efforts to amend the Constitution to affirm this in the 1960s received considerable support in Congress and may receive more in the 1980s.[10]

Between 1730 and 1830 Americans moved 180 degrees from a patriarchal to an egalitarian view of politics, or, as some would put it, from a deferential social order to an essentially individualistic one. In that process they dramatically redefined their understanding of nature, of human nature, and of the locus and operation of God's power. They did not, however, reject the European belief that loyalty to the state required loyalty to the religion of the sovereign of the nation. Sovereignty in British North America rested in the king as God's vice-regent on earth; sovereignty in the United States of America in 1830 rested in "the people," or at least in the majority of them. While Americans concluded in theory that there could be no true religious liberty without civil liberty (and therefore threw off the tyrant king and his established church system in 1776), nevertheless they were unable to conceive of a nation that did not have a common belief and practice "under God." The founding fathers and the first six Presidents (chosen until 1828 by the deference of the lower orders to their betters) sought by checks and balances to restrain the tyranny of the majority. However, as romantic ideology, romantic nationalism, and romantic Christianity gradually gained power, the will of the nation came to rest in precisely the same place as the spirit of God, namely, in the people. Under the epistemology of romanticism, external checks upon the people seemed unnecessary. By 1830 it was agreed that every individual heart resonated to the same moral chord at the center of the universe. "There is a *spirit in man* . . . ," wrote George Bancroft in 1855, "which is the guide to truth" and "which places us in connection with the world of [divine] intelligence."[11] Thus the voice of the people became the voice of God and of the nation. From this there could be only limited dissent, mere tolerance, not true religious liberty. The new nation, as de Tocqueville saw, substituted one form of tyranny for another, and when John Marshall ruled that the Bill of Rights applied only to the acts of Congress, then the First Amendment freedoms had no bearing upon what the sovereign majorities within each state wished to prescribe as orthodoxy and patriotism.

Between 1730 and 1830, then, while there was a change in the flow of God's power (from the top down to the bottom up), the principle of *cuius regio, eius religio* remained the same. The full irony of this turn of events can be understood only if we trace the trajectory of democratic enthusiasm from the first Great Awakening through the second.

Formerly described as an inexplicable religious phenomenon, the first Great Awakening is now considered by most historians as the starting point of a distinctly American identity. It is also described as the unconscious social rebellion of the common man against the prevailing structure of authority. Rhys Isaac calls it "a radical social revolt indicative of the real strains within society," "a search for more powerful popular models of proper conduct" and "the quest for a system of social control centered in the people." In short, "a revolt against the traditional system."[12] Richard Bushman argues that with the increasing economic opportunities in the eighteenth century, "the energies released exerted irresistible pressure against traditional bounds. When the Great Awakening added its measure of opposition, the old institutions began to crumble. By 1765 . . . the most perceptive leaders were looking for new methods of ordering society in an age when human loyalties would be forthcom-

175

ing voluntarily or not at all."[13] As early as 1730 patriarchal authority was proving dysfunctional in the New World. The first Great Awakening initiated a three-phased movement by Americans to break away from the organic world view imbedded in the feudal institutions of the corporate state. Spiritual rebellion was justified from 1730 in terms of God's unmediated power to release individuals from Satan's chains of spiritual bondage through a direct, personal conversion experience. The Revolution constituted the second and political phase of this popular movement culminating in what Gordon Wood calls "Republican regeneration."[14] The second Great Awakening from 1800 to 1830 brought the third phase as the Arminian doctrines of free will and free grace replaced Calvinistic predestination while the Jacksonian faith in "the omnicompetence of the common man" (and what Bancroft called "the sagacity of the many") replaced Jefferson's "rule by the aristoi." If God's power could flow unmediated and immediately into and through the hearts of the people, then "popular sovereignty" was God's means for redeeming the world. Despite the fears of conservatives like Hamilton, de Tocqueville, or Calhoun, this could not be "the tyranny of the majority" but only the righteousness of the chosen. As Bancroft, the intellectual spokesman for the Jacksonian common man, explained to such conservatives,

> It is hard for the pride of cultivated philosophy to put its ear to the ground and listen reverently to the voice of lowly humanity; yet the people collectively are wiser than the most gifted individual, for all his wisdom constitutes but a part of theirs. . . .
> If reason is a universal faculty, the universal decision is the nearest criterion of truth. The common mind winnows opinions; it is the sieve which separates error from certainty. . . . A government of equal rights [civil and religious] must therefore, rest upon [the common] mind . . . the sum of the moral intelligence of the community should rule the State.[15]

What Bancroft here calls "the universal faculty of reason" is not, of course, the faculty of intellect which the Enlightenment philosophers called "Reason" (or Rationalism). Bancroft is using the term as Kant, Coleridge, and Emerson used it. For the Romantic philosopher reason was the intuitive moral sense of the people, the heart, conscience, or soul of humanity. "Where the Jeffersonians rested their case [for democracy] on the power of man's mind," writes John William Ward in *Andrew Jackson, Symbol for an Age*, "the Jacksonians rested theirs on the promptings of man's heart." The change in epistemology was profound in that century from 1730 to 1830. Not only did Americans change the definition of God but they also altered the prevailing conception of how God operated. The sharp dualism between nature and the supernatural broke down; the line between this world and the next, between man and God, vanished. "Most of Emerson's contemporaries agreed with him," Ward says, "that there was an intimate correspondence between the inner nature of man and the outward nature of the universe."[16]

It may help us to understand this revolution in philosophy, moral values, and social structure which constituted the birth of the new nation if we can think of religion as the sociologists or cultural anthropologists do rather than in terms of theological doctrines or ecclesiastical institutions. According to a common sociological definition, religion is concerned with power. Power, though divine in origin, ultimately manifests itself in the political structure which gives order and maintains values for daily life. Anthropologist Kenelm Burridge explains religion in these terms:

> All religions are basically concerned with power. They are concerned with the discovery, identification, moral relevance and ordering of different kinds of power. . . . From [those self-evident "truths" which "command consensus" in any society] are derived the sets of moral imperatives, obligations, and rules of conduct to which men subject themselves. . . . religious activities will change when the assumptions about the nature of power, and hence the rules which govern its use and control, can no longer guarantee the truth of things [and lose that consensus which gives them legitimate moral force].[17]

Gordon Wood states in *The Creation of the American Republic* that "the Revolution was designed to change the flow of authority" or power in the colonies.[18] As such it was the fulcrum upon which the seesaw of American religion tilted between 1730 and 1830, but the momentum begun in the first Awakening was not completed until the seesaw came to rest upon the ground of the common man at the end of the second Awakening. To comprehend how this reversal of the flow of power changed a patriarchal consensus into a democratic consensus, we must go back to the beginning.

While the first Awakening had few overt aspects of political revolution, it can be seen in the larger perspective as the unconscious expression of revolt against those beliefs and institutions which had ceased to meet the needs of a great many colonists and were in fact preventing the full and free expression of the energies unleashed by new economic opportunities, westward expansion, and increasing population. Because this frustration, anger, and distrust of authority were expressed at first in spiritual reactions does not mean that the reactions were apolitical; they were clearly critical of traditional authority. The rebellion of ordinary churchgoers against the teachings of duly ordained and learned ministers (whether in Congregational New England, Anglican Virginia, or the heterodox Middle Colonies) demonstrated what sociologists call

177

"a crisis of legitimacy," a loss of faith in the established order of things. In New England the established churches managed, after an initial period of turmoil, to contain this spiritual rebellion, largely because most of the ministers capitulated to the New Light views of George Whitefield and Jonathan Edwards. Even so, dissenting denominations grew dramatically after 1750. In the Southern Colonies, as Rhys Isaac and John Boles have shown, the New Light movement seriously undermined the Anglican establishment. In the Middle Colonies, according to L. J. Trinterud, a distinctly "American tradition"—or acculturation of Scottish, German, and Dutch denominations—evolved, separating the New World believers from Old World ways.[19]

C. C. Goen, Alan Heimert, and Ernest Tuveson maintain that the new interpretation of millennialism which evolved in this Awakening marks a "watershed" in religious and intellectual thought equal to that of the Revolutionary era. What "government by the consent of the governed" meant for the political revolt of the 1770s, postmillennial faith that God had renewed the covenant with the chosen people "in America" meant for the religious revolt of the 1740s. Prior to 1740 Americans had been premillennialists, waiting upon God's will for the Second Coming and fearful that mankind would be subject to immense tribulations and sufferings prior to that day. After 1740, they became postmillennialists, convinced that they could themselves advance the kingdom of God on earth because God had especially selected Americans as God's agents in that process. Edwards preached that the kingdom of God was to be "advanced" through the prayers of Christians and by the missionary zeal of the converted, not by political action. Nonetheless, he also said that since God answered prayer for revivals, God is "at the command of the prayer of faith and in this respect, as it were, under the power of his people."[20] "Power to the people" is a revolutionary slogan even when it is stated simply in spiritual terms. Subsequent answers to Americans' prayers in a continuing series of crises after 1740 convinced them that God's power was indeed directly available to them. There is, it seems to me, a direct line from Edwards to Emerson (or Bancroft) in this respect. Heimert and Tuveson have traced this through the zeal of the Evangelical New Lights; Nathan Hatch and John Berens have shown that it is equally important among the Old Lights, rationalists, and Arminians. "The rising glory of America" was, in effect, the tilt toward self-confidence, optimism, and postmillennial faith released by the energies of a colonial people unwilling any longer to take orders and direction from the authorities "at home." Previous to the first Awakening, the preachers of America saw England as God's chosen

178

nation and expected the millennium to occur "at home," in Europe. After 1740 the colonists became convinced that God had passed the torch of human progress to them and that the millennium would occur in the New World.

The providential signs of the coming of the millennium in America have been described by Nathan Hatch in *The Sacred Cause of Liberty* and by John Berens in *Providence and Patriotism in Early America*. To the colonists their triumphs over adversity were nothing short of miraculous interventions of God specifically on their behalf. First came the series of victories over the French and Indians from 1745 to 1763 which finally drove Catholic power out of Canada. This demonstrated that God's covenant was, as Whig ideology had long held, with English Protestants: "Tracing providential history as the continuous battle of liberty versus tyranny, they centered their attention on the British constitution—'the admiration and envy of the world.' In sermon after sermon they lifted up the standard of British liberty against the aggressive tyranny of Roman Catholicism." Thus, "by the end of the French wars the preachers often referred to God's British Israel and included Britons among God's covenanted people."[21] From hindsight this colonial adulation of Britain resembles that stage of adolescence when the desire to break from parental guardianship is masked by the intense concern with pleasing the parents. Excessive admiration is latent resentment. Americans asked, "Am I a child of the King or a child of God?"

Adulation was mixed with awareness of parental weaknesses. Even as Wolfe's defeat of Montcalm ended French rule in America, there were feelings that something was wrong in the British Israel. The movement after 1760 to send Anglican bishops to America was resented as an infringement of rights, a lack of trust, a potential tightening of bonds that should be loosening as the obedient, loyal son neared his majority and demonstrated his mettle. Similar fears came from Parliament's seeming effort to undermine local self-government among the colonists. From the Stamp Act to the king's "murder" of "his children" at Lexington and Concord, a new series of providential signs pointed to God's protection of Americans against a tyrannical father as well as toward the British people's betrayal of their own covenant with God (similar to that of the Jews' betrayal when the Messiah arrived the first time). Nathan Hatch specifically notes how the American clergy (Liberals and Evangelicals, Rationalists and Pietists), having first attached the label of "Antichrist" to French Canadians, gradually shifted it to Parliament and the king after 1763. The Quebec Act in 1774, granting religious equality to Roman Catholics in Canada, constituted final proof that the king had broken his Protestant covenant. As John Adams had

179

predicted in 1765, George III seemed bent upon imposing "the canon and the feudal law" upon his most devoted subjects in America.

Once Americans identified the king and Parliament with "Antichrist," it was but a short step to the conclusion that the thirteen colonies must be "God's New Israel" to carry on the great work of human redemption. England, by 1775, was identified with Babylon or Egypt out of which heroic leaders chosen of God must lead the captive Israelites. The political liberty of America thus became essential not only to its civil and religious liberty but also to its divine destiny. As John Witherspoon, president of the New Light College at Princeton, said in 1776, "There is not a single instance in history in which civil liberty was lost and religious liberty preserved entirely."[22] Those unwilling to fight for one lost the other by default.

Redefining the nature of authority and the meaning of history, the colonists needed to forge a new rhetoric and new symbols to identify their separate destiny. Harry S. Stout has shown us how itinerant revivalism after 1740 provided a new "mode of communication" and a "new language" and style which created the broad popular base essential for successful revolution.[23] While Stout admits that "there is no clear and consistent link between revivalism and republicanism on the level of ideas," he contends that "the revivalists' repudiation of polite style and their preference for extemporaneous mass address cut to the very core of colonial culture by attacking the deference to the written word and to the gentlemen who mastered it." Any revolution in worldview "requires a new rhetoric." There was a close link between the mode and style of the itinerant revival preachers of the Awakening and that of the popular patriotic gatherings around liberty poles during the Revolution. "Itinerancy was by nature disorderly," Stout notes, because it was rootless, democratic, outside traditional bounds. Men (and even some women, like Ann Lee and Jemima Wilkinson) who felt an "internal call" to preach the gospel carried it through the highways and byways regardless of their lack of theological training, ordination, or license from local authorities. They went where the Spirit moved them; spoke to the common people in their homes, marketplaces, barns, or fields; and used the vernacular to convey their truths. "At the center of the Evangelical rhetoric," Stout says, "was the 'celebration of the union of the minister and people'" irrespective of social location, parish boundaries, or ecclesiastical hierarchies or prerogatives. The itinerants had no respect for the "Spirit-restraining" laws of the established order nor were they, any more than God, "respecters of persons" or station.

In other words, itinerant exhorters were radical egalitarians. As messengers of God, prophets with a direct link to the Almighty's power, they did not preach "down" from a high pulpit or "at" the people from a high horse, but "to the people"—man-to-man and eyeball-to-eyeball. The result was a new emotional vitality, spontaneity, immediacy in religion which totally reversed the older, formal, hierarchical understanding of how God's spiritual power moved in the universe.

> Aware that the traditional religion of covenant and hierarchy no longer spoke to the realities of a changed society, Evangelicals not only restated in new forms the ultimate ideas regarding Christ and salvation, but they also translated those new forms into a different ideology altogether, not religious but secular, one that spoke necessarily along religious lines of a utopia on earth. . . . Partly through doctrine, but even more through rhetorical strategy necessitated by that doctrine, the effect of the revivals [which continued up to the Revolution throughout the colonies] was to present for the first time on a national level, a revolutionary language and rhetoric that questioned the previously taken-for-granted status of hierarchy and submission, and offered a mass, voluntary system as a substitute basis for authority and social order.[24]

Referring to the itinerant evangelism and the formation of new churches among the Baptists of Virginia in the decade prior to the Revolution, Rhys Isaac described them as a "popular response to mounting social disorder." But their thrust was positive. Behind the revivalism "can be discerned an impulse toward a tighter, more effective system of values and of exemplary conduct to be established and maintained within the ranks of the common folk." The Awakening was an "emotional mass movement" seeking "to create an orderly moral community" on the expanding frontier in the South. "The Baptists' salvationism and sabbatarianism effectively redefined morality and human relationships; their church leaders and organization established new and more popular foci of authority and sought to impose a radically different and more inclusive model for the maintenance of order in society."[25] Behind the expansion of itineracy and of dissenting churches lay not only spiritual fervor but also a willingness to sacrifice the self for the well-being of the community in the name of a higher law and a higher destiny. As we shall note, this same folk movement continued—or revived—in the second Great Awakening and carried out the democratic logic of the Revolution.   181

Once this new spiritual force meshed with the Commonwealth ideology espoused by Jefferson, Madison, Patrick Henry, Thomas Paine, and Sam and John Adams, common ground was formed between the folk and the elite for what Gordon Wood has called "the republican ideology" of a "chaste moral order" based upon individual virtue in the name of government by the consent of the governed.[26] Lockian political theory, Enlightenment benevolence, neoclassical Stoicism, and the desire to advance God's kingdom by rescuing the colonies from the debilitating corruption of Britain all combined after 1775 into a new rhetoric of revolutionary millennialism.[27]

Because religion is the core of any cultural ordering, it affects all social institutions. Historians are just beginning to grapple with the ways in which religious attitudes affect family patterns and child-rearing methods. Philip Greven provides the first major effort to correlate the religious beliefs of parents with their child-rearing practices in colonial America. Greven's study deals essentially with different conceptions of paternalistic power among different kinds of families. The power of parents over children is similar to that of ministers over churches and rulers over subjects or citizens. Like political authorities, parents claim to derive their power from God; obedience to parents is one of the Ten Commandments. Leaders of local government were spoken of in the eighteenth century as "the town fathers"; the king was the father of his people; colonial magistrates were "nursing fathers" of the commonwealth; ultimately George Washington became "the father of his country." Different ideas about the nature of God and divine relations with humanity produce different parental attitudes toward children. If humanity has inherited Adam's sin against divine authority, the innate tendency of children is rebellion against authority, and they need to be taught submission to parental (and all other) authority at the earliest possible moment; otherwise God's anger will be vented upon indulgent parents. But if Adam's sin is not inherited, if persons are free moral agents responsible for their own salvation, and if God is benevolently disposed toward them, then children will be treated by parents as reasonable beings. Between 1730 and 1830, as Calvinistic concepts of total depravity and predestination gave way to a belief in Arminian concepts of free will and free grace, attitudes inculcated by parents toward authority figures in the home, the church, and the state changed also.

Calvinistic parents (as most parents were in the colonies) sought to subject their children to authority within the first two years of infancy. Such children grew up with profound inner tensions between their outward love, admiration, and obedience towards their parents and their own inner self-hatred, insecurity, and lack of self-worth. The conversion process (facilitated by the new preaching style of the first Awakening) helped them to transfer their manifest feelings of love from their parents to God in an experience of total self-abasement and surrender, but they nonetheless retained latent fear and hostility toward human authority. Such persons, Greven finds, tended to be ardent patriots in 1776 because they heaped upon the king, Parliament, and royal governors all their own self-loathing, their distrust of authority, their intense concern for purity and order.[28] Patriots of this evangelical-Calvinist stamp were outraged by the king's injustice toward them and became "extraordinarily vocal and active in expressing their hostilities and fears. . . . Politics provided many with an outlet for their buried feelings. . . . For evangelicals, the mother country and the father-king became symbolic representations of the dangerous, seductive, and powerful tyrants of their childhood."[29]

Edwin G. Burrows and Michael Wallace confirm Greven's view in their study "The American Revolution: The Ideology and Psychology of National Liberation."[30] They find an almost paranoid tendency among Americans after 1775 to denounce the king and mother country as "unnatural parents who have turned upon their children, abusing and mistreating them when it was their duty to protect and nourish them." A large part of the appeal of Thomas Paine's *Common Sense* sprang from his ability to reduce the king to human scale—actually to demythologize his status—in language which (like that of itinerant revivalists) spoke in the accent and to the emotions of the common people. The king, Paine said, was nothing but a "royal brute" whose title was not derived from nobility but from "a French bastard landing with an armed banditti" in 1066. Such a kingship "certainly has no divinity in it," Paine argued. Using biblical analogies, he called George III "the hardened, sullen-tempered Pharaoh of England," a man who would keep the chosen people of God in unjust bondage: "I disdain the wretch that, with the pretended title of father of his people, can unfeelingly hear of their slaughter [at Lexington and Concord] and composedly sleep with their blood upon his soul." As a spokesman for the Commonwealth ideology and an ardent advocate of republicanism, Paine also noted that Israel in its early days had been a republic and that its monarchy could be considered a punishment for the sins of its people.[31] It is significant, Burrows and Wallace note, that the Patriots, in their effort to justify the parricidal doctrine that "rebellion to tyrants is obedience to God," had in the end to argue in terms of John Locke's abstract theory of natural rights and social contract, for there was little in British constitutional law they could cite against the king and Parliament.

183

When Sam Adams said in 1780 that the new American nation should become a "Christian Sparta," he expressed, as Gordon Wood points out, the conjunction of neoclassical rationalism and evangelical pietism.[32] A Christian Sparta would be both republican and millenarian; it would unite the spiritual freedom, brotherhood, and holiness of the Christian ideal with the self-discipline, public virtue, and harmony of the Greco-Roman ideal. It would be voluntarist, reformist, activist, and individualist; yet it would also be a united and chosen people acting together under the providential care of God. The doctrine of "disinterested benevolence" perhaps best describes the ideal ethical value of the republican ideology.[33] It derived from the Scottish Common Sense philosophy, from Jonathan Edwards, and from his chief disciple, Samuel Hopkins. It also fit neatly into the Enlightenment concept of philanthropy (love of one's fellowman, self-sacrifice for the general welfare) which deists like Franklin and Jefferson espoused.

Sidney Mead has pointed out the many ways in which the pietistic and rationalist world views coincided in the Revolutionary era.[34] Even Jefferson found the teachings of Jesus the most sublime moral ethic ever spoken; Franklin believed that all men must accept certain fundamental truths—the existence of God, the immortality of the soul, the belief in rewards and punishments hereafter, the necessity of treating one's neighbor as one's self. The inconclusive debate over tax-supported education and tax-supported religion in the decades after 1776 indicates the difficulty Americans had trying to locate and routinize moral, spiritual, and civil authority in the new nation despite their broad areas of agreement on politics and divinity.

In those years, when the various states had to resolve the question of an established church system, it was agreed everywhere that the safety and prosperity of the republic rested upon public morality, piety, and virtue. It was also agreed that these virtues needed to be diffused, inculcated, taught regularly to the common people and the rising generations. Disestablishment debates hinged in part on whether churches or public schools were the most effective means of diffusing morality. Most people thought that both were necessary. Few denied that public schools should be supported by taxes on all, but it no longer seemed feasible to lay taxes to support only one denomination. Yet it was not clear whether voluntarism would suffice to support public morality and religion. The general run of the populace was too selfish (and often too poor) to support voluntarily such expensive institutions as churches. The long debate over a general assessment tax for religion (continuing until 1833 in Massachusetts) included essentially the same arguments in the former Anglican colonies as in the old Congregational ones.

Several explanations have been offered for why New Englanders agreed to continue religious taxes (distributed proportionately among all bona fide Christian sects) while Southerners took the opposite view. The most common explanation holds that it was easier to sustain a general establishment in New England because, although Congregationalists stood to gain most by it, (1) the established clergy had been loyal to the Patriot cause; (2) they had a long tradition of public service and respect so there was little anticlericalism; (3) there was more homogeneity in the population and a closer link between township life and ecclesiastical life (i.e., the towns laid the religious taxes on themselves, not any vestry and not the state legislature); (4) Congregationalists since 1728 had exempted the major dissenting sects from religious taxes; hence, there was less reason to suspect them of unfairness; (5) local control left open the option of disestablishment, for a town did not have to lay religious taxes on everyone if it did not want to; (6) the Congregationalists had a majority of the votes.

In the South, however, the effort to create a general assessment tax for religion from which the Episcopal Church stood to gain most (though this was supported by Patrick Henry and George Washington) failed because (1) the established clergy had been Tories; (2) they had not served the common people well in the past; (3) parish taxes had been laid by the vestries as required by the king as head of the church and the vestries were self-perpetuating oligarchies; (4) there was a serious split among the upper class which brought men like Jefferson and Madison forward as spokesmen for voluntarism and gave a powerful leadership to the dissenters which was lacking in New England; (5) lukewarm (rationalist) Episcopalians and dissenters together may well have been a majority of the voters; (6) the establishment had persecuted the dissenters until the very outbreak of the Revolution.

In addition, it was very difficult to devise a system of public support for religion which would be fair to all sects, great and small. The larger denominations would certainly obtain the lion's share of any religious taxes; new sects would have difficulty getting recognized; and no one knew what to do about the vested property rights already in the hands of the old established churches. Prudence and caution suggested that drastic change within the new nation should be avoided. "A republic was a delicate polity"; it "demanded an extraordinary moral character in the people," as 185 Wood notes, "because virtue was truly the lifeblood of the republic." Many leaders were not yet ready to trust the common people to act wisely. "'There must be,' said John Adams in 1776, 'a Decency, and Respect, and Veneration introduced for Persons in Authority, of every Rank, or We are undone.'"[35] Hence, during "the Critical Period," when the masses seemed to support Daniel Shays, paper money, and thriftless self-indulgence, the wise and the well-born used every ounce of their prestige and power to persuade the citizenry to accept a constitution with carefully built-in checks and balances against "a factious, turbulent democracy." From 1789 to 1828 the common man continued to accept as leaders those who were better educated and more experienced because he did not yet quite trust himself with the power that lay within his grasp. Calvinistic self-doubt died hard even under the optimism resulting from a successful revolution and a postmillennial faith.

Jefferson's election marked the beginning of a departure from this prudent republicanism. The second Great Awakening effected its final rejection. Nathan Hatch has described this Awakening in terms of the development of a truly "democratic theology," an explicitly "egalitarian religion" and an effort to create "a revolution within the church that would place laity and clergy on an equal footing" stressing "a populist hermeneutic premised on the inalienable right of every person to understand the New Testament for themselves."[36] Theologians have referred to the Awakening in terms of the breakdown of Calvinism and the rise of Arminianized Evangelicalism. Sidney Mead credited Nathaniel W. Taylor with redefining New England theology so as effectively to repudiate predestination, original sin, total depravity, and a limited atonement. The moral responsibility of the individual required under "Taylorism," or "the New School" theology, that a person must have the power to choose between good and evil (because deists, like Jefferson, Paine, Ethan Allen, were equating Calvinism with fatalism and ridiculing a view of God which made God the author of sin and a tyrant who damned innocent children to eternal hellfire because of Adam's fall).

In the new theological worldview of the second Great Awakening, God became not an angry, vengeful father, but a loving, nourishing parent; Christ died not just for the elect but for all men and women; God created the world not for his own glory but for human happiness; children were not born totally depraved but free moral agents who needed to be treated with respect (for they came "trailing clouds of glory"; the child was parent to the adult, not a child of the devil to be submissive to parental authority). Grace was not irresistibly forced upon persons, and even saints might backslide; grace was freely offered and, upon true repentance and faith, freely acquired; persons consented to God's government as they did to their own government and worked for it out of their own self-interest; sovereignty might now be trusted to the common people because they were not worms or loathsome spiders but children of God, capable of self-discipline, self-control, who innately and intuitively responded to the presence of God in nature; persons

186

were not only to be trusted with power (regardless of property qualifications or education) but they were also omnicompetent in their potential for self-development; therefore, no one was more fit to rule America than "a man of the people"—a symbol of their will because he embodied their spirit.

Dickson D. Bruce, John Boles, and Donald Mathews have demonstrated how Methodist concepts of free will and free grace became the folk religion of the frontier west of the Appalachians after 1800 because they appealed to a people ready to accept their own responsibility for success or failure in this world.[37] Mary Douglas has noted that a religion which deemphasizes ritual and hierarchy requires the parents to explain to the child "the consequences of his acts" and to persuade him to self-discipline. Such personalized religion celebrates "the autonomy and unique values of the individual."[38]

In order to combat the anticlericalism of the Enlightenment, the Calvinist ministry had to prove that Christianity was more reasonable than deism. A world constructed by a clockmaker God and run by natural laws with which God never interfered was, as Taylor, Beecher, and Finney said, more fatalistic than the Christian world in which God played a daily and active personal part performing miracles of transformation for those who believed all things were possible in Christ. The miracle of conversion wiped the slate clean for the worst of sinners and gave him or her a brand-new start in life. Through miraculously transformed individuals, the world itself might be altered, reformed, and made ready for Christ's return. Furthermore, a world run by natural law was less democratic than one in which God's will and power were immediately available through grace and intuition to every person; only a learned individual with the wealth and leisure to study at the colleges could ever master the scientific intricacies of nature. A democratic nation needed an egalitarian religion.

The final stage in America's "change in the flow of authority" took place between 1800 and 1830 through a belief in miracles. Deferential politics waned and egalitarian democracy increased because Americans felt the need for a God who was directly available to serve their needs and solve their problems, to inspire them with faith in themselves and hope for the millennium regardless of their status, family background, or educational attainments. This awakening, Wood says, "Christianized" the classical republicanism of the Revolution; it united "piety and patriotism" into a totally new concept of *e pluribus unum,* and it reversed the epistemology of Lockian sensationalism for the intuitive epistemology of Scottish common sense.[39] Perry Miller saw this Awakening as the search for

187

national unity and community through a transcendent evangelical faith which cut across all denominational and sectarian divisions; by 1830, despite the proliferation of new denominations, the new nation felt it had achieved "a union of intelligence, public spirit, and moral principle" which made it culturally unique; "that sort of union," said the president of Amherst College in 1831, "makes every patriot a Christian, and every Christian a patriot."[40] Wood concludes that "the great revival [of 1800 to 1830] was thus working out the Revolution in religion. By popularizing religion as never before and by extending organized Christianity into the remotest areas of America, the revival marked the beginning of the republicanizing and nationalizing of American religion."[41]

How did it come about? John Berens, like Miller and Wood, finds the years after 1800 crucial to "the sanctification of American nationalism" because Americans once again found God's Providence at work both in their ability to surmount political and military crises as well as in continued showers of spiritual blessing. The Napoleonic wars brought the nation to the brink of war with France in 1798 and almost led to the secession of New England after the Embargo Act of 1807. A two-party system evolved which threatened to divide the nation politically while regional divisions seemed to anticipate a split between North and South or East and West. Both Federalists and Democratic-Republicans laid claim to being the only true expositors and guarantors of America's mission; each denounced the other as a faction whose principles would undermine the whole experiment in freedom. When war came in 1812, the Federalists declined to cooperate and only divine intervention stopped the Indians (at Tippecanoe and Horseshoe Bend) and the British (in New Orleans). The Hartford Convention cast an odium upon the Federalist leaders only a "little short of treason," while God guided the frontiersmen of Kentucky and Tennessee to victory under the frontier hero, Andrew Jackson. Jackson was obviously the embodiment not only of the popular will but also of God's will.

Nathan Hatch argues that the new Christian denomination, founded in the West by Barton W. Stone and Alexander Campbell in 1830, was the epitome of the second Great Awakening. This radical religious movement represented "the exaltation of public opinion as a primary religious authority," for its preachers and followers were convinced that "biblical authority could emerge from below, from the will of the people."[42] The Christians were "venting their hostility not against Calvinism in some narrow sense," but sounding "the death knell for corporate and hierarchic conceptions of the social order." What Hatch attributes to the Christians, Wood attributes to the Mormons:

Some radical evangelicals thought they could end the religious chaos by appealing to the Bible as the lowest common denominator of Christian belief. The Scriptures were to be to democratic religion what the Constitution was to democratic politics—the fundamental document that would bind all American Christians together in one national community. The biblical literalism of these years became, in fact, popular religion's ultimate concession to the Enlightenment—the recognition that religious truth now needed documentary "proof."[43]

Joseph Smith, noting that differences in biblical interpretation tended "to destroy all confidence in settling the question by an appeal to the Bible," realized that a new prophetic revelation was necessary, and when it came, it came to one of the common folk.

Even before the Mormon revelation and the founding of the Christians, James O'Kelly, Peter Cartwright, and Charles G. Finney had broken the stranglehold of Calvinism upon American thought. O'Kelly and Cartwright spoke for the Methodists in the Southwest who, though Arminians since 1740, had suffered under the cloud of John Wesley's Toryism during the Revolution. Finney spoke for the New School divinity of Presbyterians and Congregationalists in its most radical and forthright form in the Middle West. Flatly rejecting Calvinism, where Taylor and Beecher had tried simply to redefine it, Finney proclaimed in 1828 that it was manifestly "unreasonable" for God to require the performance of the duty of making a new heart (as he does in Ezekiel 18:31) if "at the same time He knows we have not the power to obey." The Westminster Confession of 1648, the basis of Calvinism in New England, was a fraud upon Christianity, Finney concluded. Jonathan Edwards had led men astray with his attacks upon freedom of the will. "As therefore, God requires men to make to themselves a new heart on pain of eternal death," Finney preached, "it is the strongest possible evidence that they are able to do it."[44] Furthermore, Finney claimed to have discovered the spiritual laws by which God operated just as Locke and Adam Smith had discovered his laws of politics and economics. God worked through the religious affections and used the words of the preacher to excite and transform the hearts of men. Revivals were not "miracles prayed down" from heaven but psychologically "worked up" by skillful evangelists using the means prescribed by God. If man could engineer revivals, he could convert the world, and if he could convert the world, he could make it into a millennial Paradise fit for Christ's triumphal return. The true spirit of the Christian, Finney said, "is necessarily that of the reformer. To the universal reformation of the world they stand committed."[45] Their reforms were to be undertaken voluntarily through benevolent associations and by these engines of "universal reformation,"

189

Finney told Jacksonian America in 1835, "the millenium [sic] may come in this country in three years."[46]

Finney was a perfectionist, and most American evangelicals after 1830 became perfectionists of one sort or another. The New School theology taught them to take the Word of God literally, and God said, "Be ye therefore perfect even as your Father in heaven." Those outside the church believed this as firmly as those within it. Millennialism became not simply a hope or a doctrine but a plan of action, a national commitment. Andrew Jackson, though not a member of any church, spoke for "the nation with the soul of a church" when he said in his first inaugural in 1828, "I believe man can be elevated; man can become more and more endowed with divinity; and as he does, he becomes more Godlike in his character and capable of governing himself. Let us go on elevating our people, perfecting our institutions, until democracy shall reach such a point of perfection that we can acclaim with truth, that the voice of the people is the voice of God."

Implicitly, America itself was the church of God in action; its voters (whether members of any specific denomination of Christians or not) spoke as God's chosen people, for the United States itself was the embodiment of God's purpose. Power had come to the people at last in its fullest form. "This vast transformation," says Wood, "this move from classical republicanism to romantic democracy in a matter of decades, was *the real American revolution.*"[47] Americans had become as gods. The revolt against a patriarchal, hierarchical, corporate feudal world that began in 1730 had been resolved in a new consensus which constituted the true birth of the nation in 1830. Civil and religious liberty, as understood by the common man, was the will of God, as Bancroft explained. The expansion in power, prosperity, and territory of America was "the manifest destiny" of God for God's people. The idea of religious liberty had, for the time being, found a new equilibrium in civil liberty. Temporal and spiritual power were fused even while Americans proclaimed to the world that they were the first nation on earth truly to understand that religious freedom meant the separation of church and state. Perry Miller concluded that by 1830 "religious liberty opened the highway to a greater uniformity than the Church of Rome ever contemplated."[48] Such are the unintended consequences of purposive action. Ever since, from the Mormons to the Creationists, we have been testing the limits of religious liberty under popular sovereignty.

NOTES

[1]Bernard Bailyn, "Religion and the Revolution," *Perspectives in American History*, vol. 4 (1970), pp. 85-169.

[2]Nathan O. Hatch, *The Sacred Cause of Liberty: Republican Thought and the Millennium in Revolutionary New England* (New Haven, Conn.: Yale University Press, 1977); John F. Berens, *Providence and Patriotism in Early America, 1640–1815* (Charlottesville: University of Virginia Press, 1978); Carl Bridenbaugh, *Mitre and Sceptre* (New York: Oxford University Press, 1962); Ernest L. Tuveson, *Redeemer Nation: The Idea of America's Millennial Role* (Chicago: University of Chicago Press, 1968).

[3]Sidney E. Mead, *The Old Religion in the Brave New World* (Berkeley: University of California Press, 1977); Alice M. Baldwin, *The New England Clergy and the American Revolution* (New York: Ungar, 1965); Henry F. May, *The Enlightenment in America* (New York: Oxford University Press, 1976).

[4]Alan Heimert, *Religion and the American Mind* (Cambridge, Mass.: Harvard University Press, 1966); W. G. McLoughlin, *New England Dissent* (Cambridge, Mass.: Harvard University Press, 1972).

[5]Winthrop S. Hudson, *The Great Tradition of the American Churches* (New York: Harper & Row, Publishers, Inc., 1953), p. 43. Hudson credits Ernst Troeltsch with making this observation.

[6]Perry G. E. Miller, "The Contribution of the Protestant Churches to Religious Liberty in Colonial America," *Church History*, vol. 4 (1934), pp. 57-66; Gordon S. Wood, *The Creation of the American Republic, 1776–1787* (Chapel Hill, N.C.: University of North Carolina Press, 1969).

[7]Evarts B. Greene, *Religion and the State* (Ithaca, N.Y.: Cornell University Press, 1941); J. Franklin Jameson, *The American Revolution Considered as a Social Movement* (Princeton, N.J.: Princeton University Press, 1926).

[8]Heimert, *Religion and the American Mind,* see Introduction.

[9]See Hatch, *Sacred Cause of Liberty,* p. 144; Tuveson, *Redeemer Nation,* pp. 20-25.

[10]John Anderson, 1980 presidential candidate, admitted voting for such an amendment on two occasions as a Congressman. For the Christian Amendment Movement see Louis Gasper, *The Fundamentalist Movement* (The Hague: Mouton & Co., 1963), pp. 146-147.

[11]George Bancroft, "The Office of the People in Art, Government and Religion (1835)," *Social Theories of Jacksonian Democracy,* ed. Joseph L. Blau (New York: Hafner Publishing Company, 1947), p. 263.

[12]Rhys Isaac, "Evangelical Revolt: The Nature of the Baptists' Challenge to the Traditional Order in Virginia, 1765–1775," *William and Mary Quarterly,* 3rd series, vol. 31 (July, 1974), pp. 358, 361, 362.

[13]Richard L. Bushman, *From Puritan to Yankee* (Cambridge, Mass.: Harvard University Press, 1967), p. x.

[14]Wood, *Creation of the American Republic,* pp. 118-124.

[15]Bancroft, "The Office of the People," pp. 269, 266, 267.

[16]John W. Ward, *Andrew Jackson, Symbol for an Age* (New York: Oxford University Press, 1953), pp. 49-50, 72.

[17]Kenelm Burridge, *New Heaven, New Earth* (New York: Shocken Books, Inc., 1969), p. 5.

[18]Wood, *Creation of the American Republic,* p. 67.

[19]L. J. Trinterud, *The Forming of an American Tradition* (Philadelphia: J. B. Lippincott Co., 1949).

[20]Quoted in Heimert, *Religion and the American Mind,* p. 81.

[21]Hatch, *Sacred Cause of Liberty,* p. 48.

191

[22] Quoted in *ibid.*, p. 63.

[23] Harry S. Stout, "Religion, Communications, and the Revolution," *William and Mary Quarterly*, 3rd series, vol. 34 (1977), pp. 519-541.

[24] Harry S. Stout, "Religion, Communications, and the Ideological Origins of the Revolution," unpublished manuscript.

[25] Isaac, "Evangelical Revolt," p. 362.

[26] Wood, *Creation of the American Republic*, pp. 117-120.

[27] See May, *Enlightenment in America*, chapter 3.

[28] Philip Greven, *The Protestant Temperament: Patterns of Child-Rearing, Religious Experience, and the Self in Early America* (New York: Alfred A. Knopf, Inc., 1977), pp. 12-13.

[29] *Ibid.*, pp. 339-340.

[30] Edwin G. Burrows and Michael Wallace, "The American Revolution: The Ideology and Psychology of National Liberation," *Perspectives in American History*, vol. 6 (1972), pp. 167-300.

[31] Thomas Paine, *Common Sense*, ed. N. F. Atkins (New York: Liberal Arts Press, 1953), pp. 15-27.

[32] Wood, *Creation of the American Republic*, pp. 114-118.

[33] See Garry Wills, *Inventing America* (New York: Doubleday & Co., Inc., 1978), pp. 192-206.

[34] Sidney Mead, *The Lively Experiment: The Shaping of Christianity in America* (New York: Harper & Row, Publishers, Inc., 1963), pp. 39-52.

[35] Wood, *Creation of the American Republic*, p. 67.

[36] Nathan O. Hatch, "The Christian Movement and the Demand for a Theology of the People," *Journal of American History*, vol. 67 (December, 1980), pp. 545-567.

[37] Dickson D. Bruce, Jr., *And They All Sang Hallelujah* (Knoxville: University of Tennessee Press, 1974); John Boles, *The Great Revival, 1787-1805* (Louisville, Ky.: . Kentucky University Press, 1972); Donald Mathews, *Religion in the Old South* (Chicago: University of Chicago Press, 1977).

[38] Mary Douglas, *Natural Symbols* (New York: Vantage, 1973), p. 47.

[39] Gordon Wood, ed., *The Rising Glory of America, 1760–1820* (New York: Braziller, 1971), p. 77.

[40] Perry Miller, *The Life of the Mind in America* (New York: Harcourt Brace Jovanovich, Inc., 1965), p. 67.

[41] Wood, *Rising Glory*, p. 77.

[42] Hatch, "The Christian Movement," pp. 558, 566.

[43] Gordon Wood, "Evangelical America and Early Mormonism," *New York History* (October, 1980), p. 378.

[44] Quoted in William G. McLoughlin, Jr., *Modern Revivalism: Charles Grandison Finney to Billy Graham* (New York: The Ronald Press Company, 1959), pp. 67-68.

[45] Quoted in *ibid.*, p. 106.

[46] Quoted in *ibid.*, p. 105.

[47] Wood, *Rising Glory*, p. 9.

[48] Miller, *Life of the Mind*, p. 68.

"A Nation Born Again": The Union Prayer Meeting Revival and Cultural Revitalization

Leonard I. Sweet

For quite some time Timothy L. Smith and J. Edwin Orr[1] have been nudging other historians to sit up and take notice of a revival that is so haphazardly interpreted that there exists little unanimity on what even to call it: "Laymen's Revival," "Holiness Revival," "YMCA Revival," "1858 Revival," "Businessmen's Revival," or "Prayer Meeting Revival." The eyes of contemporaries, however, saw no such cloudiness. They called this revival that so enthralled them "the most extensive and thorough ever experienced in the United States," "the most remarkable ever known in the history of the Christian church," "The Great Revival," "The Great Awakening," or simply but strongly "The Revival."[2]

Much of the treatment that has been given to the Union Prayer Meeting Revival addresses the issue of origins: who or what started it. The favorite candidate both now and then is the economic collapse of 1857, which gave laity the leisure to ponder laying up treasures in heaven, where depressions do not break in and steal and where inflation does not panic and corrupt.[3] Other observers, both then and now, denied that the revival was triggered by the autumnal commercial convulsions.[4] Instead they traced its origin to the union prayer meetings sponsored by America's YMCAs,[5] the strategies for evangelism adopted in 1856 by many New York City churches,[6] Charles G. Finney's Boston revival,[7] and Phoebe and Walter Palmer's Ontario and Quebec revivals.[8]

The historical dimensions of this revival are only beginning to be appreciated. Richard Carwardine has analyzed its transatlantic context, and J. Edwin Orr has written a book measuring the revival's worldwide proportions.[9] Scholars have yet to discover the role of team ministries in spreading and shaping the revival (Charles and Elizabeth Finney, Phoebe and Walter Palmer, Catherine and William Booth, Mary and William E. Boardman, Ellen Louis and B. T. Roberts).[10] Somewhat paradoxically, furthermore, we need to study why the masses of church women took a backseat in the revival itself, an unusual sight in the history of nineteenth-century evangelism, and why the percentage of heads of families converted appears larger in this revival than before.[11] In short, the Union Prayer Meeting Revival needs to be examined within the whole context of nineteenth-century patterns of revivalism.

The focus of this essay is limited to a preliminary probing of the cultural significance of the Union Prayer Meeting Revival. Timothy L. Smith, in his engaging and engaged book *Revivalism and Social Reform*, has argued that the revival helped to prepare the churches and the country not only for the approaching political conflict which produced the Civil War but also for the approaching industrial strife which produced the social gospel movement. The revival geared the nation for the assault on slavery and "rejuvenated as well the crusades against intemperance, Sabbath desecration, and neglect of the poor."[12] William G. McLoughlin, on the other hand, argues that the revival was concerned with "personal perfection, not social reform," and as an urban, northern phenomenon of 1858 "exacerbated sectional animosity" and "helped tip the secular businessman toward the importance of maintaining the Union at any cost."[13] The possibility that the revival was "a concerted effort by Americans, North and South, to relieve the social tensions of the slavery and secession crisis and to assert some new sense of national identity that could create the climate for yet another sectional compromise by Whigs and Democrats," a hypothesis McLoughlin raises and then flatly dismisses,[14] is the exploration of this paper.

Historians are easily misled concerning the effects of the Union Prayer Meeting Revival because the conventional historical judgment has interpreted the revival as a mere spasm of religious awareness, a northern, urban, businessmen's response to economic adversity that dissipated in the air of prosperity. All this is subject to criticism. In his provocative look at *The South and the North in American Religion*, Samuel S. Hill, Jr., accents the similarity of religious praxis throughout the regions in antebellum America and argues that religious interaction was "vigorous" and "commonplace, right through 1860."[15] This essay suggests that the Union Prayer Meeting Revival was not an exception to Hill's observation about the "nearness" of the two regions except as it demonstrates one of the few examples of the North looking South rather than almost always the other way around. For the span of roughly a year in most locations and much longer in others, the revival exerted a unifying force on the American nation, making "third cousins" (Hill's description of North-South kinship patterns) feel that they were back into relationship together, if not as chums, then at least as "first cousins."[16]

194

A national drama of reconciliation and unity was played on the stage of religion. Instead of preparing the way for war, as the revival is usually construed, the first phase of the revival functioned as a preventative. Just as American religion, beginning with the Methodists and Baptists in the 1840s, "rehearsed" secession through splitting into northern and southern entities, so beginning in 1857 religion served briefly to halt division and restore a fragile sense of identity to the nation. The prime offender in modeling secession now styled itself the major redeemer in maintaining union. The Union Prayer Meeting Revival tapped deep but increasingly desperate streams of religious hope that a baptism of Christian unity could avert a baptism of blood.

I

Americans greeted the Union Prayer Meeting Revival with extravagant claims and expectations. For the secular press like the New York *Evening Post* or *Daily Tribune*, the revival was the number one news story of 1858 and "the most striking phenomenon of the day."[17] The religious press wondered whether the millennium had not begun. "One would think," wrote a correspondent for the Nashville *Christian Advocate*, "that the great day of the Lord was at hand, and the whole world would soon be filled with his glory." As the revival's transatlantic sprawl became more apparent, the predictions were pitched even higher. "We are to see such an outpouring of God's Spirit and grace as we have never seen in all past and present, far surpassing in depth and power anything the world has ever seen, to pervade not only our cities and cities only, but our land and all lands."[18] The Chicago *Christian Times*, in a front-page treatment of the revival entitled "The World Can Be Converted," contended that Americans were experiencing a "foretaste" of the coming "millennial glory."[19] Harriet Beecher Stowe, prompted by the sight of theaters functioning as churches, houses of vice being turned into schools of virtue, and businessmen willing to leave their businesses in the middle of the day and attend to God's business, composed an article comparing biblical prophecy about "characteristics of millennial times" with the promise of the revival to sacralize the secular in American society.[20]

English commentators were often equally enthusiastic. Awed by the power of the revival's growing presence in the two leading nations of the globe—"Whatever England and America are for the next twenty years, the world will become"—they found in the revival's birthplace in the New World confirmation of America's chosen status and "rational expectation" of a "worldwide revival hailing the millennial dawn."[21] The journal of the Evangelical Alliance printed a report from its Philadelphia correspondent specu-

195

lating that "the revival that is to introduce the millennium, with all its power, sublimity, and glory, may now have fairly set in."[22] Even doubters like the southern preacher William F. Broaddus, who hedged his hopes by saying, "I do not say we are in the midst of a millennium," went on to lecture that if Americans would roll the revival across the Atlantic, the millennium would ensue. "We are in the midst of eventful times, and a fearful responsibility waits on us." The world never would be converted by individual conversions. Only the shaking of social foundations by powerful spiritual upheavals could usher in God's kingdom.[23]

The Union Prayer Meeting Revival rejuvenated America's self-image as a chosen nation and America's millennial ambitions. At a time when the whole nation was fragmented over slavery, gripped in the clutches of secessionist sentiment, just when many Americans had despaired of Christianity's ability to perfect history and advance civilization, when the American moral landscape was a graveyard of unburied hopes, when many feared America's "mania" for money had dried up its heart,

> our whole nation seemed to be born again, in a day. We are as men that dreamed . . . without expectations, without special measures, without distinction of sect, or sex, or age, or climate, or erudition, religion comes home to the bosom of all men. A mysterious and sudden solemnity pervades every haunt of business and pleasure. . . . Never since the day of miracles, was there such a demonstration of supernal power, in the religion of Jesus.[24]

Like the Princeton professor who, before students at Oxford Female College, made the preceding analysis of the significance of the awakening, the American public and press found it of great significance to America's future that when everyone least expected it, God visited the nation with a sudden, spontaneous awakening that was free of overheated emotionalism, human management, organized opposition, and sectarian rivalry.

Unlike many other revival eras, Americans were conscious they were living through a revival and self-conscious about it being a "national awakening"—almost as if they were trying too hard, trying both to make it come true and to see it come to pass. Some indeed were, as one periodical observed of a contemporary chronicler of the revival whose claims for the awakening, if true, "would make the earth almost millennial."[25] Yet the issue was less whether the millennium was coming than whether America would be its site when it arrived. Only religious forces were deemed strong enough to restore America's millennial perceptions of itself which had rusted from the corrosive forces of sectional strife and moral dispute. When congregations heard admonitions about "the great alternative

196

set before you: turn or die; repent or perish; believe or be damned,"
they appropriated these words to the nation as well as to themselves.[26] James W. Alexander, former church history professor at
Princeton and pastor of the Nineteenth Street Presbyterian Church
in New York City, preached a sermon during the revival on America's greater need for revivals than any other Christian nation. If
America's privileged status among the nations of the world were
to be saved from "sectional feud, factious division, disaster and
desolation" and if the nation were to become once again a "Holy
Flock," America must become as religious and righteous as it has
become large and wealthy.

> Our nation! There used to be magic in the word. Our country
> was the watchword that passed with magnetic swiftness and power
> through the lines of our forefathers. Has it ceased to charm their
> sons? Have we sunk into unpatriotic selfishness? Have Christian
> souls forgotten—can they forget—what it is that blesses a country—
> that righteousness exalteth a nation—that the Gospel only can
> redeem us from violence, vice, and damning falsehood?[27]

The revival had come, the Chicago *Christian Times* pealed forth on
its front page, to cleanse the nation from its sins by purifying its
businesses, politics, literature, churches, and by checking its spirit
of "worldliness and money getting." The revival exhibited God's
plan to save America, "to save our country from ruin, . . . to
regenerate public opinion, and change the course of our nation."[28]

Certain unique features of the Prayer Meeting Revival, believed
by its contemporaries to be different from every other religious
awakening in history,[29] fanned the hopes of renewal for the nation's
millennial vocation. The unprecedented places of origin and rapidity
of spread startled everyone into respect. The windows of heaven
seemed to open almost simultaneously on America's three largest
and most "wicked" cities—New York (Fulton Street Church), Philadelphia (Jayne's Hall), and Boston (Old South Church). Much as
in the time of the early church and its urban centers of Jerusalem,
Antioch, Ephesus, Rome, and Corinth, cities were hit first during
the Prayer Meeting Revival. The business centers of America, once
hotbeds of commerce, had now become hotbeds of conversions.

Except for J. Edwin Orr, historians have found it difficult to 197
disagree with contemporaries like revivalist Charles G. Finney or
Cincinnati Congregationalist C. B. Boynton who contended that
slavery was such a sludge in the South's soul that showers of
blessing could not penetrate it. Even northern churches which were
silent on the slavery issues, they argued, were immune to revivals.[30]
Yet the claim that the revival did not touch the South like the rest
of the nation, or that its progress depended on anti-slavery senti-

ment, will not bear up under close scrutiny. One reason why the southern end of the revival escaped being headlined in the press or heralded over the wires, as southern bishop and college president Warren Akin Candler pointed out, was that the South had few large cities as compared to the North, and the revival was widely scattered over southern rural populations. How much Candler was given to exaggeration in his statement that, proportionately, revivals were "greater in the South than in any other section" is difficult to determine.[31]

Newspapers in cities like Cincinnati, Louisville, Charleston, Savannah, Nashville, Mobile, Vicksburg, New Orleans, and St. Louis bear testimony to the revival's indiscriminate geography. The revival began in cities of the northeastern axis, but within a few months it had like a Mexican jumping bean hit virtually every town and hamlet in the North, South, East, and, somewhat later, West.[32] What had usually happened only to single communities in previous patterns of American revivalism was now happening to an entire nation. Revival did not wait on revivalists to carry it from place to place. "The northern, middle, western and southern states were moved as by one common mighty influence."[33] It was as if Pentecost were being repeated simultaneously in every American community and the Holy Spirit were subduing an entire nation. When the fire bells struck at noon, the prayer bells struck at America's churches, halls, hotels, shops, and schools. All America, it seemed, was going together to prayer meeting and falling on its knees.

Neither storms of winter nor vacations of summer stopped people from attending their rounds of prayer meetings, and when New York City took its annual summer migration up to Saratoga Springs, they took prayer meetings with them. New York City pastors like Theodore Ledyard Cuyler were not the only ones "kept busy for six months, night and day" when the revival was at its peak. An Atlanta, Georgia, pastor exclaimed in sublime exhaustion, "There are revivals almost everywhere," and in New Orleans the revival was billed as "an epoch-making event" with "evangelical Christianity never in so prosperous a condition in the Crescent City, as now."[34] In Chattanooga, Tennessee, even though an assortment of prayer meetings were offered every hour of the day and night, the city suspended business for a day to encourage universal participation, proclaiming the holiday a "Thanksgiving Day" for the revival that seemed to be sweeping the entire nation.[35]

Mention is often made of the revival's impact on northeastern and midwestern colleges like Yale, Amherst, Princeton, Union, Harvard, University of Michigan, Williams, and Dartmouth. What is often overlooked is that the revival also rippled through southern colleges like Oglethorpe University in Georgia, Emory, North Carolina, Wake Forest, University of Virginia, Jefferson College, and Baylor, as well as numerous male and female academies and seminaries.[36]

Doorways were choked with people trying to get into union prayer meetings in both the cities and small towns of America, making it difficult to gauge the accuracy of estimates putting the number of new converts in one year's time at one-half million.[37] "Small towns and rural communities were as powerfully affected as the great cities," Timothy Smith writes.[38] Happy rumors circulated widely about several small New England towns where not a single adult sinner was spared the assault of conversion. One brother from a small, western New York village testified that he would never have been at the prayer meeting had not "the people of Bloomfield resolved that not a sinner should be left in town."[39] Even the icy waters of the Mohawk River knew there was something unusual going on in one little town that hugged its banks when the ice was broken to accommodate eager souls impatient for baptism by immersion.[40] As one traveler boasted from personal observation, "From Omaha City, Nebraska, to Washington, *there was a line of prayer-meetings along the whole length of the road;* so that, wherever a Christian traveller stopped to spend the evening, he could find a crowded prayer-meeting, across the entire breadth of our vast republic."[41]

II

Various agencies labored to promote a revival that would engulf the entire country. The denominations themselves worked mightily to implement a national revival. Denominational presses in the South, for example, featured the evangelistic methods of the northern revival as models and motivation for southern involvement in the awakening. Denominational assemblies also featured narratives of revival progress which encouraged emulation.[42] The four Old School presbyteries representing 300 ministers, 500 churches, and 50,000 members in western Pennsylvania, eastern and middle Ohio, and northwest Virginia met in November, 1857, to deliberate how the revivals could be extended to "our whole church."[43]

Ecumenical agencies like the YMCA were even more instrumental than denominations in obtaining a national scope to the revival. YMCAs were most often one of the first, if not the first, group to conduct and coordinate union prayer meetings in cities like New York, Philadelphia, Boston, Baltimore, Cincinnati, Chicago, Milwaukee, Cleveland, Charleston, Nashville, New Orleans, and San Francisco.[44] Some friends of the YMCA complained that such general evangelistic thrusts dissipated the associations' *raison d'etre*. It was the unique mission of the YMCA to throw a net of help and holiness around young men moving into America's cities. Let the established denominations, they argued, be responsible for community evangelism, and let them guide and control the revival.[45] Yet if there were a national sponsor of the Union Prayer Meeting Revival, the YMCA was it. Although the revival overflowed its patronage, the YMCA proved to be a consistent connecting link between North and South. The New York City YMCA's "Committee on Devotional Meetings," for example, sent circulars throughout the nation inviting all Americans to unite and promote the cause of Christ, an appeal that was advertised in the South, and requested other parts of the country to correspond with them about the course of the revival.[46] Similarly, the Philadelphia YMCA published an eighty-page summary of the revival entitled *Pentecost: or the Work of God in Philadelphia* (1858) which they intended to "stimulate our brethren in Christ everywhere to more fervent prayer and increased zeal."[47]

An unwitting but potent promoter of a nationwide revival was the secular press, which gave the "Great Turning to the Lord" extensive coverage. Some even gauged public interest so high and the public interest such at stake that they devoted front-page space to the schedule of weekly prayer meetings and lent editorial endorsement to informational efforts about "The Present Religious Awakening in the World."[48] It was not only the religious press that kept tabs on which denominations were most actively sponsoring the revival, quantifying state by state the number of conversions and replacing news from Washington with news from prayer meetings as the lead articles. Newspapers which could not rely on field correspondents fed their readers' appetites for revival news by reprinting New York City newspapers' coverage of the event, especially Horace Greeley's April 3, 1858, *Extra* on "The Great Revival."[49] The Union Prayer Meeting Revival was one of the most covered religious events in the history of American journalism. By bannering the work of the Spirit, the press became one of the major advertising agencies for the national awakening.

Religious propaganda was also calculated to export the revival from northeastern urban centers to all parts of the country. Harvey Newcomb authored a handbook in lay evangelism designed to perpetuate the revival and dedicated to all "converts in the revival of 1858."[50] A history of the New York City revival quickly appeared to help extend the revival throughout America, and representative sermons from the awakening were collected and published with the hope that "Christians in other parts of the country" will be similarly moved.[51] Penny-press hymnbooks, pamphlets, and tracts were widely distributed. In fact, while other businesses complained of languishing sales during the depression, booksellers rejoiced in a booming business selling religious literature and anything having to do with "the leading topic of the day."[52] In every major U.S. city, wherever strangers might congregate, places such as hotels, railroad depots, steamboat and ferry landings, boarding houses and newspaper offices, schedules of prayer meetings were posted or handbills distributed in hopes of igniting with the flame of revival visitors whose return home would spread the fire.

The strategy of reading aloud prayer requests at meetings contributed significantly to the yearning for and development of a nationwide revival. Not uncommonly were prayers offered for the awakening to span the Atlantic to the Pacific. Letters from other parts of the country were read soliciting prayers for communities as yet untouched by the Spirit: specifically, for example, prayers were beseeched for a Virginia presbytery which was "among the few reported at the late General Assembly wholly unvisited with showers of grace."[53]

Another evidence to contemporaries of the revival's cleansing of America's calling was the universality of the Spirit's sweep through society as well as geography. "The subjects of the revival included all classes," one observer reported, "the high and the low, the rich and the poor, the learned and the ignorant. The most hopeless and forbidding were brought under its almighty power."[54] The penetration of the revival into all classes was part of a predetermined strategy. One of the unusual evangelistic techniques developed during the revival was the targeting of professions and classes for special revivalistic appeals. Aside from the prayer meetings where everyone was invited, there were special services for "workingmen," "businessmen," "boys," "ladies," lawyers, fishermen, sailors, store clerks, policemen, firemen, and others. Engine houses held daily Bible studies for their occupants, hotels accommodated prayer meetings for their waiters and workers, and one New York City publishing house every noon converted its offices into a religious chapel for the employees.[55] Most major cities and some smaller communities boasted special services for police, firefighters, and their families.[56] Appropriate texts were chosen ("Is Not My Word a Fire?") and specialized tracts printed ("To Firemen," "To Police").[57] The attendance from various Philadelphia fire companies and their families at one prayer meeting totaled an astounding 1,779, and a service for firemen in New York City's Academy of Music drew what was billed as "the largest congregation ever assembled within walls in America for Protestant religious services."[58] Ethnics and the poor were targets of special drives, with various cities having their undersides scoured by union lay visitation teams like New York City's "Flying Artillery." Philadelphia's YMCA endowed a 3,000-seat "Union Tabernacle Tent" which was dedicated to the exclusive use in oppressed sectors of the city and which featured services in ethnic languages and collected no offerings.[59] Denominations like the Episcopalians previously antagonistic to revivals climbed aboard and sat comfortably with everyone else. The doors of three of the Protestant Episcopal Church's most prestigious churches—Church of the Ascension in New York, St. Paul's in Philadelphia, and Trinity Church in Boston—were stormed open by the winds of revival and the rush to prayer meetings. Episcopalians in Washington, D. C., prided themselves in reaping a bigger harvest from the revival than any other denomination in that city reaped.[60] Universalist and Unitarian critics of former revivals like James Freeman Clarke and Frederic Dan Huntington explained that "there are revivals and revivals, and 1858 is not 1828."[61] Everyone was overjoyed with the smattering of Jewish and Roman Catholic involvement in the revival, especially its promotion by the Illinois priest, Father Charles Chiniquy, and by the usually unyielding New York Bishop John Hughes's openness to the genuineness of the revival's conversions.[62] No corner of society was to be left unswept—even the churches were changed through the revival's pervasive doctrine of holiness. It looked as if the whole American family were getting a bath.

III

It is not without significance that during the revival this word "union" became a sort of national incantation, not just a political mind-set. "Union" was the Prayer Meeting Revival's favorite word. The distinguishing and shimmering feature of the revival, wrote one participant, was "the cardinal doctrine of Christian union."[63] "Christian union," wrote another, was the singular doctrine of this fourth great revival under the gospel dispensation just as the Pentecost revival had preached the divinity of Christ, the Reformation revival justification by faith, and the first Great Awakening of Edwards and Whitefield "instantaneous conversion and regeneration by the Holy Spirit."[64] The underlying premise of "union" prayer meetings was the more inclusiveness, the better. Merchants, lawyers, and doctors stood side by side with beggars, mechanics, clerks, and omnibus drivers. Methodists, Baptists, and Presbyterians sat on the same platform with Dutch Reformed, Lutherans, and Episcopalians. Lay and clergy voices mixed in prayer, and they often grasped each other's hands for a benediction of prayer and song. At a time when congregational singing was being displaced by semioperatic performances, the singing was strong and harmonious. When northerners and westerners, southerners and easterners sang together "All Hail the Power of Jesus' Name" or "Rock of Ages" with lungs swelled to the sky, it was as if the building, not the people, were singing. Differences faded from view, and for a moment at least, all felt like they were brothers and sisters, part of a national community again. As one participant expressed it, "it seems just like family prayer."[65]

Lay Christians were equally if not more instrumental than clergy in slaking the nation's craving for unity by stirring up through the revival a sense of common identity and destiny. The "union spirit" owed its power and allegiance not to the professionals but to the people. A frequently used litany praised the laity for their efforts to bring rival denominations and jealous clergy to cooperate with one another. Horace Greeley's attempt to catapult Henry Ward Beecher into the role of "Magnum Apollos" of the revival fell with a thud as people insisted on celebrating the nameless amateurs who appeared to be teaching the professionals. Disgusted with the established sources of authority, the political and religious experts who had botched things up and led the nation to its misbegotten mess, the people took things into their own hands. Although ultimately they labored in vain, they worked to fashion "union" from the ground up.

The uniform structure of almost all union prayer meetings was designed to promote a "union spirit" among classes, regions, and denominations. Without any election of a chairperson or secretary, a lay person presided at the meetings, but the order was actually maintained by the congregation itself. Prominently posted on the walls were rules for the meetings. Prayers and exhortations could last no longer than five (later reduced to three, the limit in most places) minutes, and the five-minute rule was strictly enforced by a merciless spring bell that faithfully executed its errand. The intent behind timing prayers and testimonies, singing only a few verses of a hymn, and not reading over fifteen to twenty verses of Scripture was more than a desire to get the service over with in under an hour, though this was a clear indication that the laity was running things. Rather, it was primarily a desire to create an orchestra of harmony and spirit of unity. William C. Conant explained the difference between a service based on prayer and one based on preaching in the following terms:

203

> Rapid succession is essential to the *union* of many utterances in one unbroken chain, of many notes in one expressive melody, or many individuals in the collective majesty of a "public." A succession of prolonged tones may be never so sweet, or soft, or grand, and may vary throughout the widest compass of the scale; but they are not music, for the want of connection and unity. Instead

of a dialogue, it is a series of soliloquies, and the wonderful product of the social principle by which mere *men* become that sublime object MAN, and can in that character hold exalted converse, the whole with each, and each with the whole—is lost.[66]

Preaching, which had a history of exciting controversy and exacerbating denominational rivalry, was relegated by the laity to a backseat. And even the preaching that was done, as revealed in a collection of thirty sermons delivered during the course of the revival by clergy from diverse denominations, exhibited a uniformity of message. All preached the same truths, all shunned theological controversy, and all reflected the quest for holiness.[67] People came together not to hear eloquent sermons by polished professionals but to engage in social prayer and public testimony. The people were the preachers, which is why some proclaimed this the most democratic, most American of all the revivals.[68] Other revivals in America may have been known for greater quality of preaching. But never had America, it was believed, known a greater density of prayer.

The blurring of lay-clergy distinctions was also matched by a blotting out of ecclesiastical identities. The *New York Daily Tribune* called the revival "anti-denominational" because "the advancement of sectarian views is not tolerated in any form."[69] Persons who rose to speak were forbidden to announce their denominational affiliation, and the use of nondenominational Sunday School Union hymnbooks insured that no doctrinal peculiarities would intrude to curdle the spirit of the meeting. Some were so sensitive about the possibilities of offending anyone that they advocated the exclusive singing of "God's hymnbook," the one situated in the middle of the Bible.[70] The spirit of unity and friendship had melted down ancient feuds among the faithful to the point that a newspaper from Sandusky, Ohio, reported rather impishly that a Baptist minister offered his services to his Methodist colleague, volunteering to immerse any Methodist converts who elected that form of baptism but to baptize them as a "candidate for your church." That was unity gone too far for the Methodist. "I prefer to wash my own sheep," he replied.[71] The ecumenical slogan of the Cincinnati revival, "A Long Pull and a Strong Pull and a Pull Altogether" summed up what clergy meant when they floated from union prayer meetings on clouds of communion, saying, "Our hearts have fused, and our prejudices have been broken down."[72] But even more instructive to contemporaries and illuminating to historians was the oft-repeated story of how Baltimore tried to imitate New York, Philadelphia, and Boston and joined the revival bandwagon. At first Baltimore shunned union meetings and each denomination tried to initiate revivals themselves. Not until the city "caught the union spirit" did revival break out and consume the metropolis.[73]

A feature of the union prayer meetings which engendered the perception of America as one vast concourse of religious aspiration was the reading aloud of prayer requests. This allowed the laity to set the direction and tone of the meeting by their selections of which requests to read and for which ones to pray publicly, although in some places prayer requests were the exclusive privilege of those present.[74] The reading aloud of prayer requests for an unsaved brother in Detroit or a sick child in Atlanta helped to create a feeling of community, or what contemporaries called "social power"[75] where Americans were drawn to one another in new and tender bonds of affection and common needs. The main reason why many Unitarians broke with tradition and supported the revival, according to one Unitarian preacher, was because it paved the way for a redemption of the entire American community by making Americans "feel the restraints and the inspiration of membership in the one family."[76] Habitual recountings of personal experiences in answered prayer requests had the same effect. This revival loved to tell stories; and the more sentimental, unusual, and romantic the plot, the wider the narrative circulated. The frequency of testimonies given about the redemption of "hopeless cases" and the reconciliation of "enemies" through unceasing prayer suggests an underlying hope for the resolution of such "hopeless causes" as the healing of the American political family itself.

IV

The muting of sectional differences was accomplished in various ways. Prayer meetings were structured so as to open channels of primary communication between political and social antagonists in an embracing climate of prayer and praise. In the liturgy of each union prayer meeting an important place was reserved for visitors from other parts of the country who were expected to report on the progress of revival in their areas. Northern prayer meetings listened to southerners, southern prayer meetings listened to northerners, and through listening social frictions lessened a bit. Prayer requests, the majority of which came in writing and were mailed in from all over the U.S., had the same effect as the presence of strangers. They created a common unity of need and aspiration revolving around prayer (e.g., "A resident of Georgia requests the prayers of this meeting [New York City] for two dear brothers, that they may be brought to Christ on this day of salvaton").[77] Many parents thought they heard a portion of their prayers answered when New York's and Philadelphia's YMCAs publicized throughout the country their resolve to contact personally any son whose address was

205

sent to them.[78] When North and South stopped looking at one another and looked together in the same direction, each forgot the other's differences.

The telegraph provided the technology to unite union prayer meetings—in effect almost bringing a nation together in one prayer meeting. The successful laying of the Atlantic Cable during the height of the revival helped to make the telegraph become in the popular mind a symbol of "peace" and "unity." In sermons, speeches, and editorials commemorating the Atlantic telegraph, America's religious leaders sought to "ordain" it as a "missionary," consecrated to the "perpetual peace of the two nations which it united" and to the "approach of the millennium."[79] Seizing on this theme wherein the telegraph became a divine "Oracle of Peace" and "Unity," one enthusiast echoed many others in contending that "this great invention of the century impresses upon the mind and heart of the religious world the ideas of UNITY, and thus aids in creating a power antagonistic to the injurious separations and alienations, too long prevalent in the church. A better era is at hand. Unity is the familiar message among the religious demonstrations of Providence. Unity is the loving truth of Gospel grace."[80]

Unity was also the telegraphic message flashed so frequently between prayer meetings. Although New York City's John Street Meeting and the Philadelphia Union Prayer Meeting in Jayne's Hall displayed the most cooperation and coordination of activities,[81] large meetings routinely communicated with one another by magnetic telegraph messages of Christian love and friendship. New York City's John Street Meeting received and read, for example, a telegraph of greeting from the Louisville, Kentucky, Union Prayer Meeting which said: "One thousand in attendance, greatly increased interest. This is the Lord's doing, it is marvelous in our eyes."[82] Many telegraph offices offered free telegraphs to prayer meetings as well as to converts who wished to inform their families and friends back home of their newfound faith.[83] The cooperation of the telegraph companies and newspapers also enabled noonday prayer meetings around the country to sing the same closing hymn on the same day.[84] In short, union prayer meetings voiced expressions of fellowship and interest between America's regions that were articulated or heard few other places.

206

A climate of trust between sections was facilitated by the revival's reluctance to address directly the burning political and social questions of the day. Notices and placards hung on walls blared the warning that there were to be "No Controverted Points Discussed" in the meetings. Only infrequently were overtly political concerns made the subject of prayer requests, and then they were of the order of "Pray for the conversion of President Buchanan" or "Pray for the nation."[85] Two out of New York City's three big union prayer meetings refused to read a prayer request from a fugitive slave seeking divine benefaction on his flight to freedom.[86] The same New York YMCA which spearheaded the revival in New York City refused a year earlier to pass resolutions declaring slavery to be a sin for which New York Christians were in some way responsible, prompting abolitionists to denounce America's YMCAs as not "aggressive upon the empire of darkness."[87]

The revival's moratorium on controversial subjects enabled the southern religious press to defend the revival against southern incredulity and cynicism. The *Louisiana Courier*, for example, characterized the revival as a northern, urban phenomenon led by "Black Republican parsons" and attacked it for attempting to whip up a frenzy against southern slaveholding states. Not so, declared the New Orleans *Christian Advocate*, assuring southern doubters that the results of the revival would be moral, not social or political, and that something almost providential was taking place when a paper like Horace Greeley's *Tribune*, "free-soil" in politics and "free-love" in ethics, would put aside smiting the wicked slaveowners and take up "religious themes."[88] The moderating effect of the revival on sectional animosities came about because what one participant in Philadelphia's prayer meetings described to an English audience was true of most others: "I have not, in any one instance, heard even an unpleasing word in relation to any of the popular but more muddy subjects of the day. Politics, slavery, temperance, etc., have never been referred to except in the general terms in which we know the Gospel will cure them all."[89]

The last clause—"the Gospel will cure them all"—is extremely important for understanding how William G. McLoughlin can argue that the revival's holiness theology failed to "denounce social and political injustice" while at the same time Timothy L. Smith can trace the holiness roots of social Christianity.[90] The politics of holiness, supportive of social activism during the eighteenth-century Evangelical Revival and America's second Great Awakening, became scrambled in the 1850s, which proved to be the secret of the holiness appeal during the Union Prayer Meeting Revival. Jesus did not save people "in their sins," one revival pamphlet intoned, but rather saved them "from their sins."[91] Holiness spelled power, the power to lead a victorious Christian life, the power to change suddenly. Phoebe Palmer talked of holiness as a "shorter way" to perfection. Overnight things could be different; the slow process of decay could be overturned; and the stranglehold of sin released.

One of the reasons for the spread of holiness ideology into virtually every American denomination by 1860, which Melvin E. Dieter has called *The Holiness Revival of the Nineteenth Century*,[92] was because it provided a framework for talking about eradicating sin without necessarily specifying the sins or fingering the sinners. "Believing in Christ, you love him," preached a Congregationalist pastor during the revival, "and, loving him, you love what he loves, and hate what he hates, and this is holiness."[93] This is also haziness, and the language of holiness as it developed in the 1850s offered at least theoretically a common vocabulary which all evangelicals could interpret to suit their theological dispositions and regional patriotisms. With the Palmers' and Boardmans' irenic, introspective brand of evangelical pietism that came to define holiness in personal terms like "the higher Christian life," the social and political bite of Wesleyan perfectionism was diminished even though the bark remained. It may be that when scholars leave off wondering why holiness sentiments did not invade the South and commence studying southern pneumatology we may discover that the South did indeed have a doctrine of holiness that was not all that far from Phoebe Palmer, with the exception that in the South holiness meant purity while in the North holiness meant power.

What is clear is that when southern publications gave a front-page amen to the New York *Independent*'s hope that history would look back not at the "great revival of 1858" but at the "great *reformation* of 1858" which carried religion into homes, businesses, and politics through a spreading submission to Christ which would quicken consciences and advance social, political, and economic morality ("No revival has ever done anything for Wall St. We hope this may"), southern Christians thought they heard a politics of personal holiness that would fill the churches on Sunday and the schools on Monday, empty the jails, and visit the poor and needy.[94] This they could support, for it did not threaten the South's doctrine of the "spirituality of the church" or its retirement from pre-1830 ventures in social reform.[95] In the *Independent*'s summons to a "reformation," however, many northern evangelicals heard as well a politics of social holiness, a conviction that any genuine revival of pure religion will, as the *Oberlin Evangelist* put it, "purify the public conscience and augment the force of real benevolence" which willy-nilly leads to a deeper abhorrence of slavery and "more prayer and labor for its utter extinction."[96]

Momentarily, at least, both South and North agreed that the important thing was to put first things first, and that meant promoting a revival and encircling the country with a kind of elemental warmth. Where the revival went from there was left for God and each section to decide. As one periodical responded when asked whether the revival might go beyond interdenominational unity to organic unity, "God knoweth. It makes us happy, harmonious, loving Christians, and He will care for the rest."[97] "The results of such a singular, wide-spread, and long-continued state of things," mused another, "it is not for the world fully to know."[98] Insofar as the revival succeeds in inculcating the holiness belief that active service and duty, not feeling, constitutes true religion, *The Evangelist* asserted that the nation's antislavery sentiment would be reinforced. But that the revival should make Americans "more devoted to some one specific idea or reform, independent of its connection with all others embraced in the general notion of Christian duty, we do not expect."[99] Harriet Beecher Stowe, who wrote a series of widely reprinted articles about the revival, issued a call for a more specific accounting of the revival's significance than merely the addition of church members. In her summons for more emphasis on "Fruits of the Revival," however, the antislavery issue was downplayed.[100] By engendering unity among the Christian community, which had been weakened by sectional division and theological dissension, the power and voice of the gospel was seen to be strengthened and the forces of darkness diminished. For the Union Prayer Meeting Revival, the solution to America's plight was not the abolition of slavery or the defense of slavery. Supporters of the Revival believed that somehow if only Christians could get together, everything would turn out all right. As the title of an address delivered in 1859 before the YMCAs of both Boston and Richmond phrased it, "Christianity—neither Sectarian nor Sectional—the Great Remedy for Social and Political Evils."[101]

Christian unity may have been a good slogan, and prayer a sincere weapon, but their leverage on the social order was temporary. Religion flexed its muscles, and for a moment at least everyone took notice. But the revival's physique, though sculpted by a powerful drive for unity, and capable of inspiring admiration, had not the strength permanently to move society or alter the drift of politics. The revival's prescription for America's ailments—a nonsectional, nonsectarian Christianity fashioned by prayer—came perilously close to what critics said was the essence of Phoebe Palmer's holiness ideology—believing it makes it so. The attempt to unite America was shipwrecked on the revival's shallowness and immateriality.

Because of the revival's tendency to subsume political, theological, and social controversies under a common impetus toward unity, to speak only in general terms about the "New Era in Justice and Love in our Nation,"[102] and to get specific only about duties nearer home that lay within the direct reach of individual prayer meetings, there were some who raised critical voices about the revival's superficialities. At the regular semimonthly meeting of the New York City YMCA during the height of the revival, there were a few who groused at the absence of any new benevolent movements emerging from the revival and the lack of visible signs indicating altered behavior patterns.[103] Young Edward Payson Hammond, who led Scottish revivals in 1859–1861 after serving in 1858 as a student volunteer during the early period of the revival, found himself forced to defend the American revival against reports that it failed to rouse fully the church's powers against malignant forces in society.[104] But most outspoken of all in criticism of the revival was one of its participants, George B. Cheever, an editor of the *Independent* and pastor of New York City's famous Church of the Puritans, which itself was swept up in the revival fervor. Cheever's sermons during the revival, many of which proposed increased agitation against slavery as the litmus test of the awakening's authenticity, became increasingly political to the point where forty-eight members of his congregation, responding to his charge that slavery was being cloaked by the revival in the robings of righteousness, left collectively in disgust.[105] Cheever's position was best summarized in an article on the revival of religion and the revival of slavery in the western territories; the sermon was entitled "The Two Revivals."

> And so these two revivals are rushing on, side by side, if not hand in hand. It is a most extraordinary race; on the one side, inhumanity, crudity, injustice, dishonesty, and doctrines of devils; on the other, pure and undefiled religion, love to God and man, conversions by thousands, divine truth, grace and glory? Is there no antagonism? Are these genuine and true yoke-fellows?[106]

Most of the participants did not appreciate Cheever's raising the question. North and South seemed to have come to an amicable if not altogether abiding arrangement. Both agreed that toxins of poison had entered the arteries of American society, and nonsectarian, nonsectional Christianity was the only antidote that could restore health and vitality to the nation. Political change was to emerge out of a nonpolitical revival. Christian union would have political implications. Some revivals hit mostly youth, others mostly women, the *Oberlin Evangelist* observed. But this one roamed over every range of society and grazed especially heavily among "adult and strong men," those who occupied positions of power and could effect changes in American life. [107]

For a while it appeared as if united prayer as a political strategy was working. Evangelicals took great encouragement from the presence of legislative and judicial prayer meetings in state capitals and especially in the nation's capital. In Albany, New York, for example,

210

legislators crowded into the Court of Appeals room across from the Senate Chamber to start the day in prayer together. In Washington, D.C., a United States Senator early in 1858 called for the formation of a committee to organize morning prayer meetings near Capitol Hill, which led to a "Congressional Union Prayer Meeting" and other daily prayer services which were still being continued in Washington well into 1860.[108]

V

The Union Prayer Meeting Revival did not end in 1858. Although the novelty of the meetings had worn off by 1860 and the revival fever had broken, "the spirit of prayer seems not to decline" remarked the *New York Observer*.[109] Early in 1859 a Presbyterian periodical reported that "still every thing indicates a remarkable religious susceptibility."[110] Crowds of over a thousand were still being counted at daily services in the celebrated spots, and as late as February, 1861, there is evidence that interest was sufficient to sustain many prayer meetings. The press may have tired of the revival, and the millennial glint may have faded by the summer and fall of 1858, but in many large cities "there is now nearly, or quite as deep an interest, in reality, as there has been at any time." New York City evangelicals even sensed in the fall of 1860 a new crest of revival energy flooding union meetings.[111] Enough revival activity was under way to warrant National Union Prayer Meeting Conventions in November, 1859, and March, 1860, where representatives from union prayer meetings in over a dozen states, "from Boston to San Francisco," gathered to elect officers, establish a Committee of Correspondence to help union meetings keep track of one another, and devise a questionnaire to gather data from every community in the country on how many union prayer meetings were being conducted, what was their attendance, what was the state of religion in their area, and other such information.[112]

For the South there is similar evidence of simmering revival activity after 1858. At the beginning of the war union prayer meetings were still a prominent feature of nearly every community, and one southern historian of revivals doubted whether in any other English-speaking nation "there were as few infidels and as many evangelical Christians" as in the South.[113]

What had ended in 1858 was the "union" phase of the revival, the revival's lessening of sectional tensions and shoring up of a common national identity. The southern religious press replaced front-page news of the revival with coverage of northern preachers' attacks on the South for slavery and buried revival correspondence in obliviating back pages.[114] Both sides began to conscript Jesus as an ally to their cause, and religion served to solidify and sanctify

211

the social and political positions of each side. Whereas the first phase of the revival witnessed religion helping to revitalize American culture, the conclusion of the revival helped to send two sections toward their gruesome collision, bathing the ensuing carnage with God's blessing and benediction. In fact, those military units most influenced by the ongoing revival were characterized as better equipped to fight and more willing to die for the cause than those not equally visited.

The story of the massive army revivals that proved to be such a hallmark of the Civil War has yet to be written, although the South has fared much better than the North in historical attention to this phenomenon.[115] Only a suggestive outline can be sketched here. Described by some as the most religious fighting unit in Christian history, even surpassing in spirituality Cromwell's Roundheads, the southern army camps most resembled camp meetings with convert estimates ranging from 45,000 to 150,000. Instead of "churches praying for soldiers," "soldiers were found praying for the churches." Or, as an Alabama chaplain exclaimed, "Talk about the army demoralizing the church—I don't know any church that wouldn't demoralize my regiment."[116] At the war's end the northern Methodist bishop Matthew Simpson observed that what had been true of the South was also true of the North—religion had surfaced in the army "to an extent wholly unparalleled in history."[117] Much of the support for army revivals came from the ongoing union prayer meetings like the ones in New York City where prayers were now focused on the conversion of the troops, the promotion of army revivals, and the establishment of daily prayer meetings among the soldiers. The featured "visitors" at these services were returning soldiers who testified to the wonders God was working in the encampments where soldiers were becoming more likely to congregate at prayer meetings than around gambling tables or liquor bottles.[118]

The continuity of leadership between the prewar and wartime phases of the revival renders the character and extent of the Civil War revivals less surprising. Many of those appointed commissioners of the United States Christian Commission (USCC), actually a wartime arm of the YMCA designed to minister to the physical and spiritual needs of soldiers and sailors, were prominent leaders of the Union Prayer Meeting Revival. YMCA leader George H. Stuart and holiness theologian William E. Boardman, President and Executive Secretary of the USCC, respectively, exemplify the spillage of sponsorship from the national to the sectional phases of the revival. Amidst the agonies of war, both lay and clergy missionaries called "delegates"—some comparing themselves to Whitefield and

Wesley—sallied forth to do battle against the forces of sin.[119] In the southern army the YMCA connection was also predictive of revival leadership. Many chaplains, like J. William Jones, who led the army revivals, had been active YMCA leaders during the 1857-1858 awakening.[120] Robert E. Lee was both a moral and financial backer of YMCAs, and both armies welcomed the organization of YMCA branches within their ranks.[121]

During the wartime revivals similar revival techniques obtained in both armies. Noonday prayer meetings were conducted on the front lines even with minié balls whizzing past everyone's ears. Prayer meetings with lots of singing and testifying were more popular than preaching services. In the words of one southern chaplain, there were "brigade prayer-meetings, regiment prayer-meetings, company prayer-meetings, until one of our missionaries, Rev. J. E. Chambliss, reported to our chaplains' associations that he could find no time in Davis's Mississippi brigade to preach without conflicting with some prayer-meeting."[122] Revivals in both armies were aggressively nonsectarian, and most particularly Robert E. Lee and Stonewall Jackson incarnated the revival spirit in their own spirituality and in their insistence that chaplains not represent denominations.[123] Emotional restraint characterized conversions, and lay leadership of the revivals was much more important than historians, who have been preoccupied with studying the chaplains, are inclined to acknowledge. Even holiness theology was a staple of the soldiers' spiritual diet. One general reminisced how the "rocks and woods rang out with appeals to holiness and consecration."[124]

Nor did the revival cease when the war ended. The summer and autumn of 1865 witnessed scenes of great revivals, especially in the South, as soldiers went home and tried to warm up the chill of church religion with some of the revival heat of the camps. The cultural impact of the army revivals, which reinforced social identities and political loyalties, may have lingered longer in the South than in the North, if what one historian argues about the birth of a southern civil religion is accurate.[125] But further studies are needed before conclusions can be made with any confidence. What can be said with assurance is that the Civil War, and not the holiness crusade of the Union Prayer Meeting Revival, ultimately "sanctified" and "purified" the nation.

NOTES

[1]Timothy L. Smith, *Revivalism and Social Reform: American Protestantism in Mid-Nineteenth-Century America* (Nashville: Abingdon Press, 1957); J. Edwin Orr, *The Fervent Prayer: The Worldwide Impact of the Great Awakening of 1858* (Chicago: Moody Press, 1974).

[2]*Christian Advocate*, Nashville, September 23, 1858; *Evangelical Christendom*, December 1, 1858, p. 444; *New York Daily Tribune*, March 26, 1858.

[3]For nineteenth-century attribution of the commencement of revivals to the financial panic, see Heman Humphrey, *Revival Sketches and Manual: In Two Parts* (New York: American Tract Society, 1859), p. 276; James W. Alexander, *The Revival and Its Lessons: A Collection of Fugitive Papers, Having Reference to the Great Awakening, 1858* (New York: American Tract Society, 1858), p. 6; *The Christian Times*, Chicago, January 27, 1858; *Cincinnati Daily Gazette*, March 2, 1858; Lyman H. Atwater, "Revivals of the Century," *Presbyterian Quarterly and Princeton Review*, vol. 48 (October, 1876), p. 716. Twentieth-century historians who have argued this position include M. E. Gaddis, "Christian Perfectionism in America" (Unpublished Ph.D. Thesis, University of Chicago, 1929) and most notably William G. McLoughlin, *Revivals, Awakenings and Reform: An Essay on Religion and Social Change in America, 1607–1977* (Chicago: University of Chicago Press, 1978), p. 143, and *Modern Revivalism: Charles Grandison Finney to Billy Graham* (New York: The Ronald Press Company, 1959), p. 163. For the economic collapse itself, see David Morier Evans, *The History of the Commercial Crisis, 1857-58, and the Stock Exchange Panic of 1859* (New York: Burt Franklin, 1969; originally 1859).

[4]Samuel Irenaeus Prime, *The Power of Prayer, Illustrated in the Wonderful Display of Divine Grace at the Fulton Street and Other Meetings in New York and Elsewhere, in 1857 and 1858* (New York: Charles Scribner's Sons, 1858), pp. 14-15; Orr, *Fervent Prayer*, pp. 5-6. The most sophisticated contemporary treatment of the revival can be found in the pages of the *Oberlin Evangelist*, which analyzed eight antecedents to "The Great Revival," the last one of which was the financial distress of 1857. *Oberlin Evangelist*, March 24, 1858, p. 28.

[5]C. Howard Hopkins, *History of the Y.M.C.A. in North America* (New York: Association Press, 1951), pp. 27-28, 81-84; S. Wert Wiley, *A History of the YMCA and Church Relations in the United States* (New York: Association Press, 1944), pp. 8-10.

[6]William C. Conant, *Narratives of Remarkable Conversions and Revival Incidents*, (New York: Derby and Jackson, 1858), p. 358; *Christian Advocate*, Nashville, March 18, 1858; Talbot W. Chambers, *The Noon Prayer Meeting of the North Dutch Church, Fulton Street, New York: Its Origin, Character and Progress, with some of its Results* (New York: Reformed Protestant Dutch Church, 1858).

[7]"General Revival of Religion," *Independent*, March 4, 1858; *Oberlin Evangelist*, April 15, 1857, p. 60; April 29, 1857, p. 68; May 27, 1857, p. 85. For Finney's own assessment of the causes of the American revival, as outlined to a London audience, see *Independent*, May 12, 1858, p. 3. Finney interpreted the commercial panic as an occasion for a revival that had long been brewing, both in prayers and in preparation. This is also the position of Smith, *Revivalism and Social Reform*, p. 62.

[8]The first to champion the Palmers' role in commencing the Union Prayer Meeting Revival were the Palmers themselves, in *The Revival* (September 17, 1859), p. 63. Also see Orr, *Fervent Prayer*, pp. 2-3.

[9]Richard Carwardine, *Transatlantic Revivalism: Popular Evangelicalism in Britain and America, 1790-1865* (Westport, Conn.: Greenwood Press, 1978), pp. 159-197; Orr, *Fervent Prayer*, p. 6.

[10]For the Finneys see Leonard I. Sweet, *The Minister's Wife: Her Role in*

Nineteenth-Century Evangelism (Philadelphia: Temple University Press, 1982). For the Booths see Robert Sandall, *The History of the Salvation Army, Volume 1, 1865–1878* (London: Thomas Nelson and Sons, Ltd., 1947), pp. 7-14 and F. de L. Booth-Tucker, *The Life of Catherine Booth: The Mother of the Salvation Army* (New York: Fleming H. Revell Co., 1892), p. 305, who reveals that Catherine began preaching in public during the 1858 revival. For the Boardmans, and especially for the fact that the ideas of, if not much of the writing for, William Boardman's immensely popular *The Higher Christian Life* (1857) came from his wife, Mary, see Mary Boardman, *Life and Labours of the Rev. W. E. Boardman* (New York: D. Appleton and Company, 1887), pp. 103-105, 108. For the Palmers see Richard Wheatley, *The Life and Letters of Mrs. Phoebe Palmer* (New York: E. C. Palmer, Jr., 1876), pp. 330-345; and Phoebe Palmer, *Promise of the Father: or, A Neglected Specialty of the Last Days. Addressed to the Clergy and Laity of All Christian Communities* (Boston: Henry V. Degen, 1859). For the Roberts, see Adella P. Carpenter, *Ellen Lois Roberts: Life and Writings* (Chicago: Woman's Missionary Society, 1926), pp. 13-14, 54-61, 145; Mariet Hardy Freeland, "Women of Early Free Methodism," *The Free Methodist*, vol. 31 (May 3, 1898), pp. 11-12. One of my students, Keith E. Griswold, has discovered that Ellen Stowe Roberts came under the influence of the Palmers after she moved to New York City in 1839. See Keith E. Griswold, "Women and the Holiness Movement" (unpublished manuscript), p. 17.

[11] For observations about the smaller numbers of children and women converted in this awakening as opposed to previous ones, see *Christian Advocate,* Nashville, March 18, April 1, 1858, and L. F. Bittinger, *Memorials of the Reverend Joseph Baugher Bittinger* (Woodville, N.H.: F. W. Bittinger, 1891), p. 75. For the resentment of women's presence at noonday prayer meetings in New York City and for the surfacing of scratchy sentiments that women should be prohibited from attending those designed for businessmen, see *New York Daily Tribune,* March 9, 1858. Early in the revival women were indeed sometimes excluded from participating in New York City meetings, and those that did brave the opposition sat mainly in the galleries. In Philadelphia, Boston, and Cincinnati, where invitations to attend prayer meetings were not confined to men, the women either held their own prayer meeting for half an hour after the men had left, or else they sponsored their own Female Union Prayer Meetings (see *Cincinnati Daily Gazette,* March 1, 15, 1858). But the available attendance statistics suggest that for the most part either women stayed away in droves, or the sheer numbers of men drove women from their customary seats in church. In Philadelphia's Jayne's Hall, for example, out of an attendance of 2,000 one day, only 500 were women. In New York City's Burton's Theater the percentage of women present fluctuated from 10 percent to 33 percent (*New York Daily Tribune,* March 15, 18, 25, 1858; for similar statistics in another area see *Cincinnati Daily Commercial,* April 10, 1858; *Cincinnati Daily Gazette,* March 12, 1858). The usual percentages were 66 to 75 percent. Although women were occasionally known to speak at the noonday prayer meetings (Conant, *Narratives,* p. 386), vigorous attempts by them to exert leadership roles in the noonday prayer meeting itself were met by opposition. Harriet Olney, dubbed by the press "Screeching Harry," found this out as she made the rounds of New York City's noonday prayer meetings, tried to speak during them, and was thrown out of at least one (*New York Daily Tribune,* March 13, 17, 26, 29, 1858). I have been unable to find any locations for Olney's booklet advertised in New York City newspapers and sold in bookstores for 33¢ entitled "Christian Experience of Harriet Olney" (1858). The booklet was an obvious attempt to use her notoriety from being expelled from the Ninth Street Union Prayer Meeting as a means of gaining attention to

her ministry. Her other publication, *The Old Way of Holiness* (New York, 1857), is reported missing from its only known location, the Library of Congress.

[12] Smith, *Revivalism and Social Reform*, pp. 63-79, 148-162; Timothy L. Smith, *Called Unto Holiness: The Story of the Nazarenes. The Formative Years* (Kansas City, Mo.: Nazarene Publishing House, 1962), p. 11. A similar argument dating from the nineteenth century can be found in James Shaw, *Twelve Years in America:* . . . (Chicago: Poe and Hitchcock, 1867), pp. 172, 184.

[13] McLoughlin, *Revivals, Awakenings and Reform*, pp. 142, 143.

[14] *Ibid.*, p. 143.

[15] Samuel S. Hill, Jr., *The South and the North in American Religion* (Athens, Ga.: The University of Georgia Press, 1980), pp. 60, 73, 47-89. For recent research that stresses similarities between North and South in social, economic, and political structures see Edward Pessen, "How Different from Each Other Were the Antebellum North and South?" *American Historical Review*, vol. 85, no. 15 (December, 1980), pp. 1119-1149.

[16] See Hill's first chapter, "First Cousins Separated, 1795–1810" in *The South and the North*, pp. 13-45.

[17] Quoted by *Oberlin Evangelist*, April 12, 1858, p. 56.

[18] *Christian Advocate*, Nashville, March 18, September 23, 1858.

[19] *Christian Times*, Chicago, April 7, 1858.

[20] H. B. Stowe, "Business Men's Prayer-Meetings," *Independent*, April 8, 1858.

[21] See the sermons by two prominent English clergy and excerpted in *Oberlin Evangelist*, August 4, 1858, p. 138, and December 30, 1858, p. 4.

[22] *Evangelical Christendom*, December 1, 1858.

[23] *Louisville Daily Courier*, April 8, 1858; Heman Humphrey, *Revival Sketches and Manual*, pp. 278-298.

[24] Alexander T. McGill, "The Present Age, the Age of Women." *An Address Before the Literary Societies of Oxford Female College, at their Anniversary June 24, 1858* (Oxford, Ohio: Wrightson & Co., 1858), pp. 17-18. For the question "Can the Union Be Preserved," see *Independent*, February 11, 1858, p. 4.

[25] "The Revival," *Presbyterian Quarterly Review*, vol. 7 (January, 1858), p. 520.

[26] *The New York Pulpit in the Revival of 1858: Sermons by Various Eminent Clergymen* (New York: Sheldon and Company, 1860), p. 290.

[27] *Ibid.*, pp. 25, 26, 15.

[28] *The Christian Times*, Chicago, April 7, 1858; also see February 3, 1858, and John Hall, ed., *Forty Years' Familiar Letters of James Waddell Alexander, . . .* ed. John Hall (New York: Charles Scribner, 1860), vol. 2, p. 237.

[29] For examples of numerous comparisons between the Union Prayer Meeting Revival and the first and second Great Awakenings, to the disadvantages of the latter two, see *The Monthly Religious Magazine and Independent Journal*, vol. 19 (May, 1858), p. 33; *The Christian Times*, Chicago, March 10, April 21, 1858; *New York Daily Tribune*, March 1, 1858; *Christian Advocate*, Nashville, March 18, 1858; *Oberlin Evangelist*, March 17, 1858, p. 24; "The Revival," *Presbyterian Quarterly Review*, vol. 7 (January, 1859), pp. 495-497; *Independent* March 4, 1858. Also see William B. Sprague, *A Sermon Addressed to the Second Presbyterian Congregation, Albany, Sabbath Morning, March 14, 1858, on Occasion of the Death of Mrs. Alexander Marvin* (Albany: Van Benthuysen's Printers, 1858), pp. 28-29.

[30] Charles G. Finney, *Memoirs of Rev. Charles G. Finney* (New York: A. S. Barnes & Co., 1875), p. 444; *Cincinnati Daily Gazette*, March 15, 1858; *Oberlin Evangelist*, March 17, 1858, p. 21.

[31] Warren A. Candler, *Great Revivals and the Great Republic* (Nashville: Publishing House of the M. E. Church, South, 1924), p. 217. Also see Orr, *Fervent Prayer*, pp. 28-33.

[32] A sampling of evidence attesting to the extent of the revival in the South

and West can be found in *The Savannah Daily Republican*, October 4, December 1, 1858; *Louisville Daily Courier*, March 29, April 17, 1858; *Daily Commercial Register*, Sandusky, Ohio, March 24, 25, 30, April 9, 15, 27, 1858; *Evangelical Christendom*, May 17, 1858, pp. 250-252; *Christian Advocate*, New Orleans, April 10, 24, 1858; *Christian Advocate*, Nashville, February 4, March 11, 18, April 1, 8, 15, 22, July 1, September 30, 1858; *Nashville Banner*, March 4, 1858; *Independent*, April 15, 1858, pp. 2-3; *New York Daily Tribune*, March 7, 1858; *The Revival*, August 27, 1859, pp. 37-38; *Cincinnati Daily Gazette*, March 9, 1858; James Shaw, *Twelve Years*, p. 175.

[33] Prime, *Power of Prayer*, p. 47.

[34] *Recollections of a Long Life. An Autobiography* (New York: The Baker and Taylor Company, 1902), p. 332; *Christian Advocate*, Nashville, April 22, September 30, 1858; Bittinger, *Memorials*, p. 75.

[35] *Christian Advocate*, Nashville, February 4, 1858.

[36] For the northern schools, see Conant, *Narratives*, p. 378; *Oberlin Evangelist*, April 28, 1858, pp. 63-64; May 5, 1858, p. 67; *New York Daily Tribune*, March 16, 1858; *National Daily Intelligencer*, Washington, March 23, 1858; *Evangelical Christendom*, November 1, 1858, pp. 794-796; and a handwritten prayer request found in the Bible of Helen Peabody, principal of Western Female Seminary, in the Western College Alumni Association Archives, Oxford, Ohio. For southern schools see *Evangelical Repository*, June, 1858, pp. 31-32; *The Evangelist*, April 29, 1858, p. 6; *Christian Advocate*, Nashville, April 5, 15, May 6, 1858; *Independent*, February 17, 1858, p. 2; Hopkins, *History of YMCA*, p. 38; Orr, *Fervent Prayer*, pp. 11-12.

[37] *Oberlin Evangelist*, March 17, 1858, p. 21; Humphrey, *Revival Sketches*, p. 281.

[38] Smith, *Revivalism and Social Reform*, p. 67. For an account of how the revival touched a rural Baptist church in New Jersey, see John R. Murphy, *Memoir of Rev. James M. Challis* (Philadelphia, 1870), pp. 214-216.

[39] *National Daily Intelligencer*, Washington, March 23, 1858; *New York Daily Tribune*, March 26, 1858.

[40] *National Daily Intelligencer*, Washington, August 23, 1858.

[41] Conant, *Narratives*, pp. 374-377.

[42] See, for example, "The General Assembly of 1858," *Presbyterian Quarterly Review*, vol. 7 (July, 1858), pp. 100-101.

[43] The methods they adopted included issuing a pastoral letter, directing pastors to "preach up" the revival, initiating community visitations by pastors and elders, and prayer. See *Oberlin Evangelist*, November 11, 1857, p. 182; December 22, 1857, p. 204; January 6, 1858, pp. 5-6. Timothy Smith accents the role of the churches over other agencies in *Revivalism and Social Reform*, pp. 63-67.

[44] *Christian Advocate*, Nashville, March 19, April 22, 1858; *Christian Advocate*, New Orleans, April 10, 1858; *Cincinnati Daily Commerical*, March 22, 1858; *New York Daily Tribune*, March 1, 6, 1858. For the dispute over whether heightened religious interest in San Francisco was sufficient to call it a revival, see *Independent*, June 2, 1859, p. 2 and May 12, 1859, p. 3.

[45] *New York Daily Tribune*, March 24, 1858; Hopkins, *History of YMCA*, pp. 68-69; Frank E. Sickels, *Fifty Years of the YMCA of Buffalo* (Buffalo: The Association, 1902), p. 31.

[46] *Christian Advocate*, Nashville, March 18, 1858; Conant, *Narratives*, p. 399.

[47] Quoted in Hopkins, *History of YMCA*, p. 83.

[48] See the *National Daily Intelligencer*, Washington, April 6, 1858, which every Tuesday published the week's schedule and sites for union prayer meetings. Also see *Savannah Daily Republican*, December 1, 1858.

[49] See as an example the *Cincinnati Daily Commercial*, March 1, 4, 5, 1858. There are no known copies of the April 3, 1858 *Tribune* "Extra."

50 Harvey Newcomb, *The Harvest and the Reapers: Home-Work for All, and How to Do It* (Boston: Bould and Lincoln, 1858), p. iv.

51 Talbot W. Chambers, *Noon Prayer Meeting; New York Pulpit*, p. xi.

52 John Hall, ed., *Letters of James Waddell Alexander*, vol. 2, p. 277; *Christian Advocate*, New Orleans, April 10, 1858; *National Daily Intelligencer*, Washington, March 20, 1858.

53 Chambers, *Noon Prayer Meeting*, pp. 41, 49-57, 66, 135; Conant, *Narratives*, pp. 390-391.

54 Prime, *The Power of Prayer*, p. 47. See also the announcement that "the Religious Awakening" was prevalent "among all classes of community here" in the *New York Daily Tribune*, March 1, 1858.

55 *The Presbyterian Magazine*, vol. 8 (June, 1858), pp. 249-250. A description of a Jayne's Hall prayer meeting for sailors can be found in *The Christian Instructor*, vol. 15 (May, 1859), pp. 200-201.

56 *Evangelical Christendom*, August 1, 1858, p. 287; Conant, *Narratives*, pp. 278, 401, 407; Also see *Louisville Daily Courier*, April 1, 7, 13, 24, 1858; *National Daily Intelligencer*, Washington, March 1, 11, 1858.

57 James W. Alexander, *The Revival*, pp. 213-219.

58 *Cincinnati Daily Commercial*, March 31, 1858. Fire companies were voluntary associations that had deteriorated into unruly, riotous, drinking havens for adult delinquents and were feared as almost as dangerous to the public safety as the fires they put out. See *Evangelical Christendom*, June 1, August 1, 1858, pp. 212, 214, 287.

59 *Evangelical Christendom*, June 1, November 1, 1858, pp. 212, 396. The Cincinnati YMCA also purchased a tent and pitched it on the lot adjoining the Orphan Asylum. See *Cincinnati Daily Gazette*, June 26, 1858. For the "Flying Artillery," which was composed of thirty to forty Methodist laymen who fanned out across New York City and conducted services, see *New York Daily Tribune*, March 7, 1858.

60 See the treatment of Episcopalian involvement in *Cincinnati Daily Gazette*, June 19, 1858.

61 *The Monthly Religious Magazine and Independent Journal*, vol. 19 (May 1858), pp. 326-341, 337, 348; Frederic Dan Huntington, *Permanent Realities of Religion and the Present Religious Interest* (Boston: Gould and Lincoln, 1858), pp. 39-40; Arria S. Huntington, *Memoir and Letters of Frederic Dan Huntington, First Bishop of Central New York* (Boston: Houghton Mifflin and Company, 1906), pp. 134, 136-137. Also see *New York Daily Tribune*, March 11, 15, 1858; Conant, *Narratives*, p. 377; *Oberlin Evangelist*, 1858, April 21, p. 51; *National Daily Intelligencer*, Washington, March 30, 1858; *Cincinnati Daily Gazette*, March 10, 30, 1858. See also Smith, *Revivalism and Social Reform*, pp. 69-70, 95-102.

62 *Christian Advocate*, Nashville, April 1, 1858; Conant, *Narratives*, p. 411; *The Revival*, February 25, 1860, p. 63. Accordiing to the *Cincinnati Daily Commercial*, March 31, 1858, "The revival has extended to the sect of Papal power itself." American and European travelers to Rome, visiting chapels and cathedrals, returned home to tell of conversion experiences. For further information on Father Chiniquy's subsequent career as a Presbyterian and the problems of his KanKahee mission with the church hierarchy, see two scrapbooks on Chiniquy in the Presbyterian Historical Society and Charles Chiniquy, *Forty Years in the Church of Christ* (Old Tappan, N.J.: Fleming H. Revell Company, 1900).

63 Prime, *Power of Prayer*, pp. 107-108.

64 *The Revival*, October 29, 1859, pp. 106.

65 "The Revival," *Presbyterian Quarterly Review*, vol. 7 (January, 1859), p. 510.

66 Conant, *Narratives*, pp. 382-383.

[67] *New York Pulpit* (1860); also see *The Times*, London, September 23, 1859, p. 7.

[68] Conant, *Narratives*, p. 416.

[69] *New York Daily Tribune*, February 10, 1858. For a remarkably ecumenical definition of "union" that went beyond the bounds of devotional and benevolent exercises and stalked instead the inner corridors of sacramental and ministerial issues, see Henry A. Boardman, *Christian Union: A Sermon Preached in the Tenth Presbyterian Church, Philadelphia, on Sunday Evening, November 27, 1859* (Philadelphia: William S. and Alfred Martien, 1859).

[70] *Evangelical Repository*, vol. 17 (June, 1858), p.33; *Sing Praises—the Revival and Its Lessons: No. VIII* (New York: A. D. F. Randolph, 1858).

[71] *The Daily Commercial Register*, Sandusky, Ohio, April 15, 1858.

[72] *Cincinnati Daily Commercial*, March 27, 1858; Chambers, *Noon Prayer Meeting*, p. 244.

[73] *Evangelical Christendom*, September 1, 1858, p. 322.

[74] In less than three minutes, one hundred prayer requests were presented by one congregation. See "The Revival," *Presbyterian Quarterly Review*, vol. 7 (January, 1859), p. 514. For a detailed account of a liturgy, see "An Hour in the Noon-day Prayer Meeting," *The Christian Instructor*, vol. 15 (April, 1859), pp. 55-56.

[75] *Oberlin Evangelist*, March 24, 1858, p. 31.

[76] Theodore Tebbets, "Revivals, Past and Present," *The Monthly Religious Magazine and Independent Journal*, vol. 19 (May, 1858), pp. 333-334.

[77] Chambers, *Noon Prayer Meeting*, pp. 49-57, 65, 88; Prime, *Power of Prayer*, p. 170; *Christian Advocate*, Nashville, April 22, 1858.

[78] *The Christian Instructor*, vol. 14 (June, 1858) p. 281.; Conant, *Narratives*, pp. 399-400.

[79] Rufus W. Clark, *The Atlantic Telegraph. A Discourse, Preached in the South Congregational Church, Brooklyn, September 5, 1858* (New York: Sheldon, Blakeman & Co., 1858), pp. 5, 7, 16.

[80] C. Van Rensselaer, "Signals from the Atlantic Cable," *The Presbyterian Magazine*, vol. 8 (October, 1858), pp. 442-446. Also see William B. Sprague, *A Sermon Addressed to the Second Presbyterian Congregation, Albany, on Sunday Morning, September 5, 1858, on the Completion of the Atlantic Telegraph* (Albany: Charles Van Benthuysen, 1858), pp. 20, 23, 28-29.

[81] Conant, *Narratives*, pp. 395, 413. For the printing of an exchange between the John Street and Jayne's Hall Union Prayer Meetings, see *Oberlin Evangelist*, March 24, 1858, p. 27.

[82] *New York Daily Tribune*, March 27, 1858.

[83] *Evangelical Christendom*, May 1, 1858, pp. 176-178; Conant, *Narratives*, p. 396; *New York Daily Tribune*, March 5, 1858.

[84] *New York Daily Tribune* even listed the hymns to be sung in concert for the following week. See, e.g., *New York Daily Tribune*, March 26, 1858; Conant, *Narratives*, p. 396.

[85] Conant, *Narratives*, p. 381; Chambers, *Noon Prayer Meeting*, p. 47.

[86] *New York Daily Tribune*, March 27, 29, 1858. Also see the March 27 issue for a letter from a black New York City resident who describes how blacks who tried to attend the North Dutch Church noonday prayer meeting were shunted up to the third floor where, they were told, "the colored folks had their prayer meeting."

[87] *Oberlin Evangelist*, January 21, 1857, p. 12.

[88] *Louisiana Courier*, March 10, 1858; *Christian Advocate*, New Orleans, April 3, 24, 1858; also *Louisville Daily Courier*, April 6, 1858.

[89] This is a comment from Rest Fenner of Lewisburg University in *Evangelical Christendom*, February 1, 1861, pp. 93-95.

[90] McLoughlin, *Revivals, Awakenings and Social Reform*, pp. 142-143; Smith, *Revivalism and Social Reform*, pp. 148-162.

[91] *The Revival and Its Lessons: No. VII. My Teacher—My Master* (New York: A. D. F. Randolph, 1858), pp. 9-10. For the addition of temperance to the ethics of holiness, see John Kent, *Holding the Fort: Studies in Victorian Revivalism* (London: Epworth Press, 1978), p. 317.

[92] Melvin Easterday Dieter, *The Holiness Revival of the Nineteenth Century* (Metuchen, N.J.: The Scarecrow Press, 1980). See also Smith, *Revivalism and Social Reform*, pp. 135-147, for popularity of holiness sentiments in the late antebellum North.

[93] *New York Pulpit*, p. 200.

[94] *Christian Advocate*, New Orleans, April 3, 1858. For the social goals and strategies generated by the revival, see Prime, *Power of Prayer*, p. 41; *National Daily Intelligencer*, Washington, March 20, 26, 1858; *New York Pulpit*, p. 104; Conant, *Narratives*, pp. 412, 425-426; *Savannah Daily Republican*, July 15, 1858; Hall, ed., *Forty Years*, vol. 2, p. 277; *The Evangelist*, April 29, 1859; *Louisville Daily Courier*, March 30, 1858.

[95] Samuel S. Hill, Jr., *The South and the North*, p. 65.

[96] *Oberlin Evangelist*, May 12, 1858, p. 78.

[97] "The Revival," *Presbyterian Quarterly Review*, vol. 7 (January, 1859), p. 509.

[98] "The Religious Awakening," *The Christian Instructor*, vol. 15 (January, 1859), pp. 31-32.

[99] *The Evangelist*, June 10, 1858; *New York Pulpit*, pp. 57, 330-358.

[100] Harriet Beecher Stowe, "Fruits of the Revival," *Independent*, July 8, 1858. For a reprint of Stowe's earlier article, see *Cincinnati Daily Gazette*, March 15, 1858.

[101] Quoted in Hopkins, *History of YMCA*, p. 47.

[102] *New York Daily Tribune*, March 27, 1858.

[103] *Ibid.*, March 25, 1858.

[104] *The Revival*, August 27, 1859, pp. 37-38. Payson argued that such reports were "works of the devil" who found intolerable such rich fruits of the revival as masses coming to love Christ and masses going to serve Christ's cause.

[105] This created some controversy because, upon their requests for certificates of withdrawal, Dr. Cheever refused to dismiss them "in good standing" and the forty-eight refused to accept certificates issued any other way. See *Independent*, March 24, 1859, p. 4; *Cincinnati Daily Gazette*, June 19, 1858.

[106] *Independent*, March 4, 1858; *New York Daily Tribune*, March 5, 1858. For another periodical that argued that the verdict was still out on the penetration of the spirit of the union meetings into the "common intercourse" of the nation, see "The Revival," *Presbyterian Quarterly Review*, vol. 7 (January, 1859), p. 52.

[107] *Oberlin Evangelist*, March 17, 1858, p. 21.

[108] *Independent*, April 29, 1858, p.3; *Daily Commercial Register*, Sandusky, Ohio, March 25, 30, 1858; *Evangelical Christendom*, May 17, 1858, p. 252 and May 1, 1860, p. 277; Conant, *Narratives*, pp. 369, 375; Orr, *Fervent Prayer*, p. 19.

[109] Quoted in *The Revival*, December 17, 1859, p. 165.

[110] "The Revival," *Presbyterian Quarterly Review*, vol. 7 (January, 1858), pp. 516-517.

[111] *Evangelical Christendom*, November 1, 1859, p. 440; May 1, 1860, p. 277; February 1, 1861, p. 94. "The Religious Awakening," *The Christian Instructor*, vol. 15 (March, 1859), p. 132; *The Revival*, August 4, 1860, p. 39.

[112] *The Revival*, March 17, April 14, 1860, pp. 81, 118.

[113] J. William Jones, *Christ in the Camp: or, the Religion in Lee's Army* (Richmond,

Va.: B. F. Johnson and Company, 1888), p. 264; Warren A. Candler, *Great Revivals*, p. 217.

[114]See, for example, the Nashville *Christian Advocate*'s dropping in late October, 1858, of its section on "Revival Intelligence" and its replacement by "News from the Churches." *Christian Advocate*, Nashville, October 7, 1858; January 6, 27, 1859.

[115]Herman Norton, *Rebel Religion: The Story of Confederate Chaplains* (St. Louis, Mo.: The Bethany Press, 1961); Charles F. Pitts, *Chaplains in Gray, The Confederate Chaplains' Story* (Nashville: Broadman Press, 1957).

[116]Pitts, *Chaplains in Gray*, p. 115; Norton, *Rebel Religion*, pp., 42-53, 64-65; William W. Bennett, *A Narrative of the Great Revival Which Prevailed in the Southern Armies During the Late Civil War Between the States of the Federal Union* (Harrisonburg, Va.: Sprinkle Publications, 1976; originally 1876). pp. 16, 21, *passim; Evangelical Christendom*, August 1, 1861, p. 502.

[117]Lemuel Moss, *Annals of the United States Christian Commission* (Philadelphia: J. B. Lippincott, 1868), p. 14.

[118]*The Revival*, June 1, 8, 1861, pp. 171, 179; September 28, 1861, p. 98.

[119]*A Memorial Record of the New York Branch of the United States Christian Commission* (New York: John A. Gray and Green, 1866), p. 67; Smith, *Revivalism and Social Reform*, p. 76; Frank Milton Bristol, *The Life of Chaplain McCabe: Bishop of the Methodist Episcopal Church* (New York: Eaton and Mains, © by Fleming H. Revell, 1908), p. 146.

[120]Charles Reagan Wilson, *Baptized in Blood: The Religion of the Lost Cause, 1865-1920* (Athens, Ga.: University of Georgia Press, 1980), pp. 119-138.

[121]J. William Jones, "The Morale of the Confederate Armies," in *Confederate Military History*. ed. Clement A. Evans (Atlanta, Ga.: Confederate Publishing Company, 1899), vol. 12, p. 169; *United States Christian Commission. Third Report of the Committee of Maryland* (Baltimore: James Young, 1864), pp. 109, 246.

[122]William W. Lyle, *Lights and Shadows of Army Life: Or, Pen Pictures from the Battlefield, the Camp and the Hospital* (Cincinnati: R. W. Carroll, 1865), p. 32; General John B. Gordon, *Reminiscences of the Civil War* (New York: Charles Scribner's Sons, 1904), p. 416; Jones, "Morale of Confederate Armies," pp. 159, 167-168.

[123]Jones, *Christ in Camp*, pp. 93, 96-97, 293, 299, 304; J. B. McFerrin, "Religion in the Army of Tennessee," *The Home Monthly*, vol. 4 (April, 1868), p. 27; Pitts, *Chaplains in Gray*, p. 55; Gordon, *Reminiscences*, p. 417; Lyle, *Lights and Shadows*, p. 35.

[124]Gordon, *Reminiscences*, p. 230.

[125]Wilson, *Baptized in Blood*, pp. 6-7.

The Dilemmas of
Historical Consciousness:
The Case of Augustus H. Strong

Grant Wacker

I

From time to time Winthrop S. Hudson's *Religion in America* has been described by well-meaning reviewers as the culmination of the environmentalist interpretation of American religious history—an interpretation associated with scholars like William Warren Sweet, Peter Mode, and, off on the horizon, Frederick Jackson Turner. This is distinguished company to keep, but the characterization is far from the mark. A close reading of *Religion in America* reveals that it is a sustained refutation of the notion of American exceptionalism. The confusion arises, perhaps, because Professor Hudson works with a narrow brush and a gentle touch. His style is to evoke perceptions rather than parade them. Both of these traits—the sure sense of context and the artistry of concealed erudition—are evident, I think, in his terse profile of Augustus H. Strong, a once important but now largely forgotten actor in the fundamentalist controversy.

Like P. T. Forsyth in Britain and Martin Kähler in Germany, in Hudson's view Strong is best understood as a mediator who stood between modernists on one side and evangelicals and fundamentalists on the other. For Strong the central issue was not doctrine but authority. Persuaded that modern scholarship had proved that the old foundation, infallible Scripture, is, in fact, honeycombed with historical and scientific errors, Strong discerned that the most urgent task confronting the church was not to defend the credibility of the historic creeds, and certainly not to get embroiled in peripheral disputes about premillennialism and evolution. The task, rather, was to show that there was an authoritative foundation on which orthodox belief could be based.[1]

I once commented to Professor Hudson that I thought his treatment of Strong was highly perceptive. He protested (with characteristic diffidence) that he had never "looked at Strong all that much." I doubt that, but even if it were true, he had certainly "looked at" the right things, for the problem of finding and defending objective sanctions for religious belief in a post-Kantian world haunted Strong throughout the later years of his life. And not Strong alone. Thoughtful persons on both sides of the Atlantic wrestled with the same problem in very much the same way at least two decades before the Protestant world heard God speak with a Swiss accent.

II

Historical consciousness means different things to different persons. I use the term to refer to two closely related convictions that gained ascendency among advanced social thinkers in the United States and Europe in the closing years of the nineteenth century. The first was that history is the workshop in which society and culture are forged. This meant that everything that human beings think and feel and do is profoundly conditioned by their historical setting. The second conviction was that history changes continuously without regard to supramundane laws of direction. This meant that it is not a process of development, but simply process. There were scholars who worked in the humanities and the behavioral sciences who resisted this unflinchingly relativistic understanding of the nature and meaning of history. But not many. By 1930 historical consciousness in its most radical form had come to be the hallmark of the modern mind.[2]

It is difficult to overestimate the impact that the growth of historical consciousness exerted upon religious thought in the West. It could be argued that late nineteenth-century Protestant liberalism was effectively defined by its sympathetic response to the historical understanding of culture. Liberals made their peace with the modern world in various ways, but in the end they all insisted that God's self-revelation is mediated through the flow of history.[3] Protestant conservatives, on the other hand, invariably claimed that part of God's self-revelation escapes the grip of historical conditioning. Saving knowledge of divine things is given directly, unmediated, and uncontaminated by the context in which it is received. For the conservative this meant that revelation is subject to clarification but not development. It also meant that the biblical writers were essentially ahistorical, in crucial respects unconditioned by the setting of their lives in the Mediterranean world. Indeed, the insistence that the method and the content of revelation are not significantly affected by the particularities of time and place

224

was and continues to be one of the defining features of fundamentalism.[4]

The story is, however, more complicated than this. Often at the level of ordinary faith and practice, and occasionally at the level of self-conscious reflection, we find individuals who were torn between the historically informed world of Protestant liberalism and the ahistorical world of Protestant conservatism. They knew they could not ignore the historicist critique of all formal systems of thought, but refused to give up the quiet certitudes of the old-time religion. This deep-seated ambivalence about the ground rules of religious belief seems to have driven many Protestants to reach for modernity but never quite to embrace it. The dilemma is well illustrated by the twists and turns in the theological pilgrimage of Augustus H. Strong.

For forty years, from 1872 to 1912, Strong was president of Rochester Theological Seminary and, at one time or another, president of every major Baptist organization in the North. His *Systematic Theology* was possibly the most widely used theology textbook in America; it went through eight editions, and the eighth edition is now in its thirtieth printing. Strong could be dubbed the father of the University of Chicago, for it was he who relentlessly pressured John D. Rockefeller to establish a university principally devoted to graduate studies and advanced research. Clearly he was the most visible Baptist and one of the most influential theologians in America at the turn of the century—even though he is now an almost entirely forgotten heirloom of our religious past.[5]

Strong has been a perennial puzzle. His personality did not lend itself to clear-cut characterization, nor did any other aspect of his life. Those who knew him described him as an autocratic though lovable tyrant-father. He hired for the Rochester faculty leading liberals such as Conrad Henry Moehlman, Cornelius Woelfkin, and Walter Rauschenbusch. He also hired rock-ribbed traditionalists like Howard Osgood and Albert Henry Newman. He vigorously defended Rauschenbusch's right to assail the capitalist system and just as vigorously solicited great sums of money from Rockefeller and other "robber barons." George Burman Foster, possibly the most radical Baptist theologian of the era, was known as one of his "boys." J. Whitcomb Brougher, a major force in the fundamentalist confrontation that scarred the last years of Strong's life, was also known as one of his "boys." In 1917 Rauschenbusch affectionately dedicated his *Theology for the Social Gospel* to Strong. A few years later Ernest Gordon, in *The Leaven of the Sadducees,* a biting attack on theological liberalism, upheld Strong's work as the standard that persons like Rauschenbusch had grievously betrayed.[6]

225

It is little wonder, then, that Strong has puzzled historians—or perhaps it is more accurate to say that historians have persistently differed among themselves about where he should be pegged on the theological map. Some have called him a closet liberal, some have called him a wavering fundamentalist, and some have suggested that he was simply befuddled.[7]

To some extent this difference of judgment arises because there appeared to be distinct phases in his unusually long career. Many of Strong's contemporaries believed that he took a step to the left in the 1890s, followed by two steps to the right just before his death in the 1920s.[8] Perhaps so, but this does not solve the problem of understanding Strong, for the doubleness that he manifested can be seen at almost any point in his life. He bears an uncanny resemblance to the Giant Pooka in Mary Chase's *Harvey*, who appeared "here and there, now and then, to this one and that one at his own caprice." And this is what leads us to suspect that the difficulty is rooted somewhere beneath the surface.

The problem is, in short, suppositional rather than substantive. It lies at the starting point of his thought, in his assumptions about the sources of religious knowledge. The difficulty is not—or at least not principally—an inconsistency embedded in his concrete doctrinal formulations, which were progressive but by contemporary standards acceptably orthodox throughout his life. Another way of putting it is to say that Strong's conception of the origin of religious knowledge, and more precisely, his understanding of the role of history in the formation of knowledge, was the variable. As the years passed, he became increasingly conscious of the historical character of all things human, but at the same time he clung to the conviction that the faith once delivered unto the saints somehow stands above the vicissitudes of history.

III

The split between traditional and modern ways of conceiving the sources of religious knowledge runs like a fault line through Strong's collected writings. His mature understanding of the revelatory values in history—or differently put, the knowledge of the divine that is disclosed in the flow of ordinary events—is one of the places where this subterranean stress is particularly evident. Here his thinking displayed—depending upon his mood and audience—at least three facets.

The first was an insistence, formidably argued in his more strictly metaphysical writings, that the created universe *is* Christ, the Logos, and that Christ's manner of self-expression is intrinsically historical and developmental.

All reason and conscience, all science and philosophy, all civilization and education, all society and government, in short, all the wheels by which the world moves forward toward its goal have a living spirit within the wheels, and that living spirit is Christ.[9]

The Christological reality that animates the created universe, moreover, is the essence of the evolutionary process. "It would seem to follow by logical necessity," said Strong, "that Christ is the principle of evolution. Why can there be an evolution that is rational, useful, progressive, and that combines general uniformity with occasional unique advances? John's Gospel gives us the answer, 'That which hath come into being *was life in him.*'"[10]

The historical and developmental nature of Christ's self-expression in the world was the basis of Strong's conviction that history is continually charged with pulsations of creative energy from fountains deep within itself. The universe is not a plenum, not a block universe; rather it is a "plastic organism to which new impulses can be imparted from [Christ] whose thought and will it is an expression of. . . . Though these impulses come from within, they come not from the finite mechanism, but from the immanent God." These continual increments of divine force in the historical process mean that "through all there runs one continuous plan, and upon this all the rationality of evolution depends."[11]

The second facet of Strong's understanding of the way that history reveals the divine can be described as an expression of what William R. Hutchison has called the modernist impulse in American Protestantism. No prophet of the religion of humanity applauded the spirit of the age more vigorously than Strong. This blossoming of the modernist impulse in a man who never suffered serious doubts about the veracity of the ancient creeds—indeed, in a man who lined up squarely with the fundamentalists in the last gunfight of his career—is one of the most interesting twists in the history of American evangelicalism.[12]

Strong's roundhouse embrace of modernity was really a rollicking affirmation of progress. "Through all our modern literature and life," he asserted, "Christ is working, gradually making all things new." He saw this regenerative process preeminently in the growth of learning: the process of science and philosophy, which Christians often fear, "may be only the form of Christ coming to us . . . to rescue us." He also saw it in the expansion of the church and, still more significantly, in the "great efforts outside the church to improve government, to right social wrongs, to diffuse the spirit of kindness between employers and employed." It was an exhilarating vision.

> [Christ] is moralizing the nations, giving a new sense of commu-
> nity, increasing sympathy with the wronged and oppressed, bring-
> ing the classes and the masses together, educating the race, and
> preparing the way for freedom and true religion.[13]

This modernist impulse is ordinarily associated with liberals or
humanists like Lyman Abbott or John Fiske or Octavius Frothing-
ham, but none of these outdid the conservative Strong. "Of all days
since man trod this planet," he declared, "this is the greatest day!"
And precisely because Christ is at the "heart of the universe," the
church must come to grips with the normative power of contemporary culture. It read like a manifesto from Schleiermacher's *Speeches to the Cultured Despisers of Religion.*

> Christianity must take possession of all the culture of the world,
> or she must utterly give up claim to be divine. She must appropriate
> and disseminate all knowledge, or she must confess that she is the
> child of ignorance and fanaticism. She must conquer all good
> learning, or she must herself be conquered.

Thus, as Strong saw it, modernism is not an option. It is an obligation because the "impulse to this revision is *itself* divine; an
impulse from Christ himself." To resist the modernist yearning, in
other words, is to resist Christ. To fail to see Christ "in the whole
continuous process of history . . . [is] to substitute a sort of half-
atheism for real theism."[14]

This leads to the third facet of Strong's conception of the revelatory values disclosed in the flow of history. The first two facets—
his insistence upon the developmental, evolutionary nature of the
process and his affirmation of the modernist impulse—were clear
windows letting in the light of contemporary social thought. But
the third facet, to switch the metaphor, was an abiding conviction
that the onward, upward rush of history carries within it an old-
fashioned gospel whose truth never changes.

Even in the most progressive period of his life Strong growled a
good deal about "professedly Christian teachers who so emphasized
the element of change in the history of doctrine that all permanence
is virtually denied." For these teachers there is "no such thing as
objective truth. Ethical and religious doctrine are impossible, because both are in constant flux. Even Christ and Christianity are
held to be merely temporary phases of evolution, and both may be
outgrown." He brought down the ax: "Mistaken evolutionism," by
which he seems to have meant what I have called historical consciousness, is not only "bad theology," but also "bad metaphysics,
bad ethics."[15]

Strong was certain that "mistaken evolutionism" ensnared its
victims in the same metaphysical trap that had undone the Heraclitic
philosophers. "Becoming [cannot] be observed, unless there is an

228

abiding intelligence in the observer; only when I stand on the rock apart from the stream can I see the rush of the water flowing by." In human consciousness, in short, "we find something abiding . . . a personal identity, which subsists through change and in spite of change." He summed up his objections with the judgment that the very conception of change, if the change is not capricious and useless, implies a law behind the phenomena.[16]

"Mistaken evolutionism" issues in bad ethics as well. He insisted that it is senseless to say that the consequence of an act is right or wrong unless one recognizes that rightness or wrongness, as such, is a formal concept one brings to experience, rather than a conclusion one draws from experience. "Belief in the existence of objective right is born with us, even though our conceptions of what is right may change." Ethics of this sort, he added a bit triumphantly, is "like the play of Hamlet with the part of Hamlet left out."[17]

So there it was. A fully developed historical consciousness never had a fighting chance in Strong's world. He could write and preach with ringing eloquence about the evolutionary Christ who informs and suffuses contemporary culture with his presence. Yet underneath it all, or intertwined with it all, is the timeless and unconditioned reality that transcends the process of history. All things, "matter and mind, man and God, have underground connections . . . because all things . . . have their being in God."[18] In a way it was a theological Catch-22. At a certain point in the analysis the historical always and necessarily gave way to the eternal. Here and there Strong could easily afford to meet the new theologians more than halfway because he never believed that history is the ultimate category of understanding. "We mark the passage of time, and we write our histories," he noted near the end of his life. "But we can do this only because in our highest being we do not belong to space and time, but have in us a bit of eternity."[19]

In retrospect, it is evident that ambivalence or doubleness of this sort characterized all of Strong's mature thinking about history as the medium of religious knowledge. The relationship between history and revelation was never systematically worked out, much less harmonized. He insisted that society and culture represent the ever-unfolding self-expression of the Logos. He boldly affirmed the normativeness of the central values of modern life. Yet both of these claims were pitted against a more fundamental claim. In the final reckoning, he always seemed to say that history is only a shallow stream rippling across the bedrock of God's unchanging truth.

229

IV

Strong's position was hardly consistent, but in the late nineteenth century this was not unusual. Most of the New Theologians were trying as vigorously as he to find the eternal in the midst of the historical.[20] There was a big difference, though. Strong was determined to identify the fixed and changeless truths that could be discerned in the flow of history, not with moral values, as the New Theologians sought to do, but with the historic doctrines of Protestant orthodoxy. But here Strong had boxed himself into a corner; for a modern, historically informed understanding of the origin and nature of religious knowledge was the basis on which he tried to erect essentially metaphysical—or, at the least, radically ahistorical—doctrinal affirmations about the deity, preexistence, incarnation, virgin birth, miracles, vicarious atonement, resurrection, and second coming of Christ.[21]

The problem became increasingly acute as Strong grew older. He made more and more significant concessions to the historical understanding of culture but at the same time refused to modify a doctrinal edifice originally built on very different assumptions. The coupling of liberal epistemology and orthodox creed, in short, meant that his theological system offered something for everybody. But at a stiff price. After his death his name would be piously invoked by all factions in the modernist-fundamentalist controversy in the Northern Baptist Convention, but his most creative contribution—*Christ in Creation and Ethical Monism*—would soon be forgotten, eclipsed by the ponderous and antiquated volumes of the *Systematic Theology*.[22]

Strong's dilemma was not unique. There were many so-called fundamentalists in the Northern Baptist Convention—men like Curtis Lee Laws and Frank M. Goodchild and Frederick Anderson—who were powerfully attracted to the governing assumptions of contemporary social thought. E. Y. Mullins, Strong's close friend and president of Southern Baptist Theological Seminary, appears to have wrestled with the same issue in pretty much the same way. This was true of George Frederick Wright at Oberlin and perhaps of Robert Speer as well. On the other side of the fence, ranking liberals like David Swing, William Newton Clarke, and Charles Augustus Briggs similarly struggled to make a place for orthodox doctrine in a historically conditioned view of the world.[23]

230   Among intellectuals in Western Europe historical consciousness dawned at least a generation earlier than in the United States, and its impact seems to have been deeper and sharper. Some German theologians like Isaac Dorner and Adolf Schlatter grappled quite explicitly with the problems that historical awareness posed for orthodox belief, but in England the issues were debated in a manner that seems to have resembled the American situation especially closely.[24]

This is not surprising. Professor Hudson and other scholars have shown that throughout the nineteenth century British and American evangelicalism were densely intertwined. Names like John Nelson Darby, Charles Haddon Spurgeon, and Keswick holiness are integral to American evangelical history, while Hannah Whitall Smith, D. L. Moody, and the Scofield Reference Bible are just as integral to the British story.[25] Nonetheless, George Marsden has persuasively argued that by the early twentieth century there were significant differences of style. In the United States liberal and conservative tendencies within the old evangelical consensus tended to polarize into sharply defined modernist and fundamentalist factions. In Britain there appears to have been less polarization and fewer confrontations. This may have been due to the fact that American evangelicals, especially at Princeton, were more intellectually vigorous. It also may have been due to the fact that Romanticism had deeper roots in Britain, thus cushioning the blows of Darwinism, higher criticism, and idealist immanentism.[26] Whatever the reason, British evangelicalism did not spawn a fundamentalist movement of comparable aggressiveness, size, or cultural influence until later in the century.[27]

By and large the attempt to weld ancient conclusions into modern assumptions was carried off more gracefully by British evangelicals than American ones. Perhaps it was because they were less bitterly divided. In any event, Anglican Aubrey Moore, Presbyterian James Orr, and Primitive Methodist A. S. Peake readily come to mind as essentially orthodox men who struggled to come to terms with the historical revolution of the nineteenth century.[28] W. Robertson Smith, another Presbyterian clergyman and one of the most distinguished Old Testament scholars of the century, also readily comes to mind—but as an essentially modern man who struggled to preserve the ahistorical uniqueness of Christianity. There is a special poignancy in Smith's lament that Princeton's Charles Hodge simply "has no conception of the modern form of the problem."[29]

Hodge did not, but P. T. Forsyth did—and more clearly than anyone else on either side of the Atlantic. In many ways Forsyth, who was Congregational, resembled Strong. Both were known for intimidating erudition; both were, at heart, impassioned preachers; both died in 1921. And like Strong, Forsyth knew that the historical, contextual, and evolutionary understanding of society and of Scripture could not be dismissed with a dogmatic snort about the infallibility of the Bible. Charging that the "doctrine of plenary verbal inspiration and inerrancy" was its own best refutation, he urged the church to "reduce the burden of belief," to acknowledge frankly that some creedal inheritances are more important—much more important—than others, to see that it is better to have "a few mighty cohesive truths which capture, fire, and mould the whole soul . . . than a correct conspectus of the total area of divine knowledge." The goal, in short, is to forge "a minimal creed, an ample science, a maximal faith."[30]

Yet Forsyth also insisted that the assumptions underlying the modern world view are deceptively lethal.

> It is all over with truth when man feels himself its creator. . . . Reality gives way under our feet, and standards vanish like stars falling from heaven. . . . Man becomes his own maker and he has a moral fool for his product. . . . Thought . . . commits suicide, and mankind evolves over an abyss.

He believed that the New Theology—"religion of the breezy sort"— had largely capitulated to these assumptions. Relevance had been purchased at the price of "shallow happiness . . . endless ennui and fatted death."[31]

In Forsyth's mind personal and cultural salvation lies in the recognition that "natural process does not carry with it its own explanation or reveal its own goal." The fundamental truth about history is God's invasion of history in Christ. In Christ we have a "foothold in the Eternal." With due concessions to the "historical treatment of His religious environment," Forsyth insisted, the "connexion between [Christ] and His antecedents is not causal, but teleological. History, indeed, does not give destiny, but in Christ destiny is given in the midst of history, by the way of history, and under historic conditions."[32]

V

Brian Gerrish has proposed that the effort to relate tradition to the modern world has been a central stimulus underlying creative Protestant theology since the sixteenth century.[33] The attempt by Strong and Forsyth and so many others to mix timeless doctrines with fluid notions of historical process was a specific form of the larger confrontation between tradition and the modern world. The question is, Which half of the task was problematic? For Forsyth, despite his protestations that one should start with Goethe and end with Christ, and despite the great power of his incarnational vision, there is little doubt that the problem was to salvage tradition. This is where he differs from Strong—and this is why he is less useful than Strong for helping us understand the inner workings of theological transition at the turn of the century.

The evidence suggests that throughout most of his life Strong did not clearly understand the dilemma in which he was entangled. He

232

was not a Jonathan Edwards who towered above his age nor a Benjamin Warfield who disdained to be touched by his age, and certainly not a William James who lived ahead of his age. Rather he was a touchingly human figure: too conservative to discard the nurture of his youth, too honest to discount his own religious experiences, yet too intelligent to ignore the verdict that the modern understanding of history had rendered upon inherited orthodoxy. Above all, he was too much a man of his times to be able to see that the stress in his thought was a reflection of a vast, transatlantic process of change and readjustment that heralded the dawn of modern culture.

NOTES

[1]Winthrop S. Hudson, *Religion in America*, 3rd ed., rev. (New York: Charles Scribner's Sons, 1981), pp. 279, 370-371.

[2]The amount of literature is vast. Some of the most useful studies include H. Stuart Hughes, *Consciousness and Society: The Reorientation of European Social Thought, 1890–1930* (New York: Octagon Books, 1958); Georg G. Iggers, *The German Conception of History* (Middletown, Conn.: Columbia University Press, 1968); Maurice Mandelbaum, *History, Man, and Reason: A Study in Nineteenth-Century Thought* (Baltimore: The Johns Hopkins University Press, 1971); Henry F. May, *The End of American Innocence: A Study of the First Years of Our Own Time, 1912–1917* (New York: Oxford University Press, 1959, reprinted 1964); Edward A. Purcell, *The Crisis of Democratic Theory: Scientific Naturalism and the Problem of Value* (Lexington: University Press of Kentucky, 1973); Hayden White, *Tropics of Discourse: Essays in Cultural Criticism* (Baltimore: The Johns Hopkins University Press, 1978), especially chapter 4, "Historicism, History, and the Figurative Imagination"; Morton White, *Social Thought in America: The Revolt Against Formalism* (New York: Oxford University Press, 1947, reprinted 1957); Robert H. Wiebe, *The Search for Order: 1877–1920* (New York: Hill and Wang, Inc., 1967).

[3]Sydney E. Ahlstrom, *A Religious History of the American People* (New Haven, Conn.: Yale University Press, 1972), pp. 772-774; Gaius Glenn Atkins, *Religion in Our Times* (New York, 1932), p. 86; William R. Hutchison, *The Modernist Impulse in American Protestantism* (Cambridge, Mass.: Harvard University Press, 1976), p. 2; Claude Welch, *Protestant Thought in the Nineteenth Century, 1799–1870* (New Haven, 1972), chapter 7.

[4]Willis B. Glover, *Evangelical Nonconformists and Higher Criticism in the Nineteenth Century* (London: Independent Press Ltd., 1954), pp. 80, 106; George M. Marsden, *Fundamentalism and American Culture: The Shaping of Twentieth-Century Evangelicalism, 1870–1925* (New York: Oxford University Press, 1980), pp. 110-114, 225-227; Jack B. Rogers and Donald K. McKim, *The Authority and Interpretation of the Bible: An Historical Approach* (New York: Harper & Row, Publishers, Inc., 1979), chapters 5-6; Ernest R. Sandeen, *The Roots of Fundamentalism: British and American Millenarianism, 1800–1930* (Chicago: University of Chicago Press, 1970), p. 268.

[5]For biographical data on Augustus Hopkins Strong (1836–1921) see the entries, *sub verbum*, in *Dictionary of American Biography* (New York: Charles Scrib-

233

ner's Sons, 1935); *National Cyclopedia of American Biography* (Clifton, N.J.: James T. White & Co., 1979); and Henry Warner Bowden, *Dictionary of American Religious Biography* (Westport, Conn.: Greenwood Press, 1977). More fulsome is LeRoy Moore, Jr., "The Rise of American Religious Liberalism at the Rochester Theological Seminary, 1872–1928," Ph.D. diss., Claremont Graduate School, 1966, *passim*. The best resource is Strong's typed "Autobiography," 2 vols., American Baptist Historical Society, Rochester, N.Y. For one of many assessments of his influence see Carl F. H. Henry, *Personal Idealism and Strong's Theology* (Wheaton, Ill.: Van Kampen Press, 1951), preface and pp. 11, 13, 228.

⁶For Strong's personality and personal relationships see the essays in *Rochester Theological Seminary Bulletin: Augustus Hopkins Strong Memorial Number*, 73rd Year (May, 1922, supplement); George W. Taft, "Two Remarkable Men and Their Books: Augustus Hopkins Strong and William Newton Clarke," *Standard*, January 18, 1913, pp. 576-578, and January 25, 1913, pp. 607-608. On Rauschenbusch see LeRoy Moore, Jr., "Academic Freedom: A Chapter in the History of Colgate Rochester Divinity School," *Foundations*, vol. 10, no. 1 (January-March, 1967), pp. 64-79; Ernest Gordon, *The Leaven of the Sadducees, or the Old and New Apostasies* (Chicago: The Bible Institute Colportage Association, 1926), pp. 189, 192.

⁷Those who have stressed Strong's openness, if not nascent liberalism, include Bowen, *Dictionary*, pp. 438-439; Henry, *Personal Idealism*, p. 229; Marsden, *Fundamentalism*, p. 107; George W. Dollar, *A History of Fundamentalism in America* (Greenville, S.C.: Bob Jones University Press, 1973), pp. 146, 364. Strong's orthodoxy is emphasized in Kenneth S. Kantzer, "Unity and Diversity in Evangelical Faith," in David F. Wells and John D. Woodbridge, eds., *The Evangelicals: What They Believe, Who They Are, Where They Are Changing* (Nashville: Abingdon Press, 1975), pp. 47-48; John D. Woodbridge, Mark A. Noll, and Nathan O. Hatch, *The Gospel in America: Themes in the Story of America's Evangelicals* (Grand Rapids: The Zondervan Corp., 1979), p. 68; Gerald Birney Smith, "Theological Thinking in America," *Religious Thought in the Last Quarter-Century*, ed. Smith (Chicago, 1927), p. 103. Strong's mediatorial role is underscored in Crerar Douglas, "The Hermeneutics of Augustus Hopkins Strong: God and Shakespeare in Rochester," *Foundations*, vol. 21, no. 1 (January-March, 1978), pp. 74-75; Norman H. Maring, "Baptists and Changing Views of the Bible, 1865–1918 (Part II)," *Foundations*, vol. 1, no. 4 (October, 1958), pp. 39-40; Moore, "American Religious Liberalism," pp. 52, 62, 157, 263. Moore, however, implies that the elderly Strong was confused.

⁸See, for example, Conrad Henry Moehlman, "Dr. Strong as Teacher," *Rochester Theological Seminary Bulletin*, 73rd Year (May, 1922, supplement), p. 19.

⁹Augustus H. Strong, *Christ in Creation and Ethical Monism* (Philadelphia: The Griffith and Rowland Press, 1899), pp. 274-275.

¹⁰*Ibid.*, p. 10.

¹¹Augustus H. Strong, *Miscellanies*, 2 volumes, (Philadelphia: The Griffith and Rowland Press, 1912), vol. 1, p. 163.

¹²For Strong's doctrinal orthodoxy and ultimate alignment with fundamentalism see his "Confessions of Our Faith," *Watchman-Examiner*, July 21, 1921, p. 910. See also LeRoy Moore, Jr., "Another Look at Fundamentalism: A Response to Ernest R. Sandeen," *Church History*, vol. 37 (1968), pp. 195-202.

¹³Strong, *Christ in Creation*, pp. 108-109; *Miscellanies*, p. 310.

¹⁴Strong, *Christ in Creation*, pp. 479, 106; *Miscellanies*, p. 117, emphasis added; *One Hundred Chapel-Talks to Theological Students* (Philadelphia: The Griffith and Rowland Press, 1913), pp. 152-153.

¹⁵Strong, *Miscellanies*, pp. 290, 291.

¹⁶*Ibid.*, pp. 292, 293, 302.

¹⁷*Ibid.*, p. 295.

[18] Strong, *Christ in Creation*, pp. 53-54.

[19] Strong, *Miscellanies, p. 170.*

[20] Hutchison, *Modernist Impulse,* chapters 3-4; Winthrop S. Hudson, *The Great Tradition of the American Churches* (New York: Harper and Row, Publishers, Inc., 1953), chapters 8-10.

[21] Some of Strong's contemporaries understood his dilemma more clearly than he did. Taft, "Two Remarkable Men," pp. 607-608; Clarence Beckwith, review of Strong's *Systematic Theology,* vol. 2, in *American Journal of Theology,* vol. 12 (1908), pp. 502-504; William Adams Brown, "Recent Treatises on Systematic Theology," *ibid.,* pp. 154-155; Herbert Alden Youtz, review of Strong's *Systematic Theology,* vol. 3 (1909), in *American Journal of Theology,* vol. 13 (1909), pp. 469-470.

[22] Compare Henry C. Vedder, "What I Teach About the Bible," *Baptist,* October 20, 1920, p. 1357, with Victor I. Masters, "Dr. A. H. Strong's Terrible Arraignment of Destructive Criticism," *Western Recorder,* October 21, 1926, pp. 11-12.

[23] See, for example, Laws, "The Old and New Theologies," *Watchman-Examiner,* February 1, 1917, pp. 133-134; Goodchild, "The Bible—God's Word," *ibid.,* October 13, 1921, pp. 1299-1300; Anderson, "Dr. Anderson at Des Moines," *ibid.,* May 19, 1921, p. 626; E. Y. Mullins, "The Testimony of Christian Experience," in *The Fundamentals: A Testimony to the Truth,* ed. A. C. Dixon, *et al.,* 12 vols. (Chicago: Testimony Publishing Company, 1910-1915), vol. 3, p. 85; George Frederick Wright, "The Mosaic Authorship of the Pentateuch," *ibid.,* vol. 9, pp. 20-21; Speer, "Foreign Missions or World-Wide Evangelism," *ibid.,* vol. 12, pp. 77-78, 83; David Johnson, *et al., The Trial of the Rev. David Swing* (Chicago, 1874), p. 20; Clarke, *Sixty Years with the Bible: A Record of Experience* (New York, 1910), chapters 2-3; Briggs, *Church Unity: Studies of Its Most Important Problems* (New York, 1909), chapters 10, 11, 15.

[24] For the European and British setting, see, respectively, John Higham, *Writing American History: Essays on Modern Scholarship* (Bloomington, Ind.: Indiana University Press, 1970), pp. 90-93; and Thomas A. Langford, *In Search of Foundations: English Theology, 1900-1920* (Nashville: Abingdon Press, 1969), pp. 49, 51, 53, 88. For Dorner see Otto Pfleiderer, *The Development of Theology in Germany Since Kant,* trans. J. Frederick Smith (London: George Allen and Unwin Ltd.; New York: Macmillan, Inc., 1890), pp. 211-219. For Schlatter see his essay "The Theology of the New Testament and Dogmatics," in Robert Morgan, ed. and trans., *The Nature of New Testament Theology,* in *Studies in Biblical Theology,* 2nd series, vol. 25 (Naperville, Ill.: Alec R. Allenson, Inc., 1973), pp. 117-166.

[25] Winthrop S. Hudson, "How American Is Religion in America?" in *Reinterpretation in American Church History,* ed. Jerald C. Brauer (Chicago: University of Chicago Press, 1968), pp. 153-167; Ernest R. Sandeen, "The Distinctiveness of American Denominationalism: A Case Study of the 1846 Evangelical Alliance," *Church History,* vol. 45 (1976), pp. 222-234; Melvin E. Dieter, *The Holiness Revival of the Nineteenth Century* (Metuchen, N.J.: Scarecrow Press, Inc., 1980); Richard Carwardine, *Transatlantic Revivalism: Popular Evangelicalism in Britain and America, 1790-1865* (Westport, Conn.: Greenwood Press, 1978).

[26] Glover, *Evangelical Nonconformists,* pp. 162, 168, 175; Langford, *English Theology,* p. 22; George Marsden, "Fundamentalism as an American Phenomenon, a Comparison with English Evangelicalism," *Church History,* vol. 46 (1977), pp. 217-224; J. R. H. Moorman, *A History of the Church in England* (New York: Morehouse-Barlow Co., 1973), p. 398. For the loss of vigor among Anglican evangelicals see Langford, *English Theology,* p. 122; Ian Bradley, *The Call to Seriousness: The Evangelical Impact on the Victorians* (New York: Macmillan, Inc., 1976), pp. 17-18, 195.

[27] That a very conservative form of evangelicalism, if not fundamentalism, has

flourished in Britain since World War II is an inference I draw from the sources cited by James Barr, *Fundamentalism* (London: SCM Press Ltd., 1977).

[28]For Moore see James R. Moore, *The Post-Darwinian Controversies: A study of the Protestant struggle to come to terms with Darwin in Great Britain and America, 1870–1900* (Cambridge: At the University Press, 1979), pp. 259-269. For Orr see James Barr, *Fundamentalism*, pp. 269-270, and Jack Rogers, *Authority*, pp. 385-388. For Peake see Glover, *Evangelical Nonconformists*, pp. 261, 270-271; and Marsden, "Fundamentalism," p. 217.

[29]Smith letter to J. S. Black, 14 September 1871, quoted in Warner M. Bailey, "William Robertson Smith and American Bible Studies," *Journal of Presbyterian History*, vol. 51 (1973), p. 287, n. 10. See also W. Robertson Smith, "Lecture I: The Subject and the Method of Enquiry," *The Religion of the Semites: The Fundamental Institutions* (London: Adam and Charles Black, 1907), pp. 15-24; T. O. Beidelman, *W. Robertson Smith and the Sociological Study of Religion* (Chicago: University of Chicago Press, 1974), pp. 33, 38, 40, 52.

[30]P. T. Forsyth, *Positive Preaching and Modern Mind* (Grand Rapids, Mich.: Baker Book House, 1907), pp. 124, 125, 127. For a bibliography of Forsyth's works and works about him see Rogers, *Authority*, pp. 403-405; Samuel J. Mikolaski, "P. T. Forsyth," in *Creative Minds in Contemporary Theology*, ed. Philip Edgcumbe Hughes, 2nd ed. rev. (Grand Rapids: Wm. B. Eerdmans Publishing Co., 1966), pp. 338-339.

[31]Forsyth, *Christian Aspects of Evolution* (1905; reprinted London, 1950), pp. 11, 20.

[32]*Ibid.*, pp. 37, 38, 39.

[33]B. A. Gerrish, *Tradition and the Modern World: Reformed Theology in the Nineteenth Century* (Chicago: University of Chicago Press, 1978), pp. 186, 188. For a contrasting perspective see Erich Heller, *The Disinherited Mind: Essays in Modern German Literature and Thought*, 3rd ed. (London, 1971), pp. 270-271.

236

Index

Index prepared by David and Nancy Jones.